MY LIFE
AND
FORTUNES

The Autobiography of one of the World's
Wealthiest Men

D1570527

J. PAUL GETTY

To George, Ronald,
Paul, Gordon, and
the memory of Timothy

ILLUSTRATIONS

MY LIFE AND FORTUNES

1

IN 1914, a brawling, bare-knuckled frontier atmosphere still prevailed in the Oklahoma oil fields.

Boom towns mushroomed overnight around newly discovered producing areas. At first, these settlements would consist of nothing more than a few clapboard or raw-pine shacks and some weather-beaten tents. Then, quickly, a false-front general store, third-rate hotel, barber shop, and an assortment of gambling halls, bordellos, and thinly disguised bootleg whisky-peddlers' shops would make their appearance.

Streets and roads, even in larger and older communities, were unpaved. In spring and winter, they formed knee-high rivers of mushy clay. In summer, they became sun-baked, rutted tracks, perpetually shrouded by billows of harsh red or yellow dust. Duckboard "sidewalks" installed outside the more prosperous business establishments were viewed as the ultimate in civic refinement.

Hard-bitten men from the oil fields—wildcatters, lease brokers, rig builders, drillers, roughnecks, and roustabouts—wearing stained clothes, heavy mud-caked boots, and not infrequently one or more Colt six-shooters, swarmed through the streets and thronged the few sleazy pleasure domes in the boom towns. Most of them had money to spend. New wells were being brought in daily. Oil-field workers' wages went to eight dollars and even more per day—as much as three times the wage rates then prevailing elsewhere in American industry.

One could occasionally see Indians from the Osage, Cherokee, Pawnee, and other tribes. Some were poor and wandered about aimlessly and dispiritedly; a few among them hawked blankets, necklaces, and similar cheap souvenir trinkets. Others, newly enriched by royalties from oil wells drilled on their lands, dressed flamboyantly and often went on prodigious spending sprees.

One oil-rich Cherokee chieftain descended on Tulsa and purchased two dozen automobiles—plus four dozen dray horses. He didn't trust the new-fangled contraptions to run under their own power. Another Cherokee Croesus hired a touring carnival for his own amusement, keeping the entire troupe of men and animals on his private payroll for nearly a year.

An enterprising automobile dealer made his own fortune when he discovered that ornately decorated hearses held a tremendous appeal for wealthy Indians. The big, shiny vehicles, literally dripping with scrollwork and fancily carved angels and funerary urns, became the oil-rich brave's favorite mode of transportation. Many hearses were sold to Indians in Oklahoma between 1914 and 1917. Their owners drove them with far greater pride than skill, and their large families invariably rode in the rear, or coffin, compartments and, when convenient, slept in them.

Officially, Oklahoma had been "dry" for several years. Actually, oceans of bootlegged liquor flowed into the boom towns. U. S. Marshals and local law-enforcement officers did their best to keep the peace, but fights and even shooting affrays were everyday commonplaces.

All in all, it was very much like Bret Harte's California or Jack London's Klondike. Almost—but not quite. There were such minor differences as the presence of the automobile which, although it had by no means replaced the horse or the mule-drawn wagon, was already very much in evidence. Also—and this was the most significant difference—in Oklahoma men were gripped by a fever to find oil rather than gold. But the oil fever was no less epidemic than the gold fever had been and there were few, indeed, who were immune to the contagion.

I, for one, was not among the immune minority. At twenty-one, I had already spent three months as a wildcatting operator, prospecting fruitlessly for oil in the region around Tulsa. It wasn't until the late fall of 1915 that my luck began to turn.

Then, a half-interest in an oil and gas lease on a 160-acre property known as the Nancy Taylor Allotment was offered for sale at public auction. The property was located near the tiny Muskogee County hamlet of Stone Bluff, not too far from Tulsa. I had seen the land previously and thought it highly promising. Learning that the lease was up for sale, I decided to make another and more meticulous inspection.

I drove to Stone Bluff from Tulsa in my battered Model T Ford. As was inevitable in those days on any journey involving more than a few miles, the tin lizzy bogged down in mud en route. With long-accustomed for-bearance, I listened to the taunts and jeers of the farmer whose team I hired to drag me out of the gluey morass that masqueraded as a county road.

"Why don't you get yourself a horse, son?" the farmer cackled finally—as I had known he must, sooner or later.

Arriving at the Nancy Taylor Allotment property about an hour after-wards, I made a close and thorough study of the terrain. What I saw strengthened my belief that there was oil on the property. Returning to Tulsa, I spent the evening in the lobby of the Tulsa Hotel. The lobby, which was jammed every evening with lease brokers, wildcatters, equip-ment dealers, and others directly or indirectly engaged in the hunt for oil, was the best oil-business information center in Oklahoma.

A few discreet, offhand inquiries brought the information that several other independent operators were interested in buying the lease on the Nancy Taylor Allotment.

"Anders and Cory are out to get it, and they're willing to bid high if necessary," a reliable informant told me.

What I heard disheartened me. I didn't have much money at my dis-posal—certainly not enough to match the prices older, well-established independents such as the successful team of Anders, Cory and Associates would be able to offer without batting an eyelash.

Pondering the problem that night, I hit upon a tactic which I thought might help equalize the odds. A day or two later, I went to a Muskogee bank with which I had done some business and asked one of its officers to attend the sale and bid for me.

"But please don't let on that you're acting for me," I begged.

"I won't," the banker promised with a broad grin. He had obviously guessed the nature of my scheme and was highly amused by it.

Surprisingly enough, my rather transparent stratagem accomplished its purpose. The auction sale, held the following week in the town of Musko-gee, the Muskogee County seat, was well attended by independent oil operators, among them representatives of Anders, Cory and Associates. All seemed eager to buy the lease. It appeared that the bidding would be spirited and the final sale price high.

But the veteran wildcatters were unnerved by the unexpected presence of the well-known local bank executive who had agreed to bid for me. They automatically assumed that a banker's participation in the bidding could mean only one thing: he was acting for some large oil company and was prepared to top all offers. Thus, the other prospective buyers glumly decided it would be futile to bid at all. They let the lease go, and I secured it for five hundred dollars—a bargain-basement price.

Soon thereafter, a company was formed to finance the drilling of a well on the property. Being merely a tyro wildcatter with no capital of my own, I received a modest 11.25 per cent interest in the corporation. We spudded the well—my first—shortly after New Year's Day, 1916.

I spent all my days and most my nights on the drilling site. As the drill sank deeper into the ground, my nervousness and excitement mounted higher. Then, on February 2, the bailer—the device which cleared formation rock from the drill-hole—began bringing up quantities of oil sand. This indicated that the final stage of what had been a month-long, round-the-clock drilling operation was now at hand. The next twenty-four hours would most probably prove whether I had a producing well or a dry hole.

Being young and, in many ways, still quite green, I found it impossible to control my steadily increasing tension, which soon reached an all but unbearable pitch. Even I was close to realizing that I had become more hindrance than help to the experienced and capable men who formed my drilling crew. They, of course, recognized my symptoms and good-naturedly urged me to make myself scarce.

"Be a good boy, boss," a grizzled tool-dresser exclaimed in tolerant exasperation around noon. "Get the hell out of here before you have a fit—or make us all have one!"

The thought that I was considered a boy by the crew rankled. Nonetheless, I could see the wisdom of the advice and decided to beat a retreat to Tulsa, where I had my desk-space "office" and a six-dollar-per-week room at the Cordova Hotel. I made up my mind to wait there until the drilling was completed and the final results became known.

Arriving in Tulsa later that afternoon, I sought out J. Carl Smith, a close friend, and told him of the latest developments and the effect they'd had on me. J. Carl, who was considerably older, more mature—and far less excitable—than I, listened sympathetically. He offered to leave immediately for the drilling site and watch the work there for me. I accepted his offer gratefully, and he took the next train to Stone Bluff.

There were no telephones on the remote site where my well was being drilled. The single telephone line between Tulsa and Stone Bluff itself was seldom in working order. Hence, J. Carl promised he would return to Tulsa the next day on the late train and bring me the latest news.

I spent the night tossing restlessly on by bed in the Cordova Hotel. But sleep was impossible, and I got up shortly after dawn, took a lukewarm shower, shaved, and dressed. I had no appetite. My breakfast consisted of several cups of black coffee which failed dismally to make me feel any less haggard and exhausted.

The day—a cold and gloomy February 3, 1916—passed with maddening slowness. There was no mail for me at the hotel. I walked to my "office." The few letters that had been delivered there were unimportant; there was nothing in them to occupy my mind or even briefly shift my thoughts away from my well.

For hours, I did little but fidget and glance repeatedly at my watch. A hundred times or more, I decided to drive out to the drilling site—and a hundred times or more I rejected the idea. Somehow, I managed to wait the day through, but I was at the Tulsa railroad depot, anxiously pacing the passenger platform, more than an hour before the late train from Stone Bluff was due to arrive.

It was already dark. A chill, dust-laden prairie wind swept the platform in raw gusts that stung my face and seemed to slice right through my overcoat. But I was aware of neither cold nor wind as I did my sentry-go up and down the deserted platform. Every now and then I would stop, either to check the time shown by the large clock that clung to the depot's soot-grimed façade or to peer along the railroad track in futile hopes the train might come in ahead of schedule.

At last, after what seemed an eternity, the train from Stone Bluff racketed into the station. Several oil men I knew fairly well got off the coaches. One of them saw me.

"Heard a rumor your well came in!" he called to me. "Understand it's a good one!" Then he hurried on before I could ask him for more information.

Moments later, J. Carl Smith's familiar rotund figure emerged from the rear door of the last coach, and impatiently I ran to meet him. I saw that he was walking at a rapid pace and took this as a highly encouraging sign, for J. Carl's normal movements were deliberate, almost ponderously slow. Then, as we drew closer to each other, I could see that his plump face was beaming. My hopes and spirits soared.

"Congratulations, Paul!" J. Carl boomed when he was still several yards from me. "We brought in your well this afternoon. It's producing thirty barrels!"

My elation vanished instantly, and I stopped dead in my tracks.

Thirty barrels a day, I thought bleakly—why, that was nothing, a mere trickle.

"Yes, sir!" J. Carl chortled. Now he was close enough to grab my hand, and he shook it jubilantly. "We were getting thirty barrels an hour when I left the drilling site!"

Thirty barrels *an hour*!

That made a difference—a world of difference.

That meant the well was producing more than seven hundred barrels of crude oil a day!

But it also meant something far more important.

It meant I was in the oil business—to stay.

2

THE oil man soon learns to think and measure in terms of millions.

Nature needed several million years to build vast sedimentary deposits of animal, vegetable, and mineral matter which, sinking deep into the primeval mud, decomposed under great heat and pressure to form the greenish-black hydrocarbon called petroleum or oil.

Many thousands of years passed before man finally recognized and began to exploit petroleum's seemingly limitless potentials and men began to spend, earn, and lose millions of dollars in feverish quests for the black gold.

Today, oil is big business, probably the biggest of all businesses. Without oil, there would be—there could be—no civilization as we know it. Only food, clothing, and shelter rank before oil among modern man's essential needs, and the production of these is dependent to a very great degree on petroleum, its products, and by-products.

Even random petroleum industry statistics prove that its unit of measure is, indeed, the million.

World crude oil production exceeds seven thousand million barrels annually; global refinery capacity tops twenty million barrels daily.

This oil powers and lubricates countless million machines and vehicles— some seventy-five million automobiles, trucks, and buses in the United States alone. It heats tens of millions of homes, produces millions of kilowatts of electrical energy. Petrochemical plants in the United States turn out some twenty million tons of chemical compounds, synthetics, and other products each year.

Private capital invested in leases, concessions, equipment, plants, and facilities for finding, producing, refining, transporting, and distributing oil totals thousands of millions of dollars. For example, the assets of just one company I control—the Tidewater Oil Company—total nearly one billion dollars. But even Tidewater is a small company when compared to such petroleum industry behemoths as Royal Dutch-Shell, which has more than *ten billion dollars* in fixed assets, and Standard Oil of New Jersey (known to the oil industry as "Jersey") is bigger still.

All this has come about in little more than a century. The petroleum industry did not exist before 1859, a rather remarkable fact when one realizes that petroleum has been known and, to a limited extent, used for various purposes since the beginnings of recorded history.

Scooping crude oil from surface pools, the Babylonians mixed it in the mortar with which they cemented their walls. The Bible and ancient Greek histories make references to substances which were obviously crude oil. Long before the birth of Christ, Sicilians burned petroleum in their clay lamps, and the Japanese are known to have used "burning water" as far back as the seventh century A.D.

Medieval philosophers, seeing that oil appeared to come from the rocks, named it "petroleum," or rock oil. Oil springs or seeps abounded on the North American continent, and the Indians used the oil as medicine and in making their war paints. Boiling down crude oil, which they called *copé*, early Spanish explorers caulked their leaky ships with the gummy residue.

Various peoples at various times found surface pools of petroleum and used it in diverse ways. Yet, none recognized its potentials; when the nineteenth century began, petroleum was still an unexploited and, in fact, a virtually unknown natural resource.

In the early 1800's, wood and coal remained the world's principal fuels. Lubricants were made chiefly from animal fats. Minute quantities of crude oil taken from surface pools or oil springs were being used for lighting, but almost all artificial illumination was still provided by candle, whale-oil lamps, or, in rare instances, artificial gas made from coal.

But people, their habits and living patterns already greatly changed by the impact of the Industrial Revolution, wanted to see—and to read—more. The world wanted and needed more efficient and cheaper artificial light.

Around 1849, two processes were developed for producing illuminating oil from coal or shale. The end product of one process was marketed as "coal oil," of the other as "kerosene." Coal oil or kerosene, neither was perfect, but both proved better and cheaper than whale oil. In less than ten years, fifty-eight United States plants were producing the new illuminating oils.

In the meantime, enterprising American merchandisers had discovered a novel—and totally unrelated—commercial application for petroleum. They bottled it and sold it as medicine.

"Rock Oil—the Great Indian Remedy," was hawked by self-styled "doctors" whose medicine shows toured the expanding nation's smaller cities and frontier settlements. Glib barkers assured their audiences the "medicine" would cure anything from the common cold to cancer, and people bought the noxious stuff in great quantities. What was worse, they drank it or rubbed it on their afflicted parts, firmly convinced that "Indian Remedy" possessed miraculous restorative and curative powers. It is highly doubtful if bottled petroleum effected many cures; possibly, it did have some value as a placebo. One can only hope it did little serious harm to the gullible ill and infirm.

Whatever the ethical considerations involved in the "Indian Remedy" trade, the American petroleum industry owes a debt for its existence to Samuel M. Kier, who became a highly successful rock-oil cure-all entrepreneur. Kier, a Pennsylvanian, owned several brine wells near Tarentum. These wells, drilled to relatively shallow depths, tapped underground salt-water, or brine, pools. Salt was extracted from the brine and sold commercially.

Like other brine-well operators in the region, Samuel Kier found his subterranean salt-water reservoirs were sometimes "polluted" by petroleum. Petroleum pumped from the wells was considered worthless, a waste by-product; if a well produced too much petroleum, it had to be abandoned. Then Kier recalled that the Indians used rock oil as a medicine. Soon, the red man's miracle nostrum was available to Pennsylvania palefaces, too—in half-pint bottles.

Kier's Petroleum or Rock Oil—Celebrated for Its Wonderful Curative Powers—a Natural Remedy Produced from a Well in Allegheny County 400 Feet Below the Earth's Surface.

So read the labels on the bottles—and Samuel Kier's success was instantaneous. But he still had too much "waste" petroleum. Noting that rock oil was inflammable, he wondered if it could not somehow be refined into illuminating oil.

According to one story, Kier got the idea of distilling petroleum from seeing a moonshiner's whisky-still. Another version holds that the distilling process was suggested by a Philadelphia chemist. In any event, a still with a five-barrel-a-day capacity was built. At first, Kier sold the product as a super-medicine. Then a lamp which burned the distilled oil efficiently was designed, and he began to market the oil as improved kerosene.

Sales boomed, and Kier's own brine wells no longer supplied enough by-product petroleum to meet the demand; he sought more from other brine-producers, offering up to twenty dollars a barrel for the crude rock oil. Not surprisingly, his successful ventures attracted attention and inspired further developments. Several New Haven, Connecticut, businessmen headed by George H. Bissell formed the Pennsylvania Rock Oil Company in 1854 and leased a tract of land pocked with oil springs near Titusville. After trying vainly for nearly five years to collect petroleum by hand-digging trenches around the oil springs, the company failed and was then reorganized as the Seneca Oil Company.

Some say George Bissell made the decision to drill a well on the Titus-ville property; others claim it was Edwin L. Drake's idea. No one knows whether Seneca Oil set out to drill a true oil well or merely hoped to obtain by-product petroleum from just another brine well drilled in oil-soaked ground.

Whoever had the original inspiration and whatever the specific aim, it was Edwin Drake who organized and supervised the drilling operation. A handsome man with a soldierly bearing, Drake had worked for many years as a railroad conductor. Although he'd never seen military service, he arrived in Pennsylvania styling himself as "Colonel" Edwin Laurentine Drake. Skeptics have theorized that the military title was George Bissell's brain child, conceived as a public relations tour de force to impress native Pennsylvanians and prospective investors alike.

Bogus colonel or not, Edwin Drake inspected Samuel Kier's brine wells and decided to follow traditional brine-well drilling methods. Purchasing the necessary steam-powered equipment, he assembled a crew of experienced drillers, erected a derrick, and began work.

The era of rotary tools and high-speed rigs was still in the far distant future. Drake and his workmen had to rely on the primitive cable tools then used for drilling water and brine wells. The drilling method was simply a mechanized extension of the principles involved in making a hole in the ground by repeatedly driving a sharp-edged steel bar down into the same spot in the oil or in cutting through a granite block with hammer and chisel.

Drake and his crew found the first thirty-nine feet relatively easy going. Then they encountered solid rock. Progress was slowed to inches per day as the drilling bit, powered by the wheezing steam engine, laboriously punched its way down into the rock. At last, on August 27, 1859, at a depth of sixty-nine and a half feet, the bit broke through the subterranean rock layer and struck pay sand. Oil flowed up to within a few feet of the surface. A pump was hurriedly brought to the site, and America's first true oil well was soon producing thirty barrels of petroleum per day—a daily yield worth six hundred dollars at the then-current twenty-dollars-per-barrel price.

The well precipitated the nation's first oil rush. Within a few months, others eager to cash in on the petroleum bonanza had completed more than two dozen wells in the Titusville area, and more were being drilled almost daily.

Illuminating oil made from petroleum proved itself far superior to that made from coal or shale. Now that petroleum was available in appreciable quantities, coal-oil producers hastened to convert their plants to refine it. At the same time, new petroleum refineries were being built. Thus, for a short period, rapidly increasing demand outstripped production, but the frantic rush to drill new wells continued, and soaring petroleum output closed the gap.

In 1860, crude oil production totaled some 650,000 barrels, and prices spiraled down to two dollars per barrel, one-tenth of what they had been the previous year. In 1861, again greatly increased petroleum production glutted—and broke—the market; petroleum sold for ten cents a barrel.

These were painful birth pangs, but there could be no doubt that a great industry had been born.

Within two years after Edwin Drake completed his Titusville well, new oil discoveries were made in Pennsylvania, Ohio, West Virginia, Kansas, and California. During the same period, every coal-oil refinery in the United States had either switched to petroleum or had shut down. It is an incidental oddity that people nonetheless insisted on calling the refined petroleum product kerosene or coal oil, a habit which persists to this day.

The petroleum industry's phenomenal growth rate soon carried it into the million-measure bracket. In 1862, United States crude oil production topped 3,000,000 barrels. The Civil War served to slow the pace, and production dropped back to less than 2,500,000 barrels in 1865, while prices shot as high as fourteen dollars a barrel. By 1870, the rate of expansion had been resumed, and that year's petroleum production exceeded 5,250,000 barrels. Within the next decade, crude production jumped to

25,000,000 barrels yearly. By 1900, world petroleum output was nearing 150,000,000 barrels annually.

In the beginning, oil refineries were chiefly concerned with producing kerosene, but they were soon making lubricants as well, and chemists and engineers were hard at work seeking other uses and applications for petroleum. Unfortunately, many years were to pass before any use would be made of the first and lightest refinery fraction: gasoline. For decades, gasoline was considered waste and thrown away.

The petroleum industry as a whole was very much like Topsy; it "jest growed." It was an entirely new industry; there were few laws or legal precedents and no rule books to guide or govern it. The very haphazard manner in which the industry's basic raw material—crude oil—was obtained seemed to set the pattern of growing confusion which prevailed.

There was no organization and little order. Oil exploration and drilling was conducted by uncounted thousands of individuals who, having a little capital and hoping to make large profits swiftly, engaged in independent and un-co-ordinated searches for "black gold." If one man leased a site, drilled on it, and struck oil, hundreds of others would rush to the area and begin drilling frantically on adjoining properties. It was not unusual for a man with a producing well to have it offset by scores of others which would exhaust the underground reservoir.

The petroleum producer's problems did not end when he struck pay sand; in fact that is when they really began. Aside from the risk that others might offset his well, he had to worry about selling his crude, either at the wellhead or after transporting it to a market.

At first, most crude oil was purchased by middlemen—brokers. They sought to buy low and sell high. The price a producer received for his petroleum was often dependent on how badly he needed cash or how shrewdly he could bargain. In the middleman's hands, petroleum became a highly speculative commodity. Crude prices fluctuated insanely, with the producer at the mercy of the speculators.

Competition in all phases of the petroleum industry was tough and frequently unfair and even vicious. Furthermore, oil, like gold, held a magic attraction for the general public and still does. Unscrupulous and dishonest individuals employed patently implausible get-rich-quick schemes to swindle the gullible—and, I might add, still do. These factors compounded the confusion even further.

The construction of the first pipelines changed the oil industry's complexion somewhat. The railroads, reluctant to lose lucrative oil-freight traffic, fought the pipelines bitterly, but once the new mode of transportation became established, the pipeline companies became the largest buyers of crude oil. It was hardly unusual for these pipeline companies to squeeze the producers by rigging prices low and by engaging in any one of a hundred practices which, today, are prohibited by law. The situation deteriorated steadily into chaos. Sometimes violence flared as producers rioted in protest against rigged prices, discriminatory freight rates, and other unfair practices.

Historians and sociologists might well find a lesson applicable to the socio-political macrocosm in what transpired next in the petroleum industry microcosm.

Fantastic waste, lack of organization, widespread apathy, and selfish indifference of individuals to the plight of their fellows in the industry created conditions ideally suited for the emergence of a "strong man."

The strong man was John D. Rockefeller. Taking over a Cleveland refinery in 1865, he pyramided it with dizzying speed and terrifying efficiency into a virtual monopoly over the entire American petroleum industry. Rockefeller possessed a genius for organization; he realized what tremendous advantages and rewards would accrue to anyone who could bring an appreciable degree of order and organization to the petroleum industry.

This is what he set out to do, and he accomplished his aims so well that, at its peak of power, his gargantuan Standard Oil Company controlled up to 80 per cent of America's domestic, and up to 90 per cent of its export, trade in petroleum. Standard was the nation's biggest—and, indeed, practically its only important—refiner and marketer.

There are those who maintain the monopoly held by the Standard Oil group was broken by the United States government and the Sherman Anti-Trust Act. I'll grant this is true, up to a point. The government did take action against Standard Oil, and the United States Supreme Court did eventually order the company to dissolve.

But, as a veteran oil man looking back on history in the light of my own knowledge and experience, I'm inclined to believe that other far more powerful factors had begun to weaken Standard's hold on the petroleum industry even before the government made its initial moves. First of all, as the nineteenth century waned, gas and electricity had already started to weaken another monopoly, that held by kerosene over the world's artificial lighting. Also, a demand was slowly growing for fuel oil. Asphalt was gradually coming into general use as road-surfacing material. And the internal combustion engine had been invented.

The era of the automobile and the airplane was just around the corner. The petroleum industry would soon become a giant that no combine or trust could monopolize or dominate. Not even a dozen John D. Rockefellers and an army of corporation lawyers could stave off the inevitable. By 1900, petroleum was ready to come into its own.

3

THE severest test of a businessman's acumen and ability sometimes lies in the speed and manner with which he recognizes and grasps the opportunities presented by the vagaries of Fate.

In 1903, my father, George Franklin Getty, was a successful Minneapolis attorney. He had a lucrative law practice and served as an officer and director of the National Mutual Life Association, a large Minnesota insurance company.

A self-made man who began life as a penniless farm-boy, he had accumulated a personal fortune totaling some $250,000, a very large sum in those days. He enjoyed a fine reputation in his profession, community, and state and was active in many civic, fraternal, service, and professional organizations.

In short, at the age of forty-seven, my father had achieved considerable success; his career and position were firmly established and his future was secure. There was no earthly reason for him to think the pattern might be altered.

Then, in August, 1903, a client asked George Getty to go to Bartlesville, Indian Territory, on his behalf. My father thought it would be a routine business trip. He did not dream it would change his entire life, completely reshape his future, and eventually make him a multimillionaire.

Arriving in Bartlesville, he was astonished to find that the sleepy little frontier settlement had become a roaring boom town. Purely by chance, he'd made his trip shortly after oil had been discovered in the area. Prospectors, drillers, lease brokers, equipment dealers, and others drawn by the lure of black gold were pouring into the tiny hamlet; its normal population of nine hundred had already more than doubled.

Oil was Bartlesville's sole interest and conversational topic that summer. Rumors of new discoveries and developments flashed through the town hourly. Almost all were false or at best wildly exaggerated, but this did not prevent the circulation of new and even more fanciful reports the next day.

Attorney Getty quickly brought his client's business to a successful conclusion. By all rights, he should have returned to Minneapolis immediately.

But the oil fever that swept Bartlesville was infectious.

At that time, my father knew very little about the oil business. He did, however, have a far-sighted faith in the recently developed internal combustion engine and the still-primitive automobile. He felt the "horseless carriage" would be perfected and mass-produced much sooner than most people then believed possible and realized this would create immensely increased demands for petroleum.

My father became friendly with several oil men in Bartlesville. Among them were the brothers E. B. ("Bud") and Will Carter. Colorful characters and veterans of many great oil rushes, the Carters owned the oil and gas lease on Lot 50, an eleven-hundred-acre land-parcel in the nearby Osage Nation. They wanted to sell the lease and asked my father if he would be interested in buying it.

Oil appeared to offer both opportunity and challenge. George F. Getty recognized the opportunity, and he was unable to resist the challenge. Instinct, hunch—call it what one will—told him to buy the lease from the Carters, and he did, for five hundred dollars. The price was low, but fair. Lot 50 was located miles from the nearest producing oil well.

Father returned home bursting with enthusiasm and promptly informed Mother he intended trying his hand at the oil business in Indian Territory. Sarah Risher Getty's confidence in her husband's judgment, based as it was on twenty-four years of happy and harmonious marriage, remained unshaken by this surprise announcement. Nor was Mother at all unwilling when Father declared that, before long, she and I would make a trip to Indian Territory with him.

My mother and father came from hardy pioneer stock. They had both known hard times and adversity, but they had been brought up in the dynamic American tradition that one went where and when new opportunities presented themselves.

I, of course, could hardly contain myself when told I would accompany my parents to Indian Territory.

Indian Territory!

I was ten years old. My imagination, like that of most boys in that now remote era, had fattened on a heavy diet of lurid wild West adventure stories. Suddenly, adventure far beyond any conjured up in my most extravagant daydreams was almost within my grasp.

"When are we going?" became a ritual question asked with tireless regularity at every meal and just before every bedtime.

Normally an attentive and interested—if somewhat less than brilliant—student, I now found that school palled on me. It was impossible to concentrate on books and lessons when my mind was on my projected trip to what I pictured as the wildest of wild frontiers. Even the active outdoor games I'd always enjoyed seemed dull and boring. Play seemed silly when, in a short while, I would be encountering savage redskin hordes and living the rugged, danger-packed life of a frontiersman.

But if the days dragged slowly for me, they went by rapidly for my parents, who were extremely busy making a thousand and one necessary arrangements and preparations. Father and several of his friends and business associates, including W. F. Bechtel, W. A. Kerr, Frederick V. Brown, John W. Bell, and P. D. McConnell, formed the Great Northern Oil and Gas Company, which would conduct oil exploration and drilling operations in Indian Territory. The company was officially incorporated on October 17, 1903, which, as it happened, was also my father's forty-eighth birthday. Those among his friends inclined to superstition viewed the coincidence as a highly auspicious augury for the future of his venture.

On December 7, 1903, the same group formed a second company. Although Oklahoma would not become a state until 1907, its admission to the Union was taken for granted, as was the name it would be given. Hence, my father and his associates named the new company Minnehoma ("Minne" from Minnesota, "homa" for Oklahoma) Oil Company. Father was elected president of Minnehoma Oil and assigned the rights to the Lot 50 lease to the company.

My first business investment was made at the age of eleven years and one month, and I was among Minnehoma Oil Company's first stockholders. Using five dollars of the money I'd earned doing chores and selling magazines, I subscribed for one hundred shares, which were priced at five cents each.

"There—now you're part owner of the company for which I work," my father said when he signed the stock certificate and gave it to me. "You're one of my bosses."

I'm afraid that remark made little impression on me at the time, but

I was to understand later that it succinctly stated one of George F. Getty's fundamental business philosophies. In his view, the stockholders whose investments provided a company's capital *were* its owners. A corporation's officers were bound to consider themselves employees of the stockholders, to whom they owed loyalty and for whose financial interests and welfare they were responsible.

My father practiced what he preached. During his tenure as Minnehoma Oil's president, the company's stockholders profited handsomely on their investments. In its first year of operation, Minnehoma Oil paid shareholders a 10 per cent dividend. By 1908, the annual dividend had risen to five cents a share, equivalent to the original per-share cost. In 1918, the dividend soared to eighteen cents a share. Between 1904 and 1922, the company would pay total dividends amounting to twenty and a half times the original cost of the stock.

Father ordered drilling operations to commence on Lot 50 in late 1903. The first well—Minnehoma No. 1—struck pay sand at fourteen hundred feet before the year ended. The well came in a gusher, then settled down to producing a steady hundred barrels per day. Father was greatly encouraged, and a second well was begun almost immediately.

At last, on January 19, 1904, we finally set out on our long-awaited trip to Indian Territory. We made the overnight train trip from Minneapolis to Kansas City, where we stopped off for the night. The next day we took the twelve twenty-five train to Bartlesville.

That stage of the journey is etched clearly on my memory. As our train rolled toward Bartlesville, Father talked about oil. Mother listened with a patient, affectionate smile which betrayed the fact that, as yet, she understood very little of his exuberant and highly technical monologue about derricks and drilling rigs, gushers and dry holes.

I paid practically no attention to what my father was saying. I sat hunched forward, staring through the Pullman window, hoping to see painted Indian warriors and gallant U. S. cavalrymen locked in mortal combat on the flat prairie-land across which we were traveling.

"I haven't seen any Indians," I complained after an hour or so.

"Don't worry, son," my father assured me. "You'll be able to see quite a few around Bartlesville."

"Are they dangerous?" I asked eagerly. "Will we have to fight them off?"

"No, they're not dangerous," Father replied with a broad grin. "They're rather quiet and peaceful people. The only Indians we may have to fight off are the ones who sell pottery and blankets outside the railroad station."

These were hardly the answers I wanted to hear. Crestfallen, I turned back to the window. Forlorn as my hopes were, I was not yet willing to abandon them.

Arriving in Bartlesville late that evening, we went directly to our hotel. It was dark, and I was unable to see much en route there. I did, however, obtain a few glimpses of wooden buildings with false fronts and roughly clad, booted men I immediately decided were all cowboys, deputy sheriffs, or outlaws.

I began keeping a diary when I was eleven. I've found the practice excellent discipline, and my diary entries have often proved invaluable memory-joggers. Even the briefest notations serve to close the gulf of years or even decades and bring dimly remembered faces, scenes, and events into sharp and lively focus.

On Friday, January 22, 1904—my first day in Bartlesville—I wrote in my diary: *Fine day. The sun shone for the first time in three days. In the morning I took a walk into the woods, about four miles and back. In the afternoon I walked to a high hill about three miles away.*

Simple and childish as this entry is, it evokes clear and nostalgic recollections.

My lingering disappointment at not having seen Indian hordes and charging cavalry troopers deepened as I took my first walk around Bartlesville. There were no stockades or forts, and not a single gun battle broke the morning quiet. The cowboys, deputies, and outlaws of the night before I now saw were farmers, storekeepers, and oil men. For each false-fronted building in the town, there was one substantial frame house or business structure, and there were even a few made of brick and stone. Bartlesville may have been on the frontier and in Indian Territory, but at first sight it was discouragingly tame and prosaic.

But gradually, other impressions emerged. There were a few men who carried large Colt revolvers strapped to their waists. Heavily laden horse- and mule-drawn wagons jolted through the rutted streets, their drivers cracking long whips over the animals' heads and cursing them roundly through mouthfuls of chewing tobacco. At the edges of the town, crudely built shacks and temporary structures, adjuncts of the oil boom, had sprung up—and beyond them lay vast expanses of countryside to be explored.

My disappointment began to fade that first morning as I hiked out into the country and saw the oil derricks that dotted the landscape and encountered a few Indians in tribal dress plodding along the road.

Within a few days, I had discovered that there was much to occupy a boy's time, interests, and energies in and around Bartlesville. There were horses to be ridden, hikes to be taken, games to be played with boys my own age.

I shortly acquired a small yellow mongrel dog. I named him Jip, and we immediately became inseparable companions; he followed me devotedly wherever I went. Jip was pugnacious and utterly devoid of fear, and I shared my adventures with him, occasionally falling into streams, getting lost in the woods, or incurring the wrath of those upon whom we played our tricks.

Large cattle herds were frequently driven through the streets of Bartlesville. Jip's favorite sport was to run among the plodding beasts, barking loudly, snapping at their heels, and obviously doing his best to stampede them. This invariably brought furious roars from the cowboys driving the herds; they blistered Jip with their profanity, and me as well, for I stood on the sidelines, gleefully urging my dog on to greater efforts.

Trips to Lot 50 with my father were always a great treat. It was a two-hour drive over a rough, potholed road. On red-letter days, Father would hand me the buggy reins and allow me to drive the horses.

Operations on the drilling site were superintended by J. Carl Smith, the same J. Carl who would be my friend in need many years later. When father was busy, J. Carl took me under his wing and answered the myriad questions I always seemed to have ready.

I was greatly interested in what went on at the site. Father's second well was nearing completion, and as I watched the drillers working, I gradually began to understand the principles and techniques involved. Beyond this, I got to know and understand the men who did the work—something that would prove invaluable to me in the future.

Many colorful characters with dubious backgrounds found their way to the oil fields in the early 1900's. One of the more picturesque among them was Henry Starr, who worked for my father on Lot 50.

Not many years before, Starr had been a notorious bandit, highwayman, and stage-robber who was "Wanted—Dead or Alive" throughout the entire Southwest. Henry had reformed, however, and returned to live and work honestly in the Bartlesville area, where he had often operated during his outlaw days.

At least one story about Henry Starr achieved the status of an Oklahoma legend. It appears that at the height of his criminal career Henry had waylaid Jake Bartles, the founder of Bartlesville, on three different occasions and held him up at gunpoint. Although he was a wealthy man, Bartles seldom carried much money on his person. The three holdups netted Henry Starr only a few dollars—a state of affairs he considered utterly intolerable. During the course of the third robbery, Starr lost his temper.

"Damn it, Jake!" he swore angrily. "An important man like you ain't got no business running around carrying nothing but pennies. It's a disgrace!"

Nudging Jake Bartles's paunch with the muzzle of his six-gun, Henry then delivered a classic ultimatum.

"I'm goin' to rob you agin some night, Jake," he promised the quaking Bartles. "And I'm warnin' you. You'd better have five thousand dollars on you when I do. If you ain't, I'm gonna kill you deader'n a dead coyote!"

The next morning, an ashen-faced Jake Bartles presented himself at the bank and drew out five thousand dollars in large bills. He carried the money with him constantly thereafter.

"I'm taking no chances," Bartles explained to his friends. "Henry Starr may be a low-down, no-good, thieving skunk—but he's a man of his word!"

But, for one reason or another, Starr never got around to robbing Jake Bartles again.

Henry always declared that he deplored his earlier sins, but I recall there was always a bright and eager gleam in his eye whenever he re-counted the story of one of his countless illegal escapades.

Ex-bandits or not, almost all oil-field workers loved to spin yarns about their experiences. With a wad of well-chewed tobacco clenched between their teeth or a hand-rolled cigarette dangling fireless from their lips, they could sit for hours swapping tales which were often taller than the derricks towering above them. Naturally, as an eleven-year-old I listened to them with awe and believed every word.

They were a rare breed—tough, hard-working, and intensely loyal to any employer who treated them fairly and squarely. The members of a drilling crew might, and frequently did, batter each other to a pulp on their payday sprees, but differences were invariably forgiven and forgot-ten the next day. The self-generated morale and the degree of camaraderie that prevailed on most drilling sites was remarkable when one considers the conditions under which the men had to work. Housing consisted of shacks or tents, and food was rough fare dished up by traditionally unimaginative bunkhouse cooks the men called "slum-burners" and cursed roundly, regularly, and usually with complete justification.

A shirker or gold brick could ruin morale and wreck production, and naturally there were specimens of this type among the men who applied for work on the drilling sites. My father had what amounted almost to a sixth sense for identifying these types—and he also had a flair for getting rid of them.

When he was in Oklahoma, Father superintended the drilling of Minnehoma's wells. I recall one day on Lot 50, when he was approached by an itinerant oil-field worker who "allowed" that he was looking for a job. My father instinctively recognized that this was a gold brick seeking a rest cure with pay. He let the man talk on about his previous experience and the other jobs he'd held. Finally, the job-seeker grandly demanded to know what sort of "living accommodations" there were on Lot 50.

Keeping a straight face, Father pointed toward the nearest forested hillside.

"Just take your pick of any hollow tree over there," he replied in a matter-of-fact tone. Needless to say, the badly shaken gold brick wasted no time moving on elsewhere.

On March 1, 1904, Father's drillers proudly reported that the second well was nearing completion. Mother, Father, and I went to the site the following morning. The well came in almost as if on schedule. Oil was reached at 1,426 feet, and initial production was around a hundred barrels a day.

With two wells producing on Lot 50, my father felt he could return to Minneapolis. For the next few months, further operations could be handled by J. Carl Smith. Father had unfinished business to take care of in Minneapolis—and he was already planning new and more ambitious ventures.

We left Bartlesville two days later. I did not know it then, but the course my life and business career would follow had already begun to be shaped for me.

4

BY MAY, 1905, Minnehoma Oil Company had six produc-
ing wells on its Lot 50 lease. But petroleum prices were falling. In 1903,
Oklahoma crude sold for $1.03 per barrel. In May, 1905, the price dropped
to fifty-two cents a barrel and was heading even lower.

The immediate cause of the price-break lay in the discoveries made that
year at Cleveland, near Tulsa, and in the Glenn Pool field, both in Indian
Territory. Cleveland boosted Oklahoma production by 330,000 barrels
monthly, while the rich Glenn Pool field added ten times that—over
3,000,000 barrels—to the monthly rate.

This additional production served to drive prices down. Glenn Pool
producers, who lacked adequate storage and transportation facilities,
offered their crude at panic-prices, in some cases selling it as low as
twenty-seven or twenty-eight cents per barrel. Eventually, however, the
price stabilized at around forty cents.

Minnehoma Oil Company was having trouble finding outlets for its
Lot 50 production even at these prices. Consequently, several large storage
tanks had to be constructed on the property to store the surplus.

Under these circumstances, my father and Minnehoma Oil's other
directors agreed it would be wiser to proceed slowly with additional
drilling on the lease. There was little sense in deliberately making a bad
situation worse.

It was another one of those difficult periods for oil men. An old,
familiar, and outwardly paradoxical trend had again begun to develop in
the petroleum industry.

On the one hand, demand for petroleum was rising rapidly and steadily.
New and wider uses and applications were being found for petroleum

products. Oil was beginning to fire industrial boilers, heating and steam plants. Railroads and steamship companies had started converting to oil. For example, in 1905, the Southern Pacific Railroad consumed 2,640,000 barrels of petroleum in its Texas and Louisiana operations alone; the Santa Fe railroad had 224 oil-burning locomotives.

On the other hand, even as demand rose sharply, crude-oil prices were declining.

Why?

The answer is as simple as two plus two—or rather, two minus one. The reason was the same as it had been in 1859–61, when crude prices plunged from twenty dollars to ten cents a barrel; this reason had created parallel situations periodically ever since. Petroleum production was increasing at an ever more rapid rate than consumption.

The petroleum industry has never been an exception to the rule that overproduction inevitably invokes the penalty clauses of the law of supply and demand. Too much petroleum aboveground has always meant lower prices at the wellhead.

Oil men have been acutely aware of this since the earliest days of the industry. Yet overproduction has been the petroleum industry's recurrent chronic occupational disease.

To understand this, it is necessary to examine briefly the two principal causative factors. The first is the deep-seated, obsessive fear of oil famine which has gripped the world ever since Edward Drake brought in his Titusville well. From the very beginning, many people—experienced oil men and learned scientists, to say nothing of politicians and pundits among them—have thought and said that the world's petroleum supply was limited and would be soon exhausted.

Alarmists' predictions of the imminence of a "critical oil shortage" has always been one of the factors which inspired stampedes to locate new oil sources, to find new fields, and drill more wells.

"Find more before we run short," might be said to be the philosophy inspired by the fear of impending oil famine.

"Get it before it's all gone," is the corollary motto that stems from the second cause of chronic petroleum overproduction, from the "law of capture" concept.

A natural underground oil reservoir is invisible; one cannot determine its shape or boundaries. It might well extend for great distance in all directions from a given point aboveground. It can—and very often does—

lie beneath properties belonging to scores or even hundreds of different owners.

Throughout petroleum industry history, a man who drilled on a particular site and brought in a producing well soon saw additional wells spring up on surrounding properties. All the wells drew on the same underground source; each well-owner tried to "capture" as much of the recoverable oil as possible before the reservoir went dry.

It is, of course, crystal clear that some day oil will be found only in museums. This will not happen for decades, probably not for a century. But eventually, all the oil that exists beneath the ground will be exhausted. I do not hesitate to predict that sometime in the twenty-first century, oil will be a scarce commodity. Even though there will be synthetic oil produced from shale or coal, natural crude oil reserves will be used up, particularly if consumption of petroleum continues to expand at the present rate. Unfortunately, vast quantities of petroleum have been wasted since the days when Colonel Drake brought in his first well. It is impossible to estimate how much of this precious natural resource has been squandered through the years, but certainly the quantity, had it been saved, would have been enough to defer the day of eventual oil-famine reckoning for a considerable period.

The first decade of the twentieth century was marked by great oil strikes and rushes which graphically illustrate all these points.

Typical of these was the great oil rush which began on January 10, 1901, when Anthony C. Lucas brought in his famous 100,000-barrel-a-day Spindletop gusher. The well came in with a tremendous roar that was heard—literally and figuratively—far beyond Beaumont, Texas, the town nearest to the drilling site. For days, until it was finally brought under control, the gusher spewed millions of gallons of petroleum over the surrounding countryside.

Spindletop achieved several "firsts" and made several significant contributions to the oil industry's knowledge and future. It was the first big oil discovery of the century, the first successful well drilled in a salt-dome structure and the first important oil well drilled with a rotary rig.

Anthony Lucas, a mining engineer, had long felt that oil existed in salt-dome structures such as Spindletop, a theory previously rejected by the petroleum industry. The gusher proved him right and opened new vistas for the oil prospector and producer. Lucas's well also dramatically demonstrated the practicability of drilling with rotary tools, which were rapidly and widely adopted after Spindletop showed they could be used to drill in formations which defied cable tools.

Then, the grade of crude oil produced by the Spindletop field was ideally suited for refining into fuel oil, an application which was given great impetus as a result. In fact, it might be said that Anthony Lucas' Spindletop strike ushered in the era of fuel oil as a power source.

The Spindletop discovery also precipitated an oil rush greater than any that had been known before. By late March, 1901, Beaumont's pre-Spindletop population of ten thousand had swollen to considerably more than thirty thousand. Speculation caused land values to skyrocket. Land that had previously gone begging at $8.00 an acre and was not even near the producing area sold for $35,000. The price of land within the proved field, worth $10.00 an acre before, soared to $900,000 an acre.

Nearly six hundred companies were formed to buy leases and drill wells. Within a few months after the gusher came in, 214 oil wells—120 of them jammed into one fifteen-acre area—had been completed and countless more were being drilled. Production climbed and was soon approaching the million-barrel-a-month level.

Untold millions of barrels were wasted or destroyed through lack of proper storage facilities or in the huge fires that frequently broke out even though they could have been prevented. Despite profligate waste, the Spindletop field's output remained so great that at least some contracts were made to sell crude for three cents per barrel at the wellhead. By contrast, fresh clear drinking water was sold for five cents a cup on the drilling sites! But the men who drilled the wells at Spindletop and whooped with joy as the gushers spewed forgot that oil is a one-time crop.

Within two years, the Spindletop field's spouting wells began to play out. Too many wells had been drilled, too much oil, and particularly too much of the gas which provided pressure to force the petroleum toward the surface, had been wasted. The great field went into a decline until 1925, when new techniques and better-organized drilling and producing methods revived it. The tens of millions of squandered barrels of oil could never be recovered, however—and the story of Spindletop was repeated in scores of other fields in the years that followed.

The year 1901 saw two other great fields opened—one in California's San Joaquin Valley; the other at Red Fork, just outside Tulsa. The next significant discoveries were made in 1905, at Cleveland, again near Tulsa, and in the Osage Nation, where the great Glenn Pool strike was made.

Burgeoning United States production was glutting the market, but

American producers had to contend with foreign production too. In 1862, the United States produced 99 per cent of the world's crude oil. By 1900, United States production had increased twenty times over 1862, but its percentage of world production had fallen to 42.7 per cent.

Russia had begun exploiting its fabled Baku oil fields in the 1870's; within little more than two decades, annual Russian crude oil production was nearing seventy million barrels. By 1900, Russia, not the United States, was the world's largest oil producer; its output accounted for 51 per cent of the world's crude oil supply.

By 1905, when Oklahoma crude was selling for around forty cents per barrel, Poland was producing oil at a merry clip. Standard Oil Company, fighting a losing battle to maintain its supremacy, was investing huge sums to develop Romania's rich Ploesti oil fields. Important discoveries were made in Mexico; petroleum was being produced in such widely separated places as Canada, Peru, and the Netherlands East Indies.

Obviously, these developments cut deeply into American petroleum exports. Where United States kerosene and other petroleum products had once dominated the world's markets, by 1905 the nation's overseas petroleum trade had shriveled. The consequence was that oil formerly sold for export now remained at home, adding to the surplus.

All these factors considered, it is not at all surprising that the market was glutted and prices fell. Nor is it surprising that Minnehoma Oil Company's management was content, if not to mark time, then at least to move slowly and with caution in conducting its drilling operations and increasing its production on Lot 50's eleven hundred acres.

George F. Getty took advantage of the lull to move his family to California. He and Mother had relatives there; the climate was considerably more salubrious there than in Minnesota; and, even in those days, the Golden State held promise and attraction for those who were at all inclined to migrate.

We made our move to California in 1906, stopping off first in Los Angeles, then going on to San Diego, where my parents originally intended establishing their new home. San Diego, however, fell short of their expectations. The city was still very small, and Father guessed correctly that Los Angeles would grow at a much faster rate and become more of a metropolitan center than San Diego. Nonetheless, he was a bit hesitant to change his plans. Mother and I cast the deciding votes when we declared that we would prefer to live in Los Angeles. As always in matters involving the personal preferences of his family, Father good-naturedly deferred to our wishes, and we returned to Los Angeles.

At first we rented an apartment in the Frontenac on Grand Avenue and later a house near Sunset Park on Wilshire Boulevard. Father was determined to build a house for us in Los Angeles and started to look for a suitable homesite. It was while he was doing this that Father missed a great investment opportunity—and made one of the few mistakes of his business career.

While looking around for property on which to build, he became acquainted with quite a few real estate agents who then, as now, abounded in southern California. One realtor told him of an unusual listing: Santa Catalina Island was for sale. The entire seventy-five-square-mile island, located a few miles off the southern California coast, could be purchased for $250,000 and possibly even less. The property, the realtor pointed out, could very probably be developed and made to pay handsome profits.

My father was highly amused—and not a little taken aback—by the proposition, which he viewed as a monumental example of traditional realtor's exuberance and promptly turned it down.

"I want a lot on which to build a house, and I'm offered an island out in the middle of the ocean!" he complained to my mother. "Next thing I know, some real estate man will be around to sell me a volcano!"

The rest of the story is a California real estate classic. Santa Catalina Island was purchased by the Wrigley interests and developed into a famous West Coast resort area and tourist attraction worth many millions.

As my father, in an uncharacteristically corn-fed outburst of rueful humor, observed many years later, he had missed the boat by passing up an island.

George F. Getty didn't buy Catalina, but he did, in 1907, make an excellent investment by purchasing a 100-by-150-foot lot, which was to become an extremely valuable corner property, on Wilshire Boulevard at Kingsley Drive.

Los Angeles, though larger than San Diego, was still in its infancy. The property was outside the incorporated city limits. Much of Wilshire Boulevard, now one of the world's great thoroughfares, was still unpaved, and the area around the property was mainly ranch- or meadowland studded with occasional eucalyptus trees.

Father had a large, comfortable Tudor-style house built on the property. The house was completed in late 1907 and would remain my parents' home as long as they lived.

In 1906, I was enrolled in the Harvard Military Academy, thus resuming my schooling where it had been broken off by our move from Minneapolis. Harvard Military, then located at Crenshaw and Venice Boulevards, was noted for its high academic standards and, to my sorrow, for its discipline.

Perhaps it was because I had traveled a bit more than my classmates. Possibly, I'd absorbed a little too much of the free-and-easy attitudes of the oil fields during my visits to Indian Territory. Whatever the reasons, during my first weeks I bridled at the school's military regimen, unable to understand why a speck of dust or a slightly tarnished button would elicit such bellows of rage from the cadet-officer upperclassmen. Certainly, transgressions as minor as these didn't seem to warrant long hours of knapsack-weighted extra drill on the hard-surfaced quadrangle that lay between two of the school's several big, yellow-stucco buildings.

More because I found the alternatives distasteful than because I was a particularly adaptable creature, I eventually succeeded in acclimatizing myself to my environment. From then on, demerits and extra fatigues were rare, but I was never entirely happy in the regimented atmosphere. Still I applied myself to my studies with a fair, if not spectacular, degree of success.

I'd had a voracious appetite for reading since boyhood. My favorite subjects were and have always been history and literature. My ambitions were to become a writer or enter the United States Diplomatic Service—or, ideally, to do both simultaneously.

But the pseudo-military regimen at the Harvard Academy chafed, and I did not much relish the idea of attending a private school. I preferred the far less formal and far more democratic atmosphere of the city's excellent public schools. I discussed the matter with my parents who, to my surprise, offered no objections when I told them I would like to attend the Polytechnic High School, and I transferred there to complete my high school education.

While I was going to school in Los Angeles, Minnehoma Oil Company was continuing its program of cautious operation and slow expansion. Although Oklahoma crude prices had reached new lows, my father authorized the drilling of several more wells. Through his shrewd management, the company ended every slump-year with a profit and never failed to pay a dividend to its stockholders.

In 1909, the year I graduated from high school, more wells were being drilled on Minnehoma Oil's Lot 50 lease near Bartlesville, Oklahoma, and my father suggested that I work there as a roustabout during the summer. I accepted his offer of a vacation-period job immediately.

My job lasted only a little more than a month that year. Father made a rather sudden decision to take Mother and me on a European tour. He ordered a new Chadwick touring car and instructed me to pick it up at the Chadwick factory in Pottstown, Pennsylvania. There, as was the custom in those days, the manufacturers would furnish an instructor who would teach me to drive the car while driving it from Pottstown to New York, where my parents and I were scheduled to sail for Europe aboard the White Star liner *Baltic* on July 14.

I went to Pottstown and was delighted by the car. The Chadwick was a large, handsome touring car with a ninety-horsepower engine. It had leather-treaded, metal-studded tires which, by the way, cost one hundred dollars apiece. Pennsylvania had good macadam-surfaced roads, and I can still recall the peculiar and rather pleasant sound the metal tire-studs made as the Chadwick Company's driver wheeled it along at thirty and forty miles per hour.

I learned how to drive and handle the big touring car, and it and I arrived in New York City safely and with time to spare. I met my parents in New York and was overjoyed to hear that I would be allowed to act as their chauffeur in Europe and drive the Chadwick during our tour.

We sailed on the *Baltic*, the car stored in the hold below decks. We spent three months traveling through England, France, Switzerland, Holland, and Germany, seeing and savoring an era and way of life which, five years later, would be swept away forever by the holocaust of World War I.

5

M Y PARENTS and I arrived back in the United States during the fall of 1909. We returned to Los Angeles, where I resumed my formal education by enrolling in the University of Southern California, more generally known as U. S. C.

For a time, I had seriously considered trying for the United States Naval Academy at Annapolis. I would have liked to become a naval officer, an idea which my father opposed vigorously. He argued that the world was at peace, and that the United States had not been involved in any major war for nearly half a century. Indeed, the last big conflict had been a Civil War, and there was hardly any likelihood of history repeating itself in that regard. All in all, he could see little possibility of war anywhere in the world, a view that was shared in that period by the overwhelming majority of people all over the face of the globe. It was a time of peace, and the future looked peaceful. My father contended that I would be serving no very useful purpose by entering the Navy.

Convinced, I transferred my ambitions to the field of diplomacy and decided that I would like to enter the United States Foreign Service—the State Department. Because several fine courses in political science and economics were being offered by the University of California at Berkeley, I transferred there after a short time at U. S. C.

I fear that I was anything but the conventional, Joe College type of undergraduate. I felt that my purpose in attending a university was to study and, I hoped, to learn—not to play football, engage in campus politics, or draw cartoons for the student humor magazine. I had no particular taste for the frantic, overorganized, and tightly compartmented undergraduate social life which even then played an inordinate part in American higher education.

I resented the rigidly stratified and patently artificial class system I found operating among my fellow students. It struck me as pernicious, a direct contradiction of the American educational system's avowedly democratic principles. I preferred to choose and make my own friends—male or female—and to measure them by my own standards rather than by the traditional "Org or Non-Org?" or "which house?" yardsticks.

Also, the playground atmosphere in which undergraduates reveled seemed wasteful of time and energy. Although I had an entirely normal appetite for sports, relaxation, and wild-oat sowing, I considered these secondary to the business at hand—namely, the acquiring of an education. I was, perhaps, slightly ahead of my classmates in this regard. I'd already learned that it was entirely possible to do one's adolescent hell-raising anywhere, not solely at a university.

Again, I suppose my experiences in the oil fields influenced my views and opinions. I spent a month in 1909 and my entire summers during the next three years working in Oklahoma, first as an oil field roustabout and then, after serving a grueling apprenticeship, as a tool-dresser.

In no way would I care to belittle the benefits I derived from my university education. Certainly they were many and great and have stood me in excellent stead throughout my business career and in my private life. On the other hand, I cannot help but feel that many of the most important and valuable lessons were learned in the hard and practical schools provided by the oil fields of Oklahoma.

True, I was still in my teens, a wealthy man's son, and I worked on the drilling sites and rigs mainly during my holidays from school. However, none of this made the least difference to the men with whom I worked and lived. I, like anyone else, had to prove myself and my ability to get along with others and function with split-second precision as a member of a closely knit and extremely hard-working team.

There were many tests, no less rigorous or decisive because they were unofficial and informal, which one had to pass before being accepted by one's fellow workers in the oil fields. I learned this even during my first stint in the fields during 1909, when memories of the Harvard Military Academy's tough, arbitrary discipline were still fresh in my mind.

No cadet officers came through the weather-beaten bunkhouse on Minnehoma Oil's Lot 50 to make an inspection and gig me if I failed to clean the floor under my cot. But a disapproving glance from the leathery roustabout who occupied the next cot had as strong a remedial effect and proved as much a future deterrent as any extra drill with a full knapsack.

Nor did I need any bugle calls or alarm clocks to awaken me at 5:00 A.M. It was enough to know that late rising was equated with shirking and taken as an admission that one was unable—or, what was worse, unwilling —to stand the gaff of the standard, six-day-a-week, twelve-hour work shift. The fact that I was not yet seventeen was immaterial. I had voluntarily chosen to take a man-sized job. Hence I was expected to do a man's work—and to do it like a man, and not like a boy.

By my second year on Lot 50, I was also expected to pull my own weight and throw—and take—my share of the punches when the inevitable donnybrooks developed during payday-night visits to town. These frequently riotous affrays sprang from such earth-shaking controversies as which of two or more rival drilling crews was the best or fastest or had the greatest collective capacity for the caustic liquids then being sold in Oklahoma under the totally false premises that they were whisky. And, I might add, no breach of oil-field etiquette was considered more serious than the failure to work one's full twelve-hour shift on the day following such a battle.

I recall how my seventeen-year-old pride swelled on a hot July morning in 1910, when I was finally notified that I had passed my tests and proved myself.

"Damn it, Paul, get a move on!" the driller—the man who bossed the crew—growled at me shortly after I reported for work on the drilling site.

It was the first time that he had addressed me as "Paul" and not just as "Hey, kid!" The verbal accolade was not missed by the other men with whose at least tacit concurrence it had, of course, been bestowed. Thenceforth, I was considered, and could consider myself, a full-fledged roustabout, an equal member of the work crew.

Roustabout jobs involved varied and always strenuous tasks. Machinery had to be unloaded, assembled, shifted, and operated. Lengths of pipe had to be stacked, and pipelines laid from wellheads to storage tanks. All in all, there were a thousand and one chores, not a few of which called for rapid, monkey-like scrambles up and down the seventy-four-foot derrick or other forms of extreme physical exertion.

But the jobs called for brains as well as brawn. Mistakes could result in serious damage to expensive, hard-to-replace machinery and equipment and cause very costly delays and stoppages in the drilling and producing operations. Errors in judgment or timing could also prove dangerous to life and limb—not only to the individual who made the errors, but also to others working on the site or rig. A whipping rope, snapped cable or kicking brake could easily maim or kill, and so could a fall.

In the days of cable-tool drilling, the drilling crew proper consisted of two men—the driller and the tool-dresser. The tool-dresser, or "toolie," was not only an expert all-around oil-field worker, but also a highly specialized blacksmith. It was his job to sharpen and, when necessary, to repair and retemper the bits and other tools used in cable-tool drilling. The toolie's portable forge was always close to the rig and was in almost constant operation. Today's special-process steels were unknown at that time; the cutting edges of the bits dulled or chipped frequently, especially when drilling in hard formations. It was imperative that the tool-dresser maintain an adequate supply of freshly sharpened and serviceable bits ready for instant use.

I decided that I wanted to be a tool-dresser. The rawhide-tough, veteran toolie on one of the Lot 50 drilling crews—an old-timer whose surname, Grizzle, matched his sun-baked, grizzled appearance—offered to teach me the trade. An artisan who took great pride in his work, Grizzle was a hard taskmaster but an excellent teacher. The standards he set for himself were high, and he demanded no less from his pupil.

Countless were the occasions when Grizzle inspected a bit I had laboriously sharpened and indicated his dissatisfaction by squirting a brown stream of tobacco juice into the red-hot forge and glaring at me balefully.

"Dammit, I could chew rock faster'n you could drill it with the edges you've put on this thing!" he'd snort contemptuously. And back I would go to the forge to start all over again.

But I was genuinely interested in the work and gradually managed to master the tricks of the trade. After a time, even the exacting Grizzle admitted that I was making good progress, and by 1911, I was considered sufficiently trained and experienced to be given a tool-dresser's job on one of the Minnehoma Oil Company's drilling crews. Such was the reputation of my mentor, Grizzle, that the mere fact he had passed me out was all the recommendation I needed to be accepted as a full-fledged toolie by all the drillers and tool-dressers on Lot 50.

There was much more activity on Lot 50 in 1911 than there had been the previous year. Crude oil prices, having dipped to dismal lows, had begun to rise again. My father and his associates correctly guessed that it was time to accelerate Minnehoma Oil's rate of expansion.

Additional wells were being drilled on the eleven-hundred-acre property. My father also purchased seven new leases near Cleveland, Oklahoma, where there was a sizable oil boom; among them were the Russell and Michaels leases, each covering eighty-acre properties on which wells were drilled soon thereafter. Both properties proved productive and profitable. During the next several years, the two leases would produce more than a million barrels of crude oil and show a total excess recovery—a net profit over all costs and expenses—of some $850,000.

Crude oil prices continued to rise in 1912, and Minnehoma Oil continued to acquire more leases and drill more wells, paying its stockholders a four-cent-per-share dividend that year.

It was in 1912 that my parents approved my proposal to finish my university education abroad, at Oxford University.

I completed my summer's work in the oil fields and, in November, sailed for England.

My desire to attend Oxford had been prompted by several considerations and was the result of long and careful deliberation. I had just about made up my mind to enter the United States Diplomatic Service when I finished my schooling. To prepare myself for such a career, I felt that I needed to take the best available globally orientated courses in economics and political science. In the pre-World War I era, the United States had not yet taken its place among the world's leading powers. The curricula of American universities, like the policies of the American government and the outlook and mood of the American people, were largely isolationist, or at best "Western Hemispheric" in orientation. In those days, British diplomats were universally conceded to be the finest in the world, and they were almost all Oxford or Cambridge trained.

Then, I liked what I'd heard about English teaching methods, which varied greatly from those employed in the United States. In America, undergraduates were required to attend a certain number of formal classes and to take a certain number of formal examinations over a given period. They were, in effect, spoon-fed learning at a rate geared to the abilities of the median student. In contrast, the English universities' tutor system gave the student far more freedom and latitude, and thus more opportunity, to learn as much and as fast as he desired and was able. He was also encouraged to read and study widely, far beyond the strict limits of his "subject" or "course."

Lastly, I wanted to see and learn more at firsthand about Great Britain and Europe. I planned to take an extensive tour after completing my studies at Oxford.

Arriving in England, I established myself in simple but comfortable "digs" located above an antique shop at 14 The High, Oxford. I began my studies under the direction of a Magdalen College tutor and, for the first time, found an educational system in which I felt completely at home and at ease.

Students at Oxford were considered to be mature and responsible individuals rather than unreliable adolescents. The long-established theory seemed to be that, since a student had expressed a desire to obtain an education by enrolling in the university, he could be trusted to pursue his studies without constant, niggling supervision.

A student came and went much as he pleased. If he chose to waste time, miss lectures, or fall behind on his reading, that was his affair. Success or failure was dependent on him alone; only he would be the loser if he frittered away his opportunities.

There was much emphasis on sports and social life at Oxford, but oddly enough, both were far less formalized than in the United States. My own favorite sports were swimming, boxing, and weight-lifting and, although I was tolerably good at all three, there was absolutely no compulsion to go out for sports or to join school teams. One could enjoy sport for its own sake.

Being well aware that England was ruled by a monarch and had hereditary nobles and sharply drawn class lines, I expected social life at Oxford to be even more stratified and compartmented than in American universities. To my surprise, the exact opposite proved true. Although I was an American who spoke with what amounted to virtually a foreign accent and had worked in the oil fields, I was accepted at face value and without reservation by my fellow undergraduates. Many became close friends, and I was frequently a guest in their homes during weekends and holidays.

Surprising to me, indeed, was the free and easy intermingling of students from many and varied walks of life. There were no Greek-letter fraternities to which one had to belong as a prerequisite to participation in undergraduate social life. I recall, for example, that I was introduced to H.R.H. Edward, then Prince of Wales and now, of course, the Duke of Windsor, by a fellow student who was neither titled nor wealthy. The introduction, incidentally, later ripened into a friendship that has endured to this day.

My days at Oxford passed swiftly and pleasantly. In June, 1913, I received my diploma in economics and political science. My formal education was completed, and I was ready to top it off with a traditional grand tour.

I remained in England long enough to attend the Derby, after which I left for Berlin, spending a week there before going on to Hamburg and then to Kiel, the great German naval base.

I saw much evidence of Hohenzollern Germany's rapidly growing naval might at Kiel, but certainly there was no indication there, or anywhere else on my travels, that Europe would soon be plunged into war. If anything, there was much to assure one that the era of peace would continue for a long time to come.

Travel was very free and uncomplicated in comparison to what it would be in later years. Passports were practically unknown. Of all the countries I visited, only Russia demanded that travelers within her borders have passports. Only Russia exercised control over who came into the country by requiring visas before entry.

There were no exchange restrictions, either. One could move across borders carrying as much or as little money of any and all nations as one wished. The world was still on the gold standard, and every bank stood ready to pay the gold equivalent for banknotes and currency. Nor were there any income-tax forms to fill out or exit permits to clear with the authorities. All national currencies were as steady and strong as the Rock of Gibraltar, which still stood as the invincible symbol of the might of the British Empire.

From Kiel, I traveled by boat to Korsor in Denmark, from where I continued on to Copenhagen and thence to Sweden. I spent several days sight-seeing in Stockholm, going from there to Abo, Finland. From Abo, my travels carried me to Helsingfors. After a few days, I continued on to St. Petersburg—now Leningrad—in Russia.

In St. Petersburg, I stayed at the ornate Astoria Hotel and spent the days sight-seeing and in taking Russian lessons. After a week or so, I had mastered enough of the difficult language to get by, at least in infinitives and the present tense, and I took the train for Moscow.

No sooner had I seated myself in my compartment than I was joined by a young American married couple. Husband and wife gave me one quick glance and evidently took me to be a native Russian who understood no English. As soon as they sat down, they launched into a bitterly vituperative quarrel, angrily accusing each other of a wide variety of faults and failings. The argument went on throughout the trip, becoming nastier and more personal with each exchange of accusation and recrimination.

I was extremely embarrassed, but there was nothing I could do. Seats in the compartments were reserved by ticket and could not be exchanged. I would have read, but the only books I had with me in my bags were in English, and had I taken one of them out, the couple would have realized that I understood every word they said—and that would have been even more embarrassing for all three of us. Thus I sat in acute discomfort, staring blankly out of the window while the husband and wife continued their furious bickering throughout the entire four-hundred-mile journey from St. Petersburg to Moscow.

I remained in Moscow for a week, then booked passage aboard a Volga steamer bound for Astrakhan and the Caspian Sea. I doubt if I could have chosen a better way to see a large segment of European Russia. The boat moved slowly down the Volga, making frequent stops to take on and discharge passengers and cargo. The trip gave me the chance not only to see Russia, but to obtain a feel of the country and its people as well.

To a great extent, I shared the impressions and reactions of those who have been moved to remark about the enigma of Russia. The country was vast; the terrain often reminded me of the United States and Canada. Everything was on a grand scale. Long distances had to be traversed, and there were great stretches of flatland reminiscent of the American prairie.

There were countless apparent contradictions and paradoxes. On the one hand, there were many and very striking evidences of great wealth. There were endless rows of opulent town houses in the cities, unnumbered great estates with magnificent manor houses in the country areas. On the other hand, in such cities as St. Petersburg and Moscow, one encountered hordes of people who were shoeless, clad in rags, and who slept regularly in the streets or in the public squares. By Western European standards, the common people appeared to be very poor. I could not help but sense the strange, brooding fatalism that showed itself in the people even when they were at their gayest and most exuberant emotional peaks. I was also struck by the ennervating effect that the Czarist government's cumbersome bureaucracy had on almost every phase and facet of life. Papers— reams of papers—all properly executed, signed, countersigned, stamped, and sealed, were needed before the average Russian citizen could lawfully engage in even some of the simplest of everyday activities.

All these things and more were apparent on the surface, but at no time during my weeks in Russia did I receive any hint or inkling to make me dream that the country would be swept by bloody revolution and civil war only a few years later. On the contrary, I often marveled at the placid good nature of the peasants and workers and the complacency of the educated and more prosperous individuals I met.

Disembarking from the Volga steamer at its Astrakhan terminus, I learned that a boat was leaving later that day for Baku. I obtained my ticket and was told that I would actually have to take two boats. Astrakhan is situated on the delta formed by the Volga as it empties into the Caspian Sea. The first boat would navigate the shallow channels to the sea and then go an additional forty miles to meet a second, larger steamer which would take me the rest of the way. The Caspian there is extremely shallow, and no vessel of any appreciable draught could approach any closer than forty miles to land. In all the first stage of the journey covered some eighty miles—half through the delta channels, half to deeper water in the Caspian itself.

Transferring to a somewhat larger vessel forty miles out in the inland sea, I went to my cabin and discovered that I was to share it with a Russian prince about my own age. He spoke excellent English and we soon became fast friends, particularly after a Caspian storm sprang up on the first night out. I was a good sailor; my companion was not. I helped him as much as I could, and he expressed his gratitude and assured me that he would forever after stand ready to return the favor.

The decrepit steamer rode through the storm, but it suffered some damage, and the captain put into port about 180 miles north of Baku. My friend, whose name I have long since forgotten, and I had experienced enough Caspian Sea travel and took a train the rest of the way to Baku.

I spent several days in Baku, inspecting the great and fabulously rich oil fields there. I had many long conversations, in my by then greatly improved Russian, with the drillers, tool-dressers, and roustabouts in the Baku fields. The experience proved that oil-field workers were much the same no matter where they worked or what language they spoke.

I was traveling on a monthly allowance of two hundred dollars which I received from my father. The money was sent to me periodically at various stops on my itinerary. There was supposed to be a remittance waiting for me at Baku. I went to the appropriate bank, only to learn that no money had been received. As I was then low on funds, I cabled my father that my remittance had not arrived and asked him to trace the money.

I made two trips a day to the bank, but nothing came in. After a few days, by then practically broke, I encountered my friend and erstwhile cabin-mate, the Russian prince.

He said that he was bored with Baku and asked me if I cared to go on to Tiflis with him. I admitted that I did not have funds for the journey, but that I was expecting money from my father.

"I'll loan you all you need!" my friend exclaimed. "You can have the bank forward your money to Tiflis when it arrives."

I accepted his offer and we proceeded to Tiflis, where I again made my twice-a-day pilgrimage to the bank, without avail. The Prince laughed it all off, pressed more money on me, and we moved on, hiring a car and driver and taking the Georgian Military Road to Pyatigorsk. We took a Black Sea steamer from Novorossisk to Yalta.

To add to our financial problems, a thief entered our cabin while we slept aboard the steamer and stole the money we had in our trousers pockets. Luckily, my friend had some reserve funds in his coat, and, after reporting the theft to the police, we continued our travels together, touring the Crimean battlefields and then taking the train to Vienna. Once more, my friend advanced me the money I needed for the trip, and once more I ordered the bank, this time at Yalta, to forward the remittance to me at my next address.

I found no remittance in Vienna, and I made the now-customary two trips a day to the bank. The Russian prince did not go to Vienna and went on to Rome. He offered to advance me even more money, but this time I decided I had best wait for my allowance to catch up.

The money arrived several days later, in an envelope that was literally covered with stamps and scrawled forwarding addresses. In the envelope was a draft for $350, scarcely more than the amount I owed my friend, the Prince. As luck would have it, I received a telegram from him the same day. He said he was low on funds, and I naturally wired him the money I had borrowed. This left me with only ten dollars or so. Fortunately, the next remittance from my father arrived in Vienna about a week later.

I have never seen or heard from my Russian friend since then. I have often wondered how he survived the upheavals which soon thereafter wracked his country and its people. I hope he came through it all safely and successfully, for he was a most generous and entertaining traveling companion and a good friend whom I would have liked to have seen again.

I spent an entire month in Vienna, savoring to the full the never-again *Gemütlichkeit* of that fabulous city as it was under the Hapsburgs. My next stop was Budapest, then one of the world's most beautiful and gayest cities—the Paris of *Mitteleuropa*, the Magyars called it with every good reason.

Once more boarding a river steamer, I cruised down the Danube to Belgrade and Bucharest. From the Black Sea port of Constanza, I traveled by ship to Constantinople, now Istanbul. The unique beauty of this colorful and historic city caught my fancy, and I stayed several weeks, marveling at such landmarks as the Hagia Sophia and sipping *raki* or thick Turkish coffee in the cafés along the Bosporus.

From Constantinople I journeyed to Smyrna, now called Izmir, whence I crossed the Aegean to Greece. My long-lasting love affair with ancient Greek sculpture, which has an important place in my art collection, dates from this visit.

On December 14, 1913, I took a ship from Piraeus to Alexandria, Egypt. On the second day out, which happened to be my twenty-first birthday, we ran head-on into one of those sudden, incredibly violent storms one is liable to encounter in the Mediterranean during the winter months. The ship, a rusty, battered, three-thousand-ton Romanian steamer, the name of which I have conveniently blocked from my memory, seemed reluctant to ride out the storm. The ancient tub acted as though it was tired of trying—and for several hours, even the ship's officers agreed that there was some doubt whether the vessel would survive the savage buffeting of wind and water. Their further admission that the ship's far-too-few lifeboats were unserviceable hardly made the polyglot passengers less panicky or more cheerful. I recall that I held on grimly to my chair in the dining saloon and wondered idly if I would ever "celebrate" another birthday.

However, by some major miracle, the ship managed to remain afloat until the storm finally subsided, and eventually it limped into Alexandria Harbor. I remained in Egypt until February, 1914, viewing with awe the remnants and ruins of the great civilization of the ancient Egyptians.

Embarking finally on the Cunard liner *Franconia*, I left Egypt and went to Gibraltar, from where I made an overland tour of Spain that lasted until early in April, when I went to Paris. I remained there until July.

In June, my parents came over to Europe aboard the German liner *Vaterland*. They landed at Hamburg and toured through Germany, making their way at a leisurely pace to Paris, where it had been arranged that we would meet.

On Sunday, June 28, 1914, I was attending the running of the Grand Prix at the Bois de Boulogne race track with a party of friends. Our seats were not far from the box occupied by M. Raymond Poincaré, the President of France.

During the afternoon, we noticed a sudden stir around M. Poincaré's box. A breathless official messenger accompanied by two uniformed gendarmes made his way to the President and, after saluting smartly, handed him an envelope.

M. Poincaré tore open the envelope, took out the message that was inside, and read it hurriedly. His face showed that its contents were serious. My friends and I wondered what momentous news had been brought to the President of France. It wasn't until later in the afternoon that we saw the shrieking headlines which announced the assassination of the Austrian Crown Prince, Archduke Franz Ferdinand, and his wife at Sarajevo.

The pace of life did not change in Paris. While the French public appeared shocked at the news, there were few if any Frenchmen who imagined that the incident would lead to war.

My parents and I had an altogether pleasant stay in Paris visiting the museums and galleries, attending theaters and concerts. Although an international crisis was mounting steadily, there was little sign of it in the French capital. All attention there was focused on the Caillaux trial, a sensational courtroom carnival which stemmed from a typically Gallic boudoir-scandal-cum-murder.

The wife of Joseph Caillaux, a prominent French politician, had killed the editor of *Figaro* after the latter published some lurid letters she had exchanged with her husband before their marriage. Mme. Caillaux was on trial for murder, and each day, Parisian newspapers carried torrid accounts of the sensational revelations that had been made in court. The courtroom was always jammed, and huge crowds formed outside the doors hoping to get in. My father, presenting himself to some minor functionary as a member of the American Bar—which, of course, he was—obtained not only admission but was given a sort of guest-of-honor's chair during one trial session. Eventually, as anyone knowing French justice might have imagined, Mme. Caillaux was acquitted amidst cheers and tears from the courtroom "audience."

There was considerable talk of war—but it was still only talk when we left Paris for London on July 27. The next morning, exactly one month after the assassination at Sarajevo, we awoke in our London hotel to learn that Austria had declared war on Serbia. Within a few days, most of Europe had been plunged into war.

My father found it extremely difficult to arrange our return passage to the United States. Many liners had been taken off the Atlantic passenger runs and pressed into service as troop transports. Tens of thousands of Americans, caught abroad when the hostilities started, were clamoring for berths on all available ships. To make matters worse, in the first flurry of excitement, normal international banking procedures were suspended. It was impossible to cash letters of credit or traveler's checks.

Fortunately, my father had previously purchased return tickets on the Cunard Line. The steamship company did all it could do to honor these as quickly as possible, but the rush was so great that we didn't sail until September 12, 1914.

Our ship was the *Lusitania*, the giant Cunarder which, a few months later, would be sent to the bottom by German U-boat torpedoes, carrying with her 1,198 men, women, and children. Our own trip, however, was entirely uneventful and we arrived in New York almost exactly as stated on the sailing schedules.

As yet, the European war had made no appreciable changes in the patterns of American life. New York, where my parents and I spent a little time before they went on to California, was much the same as it had been when I last saw the city two years before. So was the rest of the country I traveled across when, in late September, I took the train to Tulsa, Oklahoma.

But if I could notice no major changes elsewhere, I could certainly see them in myself.

I was nearly twenty-two, and my student days were over forever.

It was time for me to start work, to begin a career.

6

I CANNOT honestly claim that I possessed any innate talent nor even any particular desire for a business career. I'm quite certain that if I'd had a brother or brothers interested in business, I would have gone ahead with my plans to enter the U. S. Foreign Service.

My father made no overt effort to deter me from this goal. He did, however, point out that I was an only child, and thus the logical person to carry on the business he had so painstakingly built over the years. My father was also an individualist who felt that each man could best create his future on his own rather than as a cog in the complex machinery of a large, established organization.

He maintained that my impatience with slow-moving educational systems and my fast jump from roustabout to tool-dresser were proofs that I would not be content waiting out the long years it took to climb the rungs of the government service ladder.

We did not argue over the question of my career; as always when our opinions differed, my father and I debated the matter reasonably and logically.

"You've practically grown up in the oil industry," he concluded. "You already know as much—and possibly more—about it than many men who are actively and successfully engaged in the business."

In the end, we arrived at a compromise. I agreed that I would try my hand at the oil business in Oklahoma before taking any decisive steps in other directions. For his part, Father agreed to advance me one hundred dollars per month for my personal expenses and provide funds with which I could buy low-cost leases on properties I considered promising. If I brought in any producing oil wells, we would share the profits, 70 per cent going to my father, the remaining 30 per cent to me.

I went to Tulsa, where the Minnehoma Oil Company had recently established field offices in the R. T. Daniel Building. I arrived in Tulsa shortly before the end of September, 1914, and rented a small but reasonably clean and comfortable room at the Cordova Hotel for six dollars per week. I also arranged to take my meals at a nearby boarding house, paying the proprietor another six dollars weekly.

In later years, I could recall with amusement that more than one future millionaire hungrily eyed the last chop or stuffed himself with bread and potatoes at the boarding-house table. Several of the impecunious but ever and avidly hopeful wildcatters with whom I boarded there were destined to strike it rich. Notable among them was my friend R. A. Josey, a kind and jocular man who later amassed a very large fortune in the oil fields.

Soon after I got to Tulsa, I bought a much used—and abused—Model T Ford. Decrepit and balky, it refused to respond to any but the most vigorous cranking when I wanted to start its engine. Incapable of traveling at much more than thirty-five miles per hour, even when headed down a steep grade, the wheezing lizzy could be brought to a shuddering halt only by tramping heavily and simultaneously on both the brake and reverse-gear pedals. Nevertheless, the senile jalopy provided transportation for my travels around the oil fields and long served as my mobile field-headquarters—so much so that I can, in a manner of speaking, say that I made my first million dollars in its sagging front seat.

The first stage of my wildcatting career was hardly marked by any meteoric success. Although Father's Minnehoma Oil Company was flourishing, this had no direct bearing on my own operations. I was working independently and at that time had no connection with the company, save, of course, that I was still one of its stockholders by virtue of my hundred-share purchase in 1903.

The fall of 1914 was not the most opportune time for a beginner operating on a shoestring budget. Important new oil discoveries in Oklahoma had served to raise the prices of leases and to depress the price of crude oil. The great Cushing Field, which was still being developed by such veteran producers as Tom Slick, had already reached a daily production in excess of 280,000 barrels. The Healdton Field near Ardmore, with more than 250 wells already drilled, was producing 68,000 barrels daily.

These additional floods of petroleum had their predictable effect on crude prices. Purchasing pipeline companies, mainly the Prairie Oil and

Gas Company, balked at paying the $1.05-per-barrel price to which Oklahoma oil had risen by early 1914. By refusing to buy and carry all oil produced—pegging the quantities it would buy first at 75 per cent, then as low as 35 per cent of production—the pipeline companies broke the price. Lows of 55 cents and even 40 cents per barrel were reached that year in Oklahoma.

Notwithstanding this serious price break, exploration and drilling continued at a furious pace throughout the state. Much of the activity centered on the rich Cushing Field, which lay east of the town of Cushing in a sort of no man's land between the Indian nations and what had formerly been Oklahoma Territory.

Cushing itself had become a roaring helldorado, a pattern closely followed by the four boom towns—Drumright, Dropright, Allright, and Damnright—which had sprung up in the Cushing Field itself. Of these, Drumright was the largest and would eventually become a thriving, stable, and permanent community.

But in 1914, the towns were showing no signs that they would ever achieve any degree of respectability. Cushing, its population swollen to many times its normal size, was the railhead to which oil-field supplies and equipment were delivered in freight cars and then transshipped by horse- and mule-drawn wagons to the drilling sites. Conditions in Cushing bordered on complete anarchy. Not only oil men but armies of gamblers, prostitutes, thieves, and confidence men had swarmed into the town.

Gambling establishments, cribs, and "blind pigs" sprouted along the dirt streets, which were churned into thigh-deep bogs by steel-tired wagons and the hoofs of draught horses. Housing of any kind was at a premium; at night, the tables in Cushing's pool halls were rented as beds, with two and sometimes three men sharing a single table. Fights, knifings, and shootings were common occurrences, as were holdups and robberies. In the gambling halls, heavily armed guards sat or stood on balconies overlooking the gaming tables.

A single, incredibly bad road led fourteen miles east from Cushing to Drumright. Known to oil men as "the road from Jericho to Jerusalem," it was alleged to be passable only on horseback or by Model T Ford. The road was perpetually jam-packed with freight wagons, moving with capacity loads toward Drumright and the fields, or returning empty to Cushing.

Drumright was a somewhat smaller but even wilder version of Cushing. Flimsy shacks and mud-spattered tents spread out in disorderly rows and clumps. Between them were piles of green lumber, stacks of pipe, or jumbles of machinery and equipment.

The boom town's Tiger Creek Avenue was a raucous focal point for vice of all kinds. Prostitutes, panders, crooked gamblers, out-and-out thugs all gathered there to fleece and rob the oil-field workers when they came to town on payday.

Speculators had a field day. Land values soared. Leases which had been worth a few hundred dollars were traded back and forth, and their prices spiraled up into the tens of thousands.

It was not unusual for leases on undrilled property, worth forty or fifty dollars per acre a year before, to be sold at a price of three thousand dollars an acre and even more.

Obviously, the existing situations and conditions had their discouraging aspects for the tyro, but there were also innumerable success stories to give new heart and hope to even the most luckless wildcatting operator. Several men with whom I became good friends were among those whose good fortune provided the most impressive examples.

Easy-going, good-natured Marion Lionel Travis was only twenty-eight in 1914. Starting a few years before with almost no capital, he had already made his first million.

Young Bill Roeser, who had made and lost two or three fortunes in the oil business, was busily making yet another. As proof, he customarily wore a neatly fanned-out ten-thousand-dollar bill in his buttonhole.

John Markham, then in his mid-thirties, took a gamble and bought the unproven Sarah Rector Lease in the north end of the Cushing Field. Drilling quickly showed that Markham's property was one of the richest in all Oklahoma oil history—and he was a multimillionaire.

R. M. McFarlin, a kindly, warmhearted man, had been a failure in the cattle business. With dogged perseverance, he tried again—in the oil business, where he achieved spectacular success. Part owner of the McMan Oil Company, one of the most successful oil-producing companies in the United States, McFarlin had made many millions. Despite his great wealth, he remained an extremely friendly, straightforward man who often took the time and trouble to have long talks with me, and I learned much about the oil business from him.

Many other men were also achieving swift and notable success and making large fortunes in the Oklahoma oil boom. Overenthusiastic local boosters were exuberantly predicting that the Cushing Field alone would soon be producing a million barrels of oil and a new oil millionaire each day. The prophecy was never entirely fulfilled, but new wells continued to come in, and word of each new strike would set off fresh waves of speculation and of prospecting and drilling activity.

Anyone who wished to keep posted on the latest developments went naturally to the lobby of the Tulsa Hotel. This was the unofficial headquarters for oil operating in that part of Oklahoma and a highly reliable information center. In the evening, the lobby was crowded with established oil producers, hopeful wildcatters, equipment dealers, lease brokers, and others, all trading reports and rumors and often transacting large-scale business. Some lease brokers found it unnecessary to maintain any other offices; they were able to do a brisk and profitable trade in leases without ever moving from one of the hotel's large, leather-upholstered armchairs.

I realized the value of up-to-the-minute information. In between my frequent and regular trips to the oil fields, I spent considerable time in the Tulsa Hotel lobby, where I became acquainted with a great many oil men and their methods of doing business. At first, I did far more listening than talking. Then, as my store of information increased, I discovered that I, too, could swap bits of news and frequently learn things of value and advantage.

I began doing business as a lease broker, trading in low-priced oil and gas leases on properties in and around the Tulsa, Cushing, and Cleveland areas. I started slowly, feeling my way with caution and conducting my operations on a modest scale. Consequently, my profits were microscopically small compared to those being reaped by successful wildcatting operators who had actually brought in producing wells.

This did not discourage me unduly. I knew I had much to learn—and unlearn—before plunging into actual drilling operations. Besides, I had found no leases which I felt were sufficiently promising to warrant costly exploratory drilling and yet priced within the limits of the sums available to me. I was satisfied to bide my time until I did locate a property which was at once reasonably priced and also, in my opinion, likely to produce oil.

The science of petroleum geology was still in its infancy. It had not yet gained any wide degree of acceptance, and much oil prospecting was still being conducted largely on a "by guess and by God" basis. In fact, many old-time oil men sneered openly at the suggestion that "some damned bookworm" could help them find oil. There were even those who preferred to rely on oil diviners and "dowsers" rather than to have any traffic with the newfangled scientists.

T. N. Barnsdall, a great and fabulously successful Oklahoma oil pioneer, was one who had his own, unique and rather bizarre theory about the best way to find oil.

"You sniff for it," Barnsdall declared, often and with great sincerity. "A good oil man can smell the stuff—even when it's three thousand feet under the ground!"

For my part, I belonged to the small minority that already believed in the science of petroleum geology. Let me hasten to make clear that I did not consider it an infallible science. Rather, I felt that, as with all things in nature, there must be some logical order to the manner in which petroleum was distributed beneath the earth's surface. I was convinced that geology provided the oil prospector with certain generally fairly reliable guides and indicators to aid him in the search for oil. I obtained all the printed matter I could find on the subject and studied it thoroughly, talked at length with geologists and watched them at work, and applied what I learned when sizing up leasable properties.

My first year as an independent operator in the oil business was not precisely what one could call a resounding success. Although I did manage to show a profit on my activities as a lease broker, my 30 per cent share of the net proceeds hardly added up to any monumental total.

Then, in the late fall of 1915, I made one of my customary property-reconnoitering tours, this time to Muskogee County, some distance south-east of Tulsa. In the course of my visit, I inspected a tract known as the Nancy Taylor Allotment near the town of Stone Bluff, Oklahoma, and saw that, according to all I had learned about petroleum geology, the property was highly promising.

Shortly afterwards, I ascertained that a half-interest in a lease on a part of the property—described in official registers as SE/4 Section 20-16N-15E —was to be offered for sale at public auction. I made another inspection trip to the property and came away feeling quite certain it would prove to bear oil.

I have already related how I bought the Nancy Taylor Allotment lease from under the noses of prosperous veteran oil men by having a Muskogee bank official bid for me at the sale. As I had suspected—and hoped—they might, the other potential bidders jumped to the erroneous conclusion that he represented some large oil company. Fearing that whatever sums they offered at the auction would be immediately topped, they made no efforts to bid at all, and I obtained the lease for the proverbial song, paying only five hundred dollars for it.

I was confident there was oil on the property, and I was confident that I could find it.

Nothing remained but to drill my first well, and this I was determined to do without any further delay.

7

I DID not possess sufficient capital of my own to finance the drilling of a test well on the Nancy Taylor Allotment Lease. In the time-honored tradition of the small-scale independent oil operator, I had to obtain the necessary funds by forming a company and prevailing upon others to invest money in the enterprise.

I soon incorporated the Lorena Oil Company, which I, as a somewhat romantic twenty-two-year-old, named for Miss Lorena Carbutt, a very charming young lady of my acquaintance.

Those associated with me in the company were: George F. Getty, B. A. McBridge, H. Luedinghaus, Jr., J. Carl Smith, H. W. Anders and M. S. Cory. The last two named were, of course, the Anders and Cory who had been so eager to obtain the Nancy Taylor Allotment Lease.

Anders and Cory had accepted their defeat at the auction with good humor. Holding no grudges against me for having beaten them to the lease, they willingly invested money in the Lorena Oil Company, for they owned the other half-interest in the lease and were as confident as I that we would find oil on the land.

As provided by our partnership agreement, my father owned 70 per cent and I 30 per cent of the undivided half-interest in the lease. We transferred our joint interest in the lease to Lorena Oil, receiving 37½ per cent of the company's stock in return. My 30 per cent share of this block of stock represented only 11.25 per cent of the total stock issued by Lorena Oil. Such short-end arrangements were the rule rather than the exception for wildcatting operators with slender financial resources and served as strong arguments and incentives for the "independent" to quickly accumulate as much working capital as possible.

With the formation of the Lorena Oil Company, we were ready to begin drilling operations on the Nancy Taylor Allotment Lease. The well was spudded during the first week in January, 1916. Cable-tool drilling proceeded on the customary two-shift-a-day, round-the-clock schedule. I spent most of my time on the site. Although I was ostensibly there to watch the drilling, I frequently pitched in to do my share of even the roughest and most menial work on the rig.

I have previously told how, with the bailer bringing up quantities of oil sand on February 2, my excitement and tension motivated my retreat to Tulsa. My old friend, J. Carl Smith, went to the drilling site and supervised the final stages of drilling on my behalf. Returning to Tulsa the following evening, he brought me the news that my first well had come in, with initial production exceeding seven hundred barrels daily.

Needless to say, I was greatly elated and encouraged by this success. It had the effect of proving—or, perhaps, of finally forcing me to admit to myself—that I had contracted a virulent and incurable case of oil fever. Just as my father had done some thirteen years earlier, I now fully recognized that wildcatting for oil was a supremely thrilling and exhilarating gamble for high stakes which offered opportunities and challenges I could neither ignore nor refuse.

By February 10, the daily production of my first oil well had tapered off to two hundred barrels. This rate of production decline was by no means unique. The production of new wells often drops off sharply from initial levels and settles down to a much lesser steady flow after a few days. Nonetheless, I felt it was advisable to sell the Gettys' interest in the lease.

The well had opened up a new producing area in Muskogee County and triggered a minor oil rush in the Stone Bluff region. Under these circumstances, I could expect to make a fast sale and get a good price for the Gettys' stock in the Lorena Oil Company.

I broached the suggestion to my father, and he agreed to let me follow my own instincts and counsel in the matter. Two days later, I sold our 37½ per cent stock interest in Lorena Oil to the Cosden Oil and Gas Company for a net price of forty thousand dollars.

Cosden Oil and Gas assumed the Gettys' share of the costs involved in drilling and equipping the well. As I had paid only $500 for the lease in the first place, the price represented a clear profit of $39,500. I received 30 per cent of this amount, or $11,850. It was not a great fortune, but it was a very fair return for less than four months of work.

The profitable sale of the Lorena Oil Company stock seemed to be a major milestone in my career. Almost immediately after the transaction was completed, my fortunes took a sudden and spectacular all-around turn for the better.

My lease-brokering business boomed, and I made sizable profits on a large number of transactions. I also acquired several leases on properties I intended to develop. Some of these leases were located in Noble and Garfield Counties, areas which had been totally ignored by oil prospectors for many years. A belief prevailed that since these counties lay in the "red-beds" area, it was useless to seek oil there.

"There is no oil in the red-beds area of Oklahoma."

This opinion had been voiced so many times over such a long period that it had become virtually an article of faith among Oklahoma oil men. I could find no reasonable basis for the theory and no scientific evidence to support it. It appeared to be merely one of those almost superstitious beliefs which spring up without much rhyme or reason and to which people cling tenaciously without really knowing why.

I, however, thought that geologic structures in the red-beds areas suggested the presence of oil. I retained a well-known geologist, Dr. Edward Bloesch, to work the structures, and his reports seemed to confirm my theories. Despite the derisive howls of the skeptics, I eventually went ahead with drilling on the Noble and Garfield Counties properties. I struck oil, opened up yet another new producing area, and demolished a myth.

My father was evidently satisfied that I had made passing marks in my business entrance examinations. I was first appointed a director of the Minnehoma Oil Company; then, in May, 1916, our father-son partnership was incorporated as the Getty Oil Company. My father was named president and treasurer, and I the secretary, of the new corporation. Of the one thousand stock-shares issued when Getty Oil Company was formed, my father received seven hundred and I received three hundred, thus maintaining the 70-per-cent–30-per-cent ratio that had prevailed under the previous partnership.

Incidentally, it might be well at this point to clarify the business relationship that existed between my father and me. When he provided financing for any joint ventures, we shared the profits on the 70-per-cent–30-per-cent basis. When I purchased leases or engaged in prospecting, drilling, or other operations on my own account, providing my own financing, my father did not share in the profits. Conversely, he organized and operated companies and engaged in various enterprises on his own account. I did not share in the profits from these save in instances when I invested some of my own money in them, and then my share was in proportion to my investment.

After Father and I incorporated our partnership and formed the Getty Oil Company, I went right on dealing in leases and prospecting and drilling for oil. I usually acted as my own geologist, legal adviser, drilling superintendent, explosives expert, and jack-of-all-trades.

The months that followed were extremely fortunate ones for me. In most instances, the leases I bought were sold at a profit, and when I drilled on a property, I struck oil more often than not.

There were no arcane secrets, no mystical formulas behind these successes. I operated in much the same manner as most wildcatters. The wildcatting operator had to possess a certain amount of basic knowledge and skill. He also needed experienced, reliable, and loyal men on his exploration and drilling crews. But, beyond these things, I believe the most important factor that determined whether a wildcatter would succeed or fail—whether he would bring in a producing well or wind up with a duster—was often just plain luck.

However, lest there be those who imagine that independent oil operators had little to do but wait for the wheel of fortune to spin and then reap their profits, let me say that the oil business was never an easy one. The search for oil and its production have always entailed work—hard work—and have always been fraught with innumerable financial pitfalls. Wells sometimes blew out, and profits, and often capital, were devoured with appalling speed by costly efforts to extinguish the resulting fires. Dry holes, equipment failures, and breakdowns at crucial periods, legal squabbles and litigation over leases and rights-of-way—these were a few of the dangers and setbacks which frequently drained the wildcatters' financial resources.

In addition, all of us who operated independently often found ourselves facing heavy competition and opposition from major oil firms. Some of these huge companies did not always abide by Marquess of Queensberry rules when they engaged in legal or financial in-fighting to smother an independent who appeared to be growing too big or too fast.

Wildcatters developed traits and techniques which enabled them to stay in business and do more than merely hold their own against the petroleum industry's giants. We became flexible, adaptable, and versatile, adept at innovation and improvisation, if for no other reason than because we *had* to if we were to survive.

For example, the big companies employed vast numbers of specialists and consultants, administrative personnel, and office workers, housing them in large and expensive offices. We, the independents, concentrated on keeping our overhead expenses down. We sought our experts among the veteran oil-field workers who formed our prospecting and drilling crews, or we relied on our own judgment and experience to solve our problems as they arose. We did our own administrative and paper work and held both to absolute minimums. As for our offices, these were, more often than not, our mud-splotched automobiles or tiny, desk-space cubicles in some sagging building located in a low-rent neighborhood.

As I've said, I was lucky—very lucky. The Getty Oil Company prospered, and I also embarked on numerous highly profitable ventures on my own account.

These activities kept me busy, too busy to pay more than cursory attention to how much money I was making. Then, one day, I stopped and took detailed stock of my financial situation.

In June, 1916, I suddenly discovered that I'd gone a very long way since September, 1914. I had become a successful independent oil operator and had built a business of my own in the American petroleum industry.

And, I had made my first million dollars.

At twenty-three, I was a millionaire!

The realization was a shock, albeit a most pleasant one, and I fear that it went to my head. I reasoned that I'd made enough money to meet any conceivable personal requirement I might have in the foreseeable future and could see no reason why I should exert myself further to make more. With the cocksure arrogance of youth, I made a snap decision to forget about work thereafter and to concentrate on play, on enjoying myself.

My decision was influenced, at least in part, by the fact that there was a war raging in Europe. Although the United States had not yet entered World War I, I felt certain that American participation in the conflict was inevitable. I'd already filed official applications to serve either in the Air Service—my first choice—or the Coast Artillery when and if the United States declared war. I was sure it would be only a matter of time before I received call-up orders, and I wanted to relax and have fun before they arrived.

I loved California and the easy, informal, and extremely pleasant life that prevailed there in those days. Also, many of my personal friends lived in southern California. Thus, it was only natural that I return to Los Angeles to enjoy the money I'd made in the Oklahoma oil fields.

"I've made my fortune, and I'm going to retire," I announced blandly to my startled parents when I arrived in Los Angeles.

Neither Mother nor Father were very pleased with my decision. Both of them firmly believed that an individual had to work to justify his existence, and that a rich person had to keep his money working to justify its existence. My father tried to impress upon me that a business-man's money is capital to be invested and reinvested.

"You've got to use your money to create, operate, and build businesses," he argued. "Your wealth represents potential jobs for countless others, and it can produce wealth and a better life for a great many people as well as yourself."

Admittedly, I paid little attention to him—then. Later, I was to realize the truth of what he said, but first I had to try things my own way.

I'd acquired a spanking new Cadillac roadster and an extensive ward-robe. I had all the money I could possibly need. I had made up my mind I wanted to play, and with these prerequisites, I encountered no difficulty plunging full tilt into the southern California-Los Angeles-Hollywood whirl of fun and frolic.

Although the United States entered the war, my call-up was first de-layed, then postponed by bureaucratic snarls. Finally, I was notified that my services "would not be needed." I consequently went on enjoying myself.

But a man in his twenties who has known what it is to work hard and to achieve results can attend only so many parties and dances without getting bored. He can drink only so much champagne and paint the town red only so many times before he wakes up to the realization that he's wasting a very great deal of time and energy on meaningless things.

It took me a while to reach the super-saturation point, but reach it I finally did. By the beginning of 1918, I had tasted far too much pleasure; I no longer savored my far too premature "retirement."

By 1918, I was back in the oil business, not a little abashed by the "I told you so" look I got from my father when I informed him that, having retired at twenty-three, I was coming out of retirement at twenty-five.

8

THE years 1917 to 1920 have often been referred to as the golden age of Oklahoma oil.

By 1915, Oklahoma had become the nation's leading oil-producing state, a not unmixed blessing when one considered that Oklahoma oil producers had a huge, price-weakening surplus on their hands that year.

But crude oil surpluses throughout the country began to dwindle rapidly by the end of 1916. With war raging in Europe, Allied and neutral nations found it increasingly difficult—and finally practically impossible—to obtain vitally needed oil anywhere but in America.

Naturally enough, crude oil prices started to rise. Having dipped to forty-cent-per-barrel levels and even lower in Oklahoma in 1915, they were up to $1.20 by late 1916. With the entry of the United States into the war the following year, demand increased even further, and so did prices, reaching $1.73 in 1917, $2.23 in 1918, and continuing their rise to reach towering peaks in 1920.

Obviously, anyone who owned good producing oil wells stood an excellent chance to reap a golden harvest in this seller's market. By the same token, the upward spirals of demand and prices gave new and added impetus to those engaged in the hunt for oil. By 1918, the number of oil-producing companies in the United States was rapidly approaching the sixteen thousand mark.

In December, 1916, my father sold the Minnehoma Oil Company's lease on Lot 50—the property near Bartlesville which had provided the basis of his oil fortune—to the Zola Oil Company. Lot 50 production had dropped to 120 barrels daily; he felt it advisable to sell and use the $125,-

ooo cash received from the sale to develop other, potentially more productive, properties. But the deal was held up and, in fact, almost fell
through completely because of an incident which sheds a revealing side-
light on George F. Getty's character and personality.

Among Minnehoma Oil's chattels on Lot 50 was a team of fine draught
horses named Pat and Madge. Father was very fond of the two animals,
and they were fond of him. He had only to call their names, and the
horses would come over and nuzzle him while he rubbed their heads and
ears. Maintaining that they were making a lock-stock-and-barrel purchase of the Lot 50 Lease and everything on it, Zola Oil Company
representatives insisted that Father sell them the horses which, still young
and strong, could do much draught work on the site. Father, however,
felt that Pat and Madge should be retired and refused to sell them. A
lengthy argument ensued, but when it became apparent that he would
rather lose the sale than give up the horses, the buyers gave in. Pat and
Madge were taken to one of Father's other leases, where they were allowed
to roam in perfect freedom on a rich pasture.

After the sale of the Lot 50 Lease, Minnehoma Oil still had more than
four dozen producing wells on other properties with a total output of
several hundred barrels daily. Additional leases were purchased and additional wells drilled. The company prospered, and so did the Getty Oil
Company, which paid a 5 per cent dividend in August, 1918, and another
5 per cent dividend the following January.

In 1918, the year that I came out of "retirement"—or, as my father
wryly put it, out of "post-adolescent hibernation"—development and
drilling were resumed on the Noble and Garfield Counties red-bed leases
and other properties. Several producing wells were brought in; fairly
typical among them were those on the Dively Lease, which would show
an eventual excess recovery—clear profit—of more than $400,000.

There was also considerable development and drilling in Osage County
and elsewhere in Oklahoma. Both Minnehoma and Getty Oil Companies
also continued to expand their operations farther afield, securing leases
in Kansas, where significant discoveries had boosted that state's petroleum
production to nearly forty-five million barrels a year.

Contrary to what one might have reasonably expected, demand for
petroleum did not slacken and crude oil prices did not drop after the
November 11, 1918, Armistice. On the contrary, both continued to rise
steadily. There were many reasons for this.

Largely cut off from eastern hemisphere petroleum resources during the years 1914–1918, the Allied war machines had depended mainly on American oil sources. So much so that the United States had produced more than 80 per cent of all the oil used by the Allies during the war. But British and European reliance on American petroleum did not end with the cessation of hostilities. To all intents and purposes, the great Russian oil fields, which had produced more than half the world's crude at the turn of the century, were no longer in operation.

Torn first by war, then revolution, and finally civil war, Russia was unable to get its vast Baku fields back into anything resembling full-scale production. Russia's share of world crude production, which had reached 51 per cent in 1900, nose-dived to somewhere around 3 per cent in the immediate postwar years. Other European, Middle Eastern, and Asiatic fields accounted for only some 8 per cent more.

The world had to look to the Western Hemisphere for its oil. The United States regained the position of clear-cut supremacy it had lost in the latter part of the nineteenth century. After the Armistice, the United States was producing nearly 65 per cent of all the world's crude oil. Mexico, where fabulously rich strikes had been made commencing in 1910, accounted for nearly 23 per cent of world production, a Number Two position from which it was destined to be pushed by the ruthless exploitation, reckless overproduction, and senseless waste practiced by United States and British concessionaires operating there.

Thus, it can be seen that the United States was the world's principal petroleum producer after World War I ended, the source on which most nations drew for their oil. That was one reason for continuing high prices. But there were other reasons, too.

Basic demands and uses for petroleum were far greater and more numerous than they had been before World War I, and they were growing and multiplying rapidly. In 1919, United States automobile production was double what it had been in 1915; motor vehicle registrations stood somewhere around the seven million mark and would pass nine million in 1920.

Most of the world's navies had converted to oil during the war; now the world's merchant fleets were following suit. The trend toward using oil as an all-purpose industrial and domestic fuel had been greatly accelerated. All these factors combined to keep consumption—and thus demand and prices—high.

In 1919, the attention of many oil men was beginning to turn toward southern California, where rich new producing areas were being discovered and developed. I sensed that a great new oil rush was in the making, and I was among those who wanted to be in on it from the start. Consequently, in the fall of that year, I shifted my operations to the Golden State.

Sad to relate, my first oil-prospecting venture in southern California proved to be a dismal fiasco. I began drilling a test well on the Didier Ranch near Puente in October. Drilling, with cable tools, proceeded at an extremely slow pace due to the abnormally difficult formations encountered. I did not supervise the operation personally, and after nearly seven months of drilling, the well had gotten down only two thousand feet. When more than ninety thousand dollars had been spent on fruitless drilling, I transferred the lease on the property back to its original owner. He stubbornly carried on where I had left off, but without any more success than I had encountered.

At about the same time that I acquired the lease on the Didier Ranch property, I was approached by a group of wealthy bankers and financiers who were eager to "get into the oil game." With crude oil prices edging up toward the three-dollar-per-barrel level, they seemed to feel that investment in an oil company was an excellent way to make large profits. I made it as clear as I could that oil ventures were at best risky and warned that while I expected crude prices to go slightly higher, I also anticipated that there would be a sharp break in the not-too-distant future. Nonetheless, they were insistent and assured me that I would have a completely free hand to manage any company we formed.

We incorporated a company capitalized at five million dollars early in 1920 and began prospecting for oil in Oklahoma and California. Some producing wells were brought in on various leases purchased by the company.

The venture, upon which I had embarked with some faint misgivings and reservations, did not prove to be a particularly successful one. Part of the trouble lay in the fact that my associates were totally unfamiliar with the oil business and inclined to be impatient. It soon became clear that they expected to make huge profits practically overnight. They seemed unable to grasp the fact that it did, after all, take time and cost money to drill oil wells and that not every well could be a great gusher.

The situation was further complicated by the advent of the crude oil price drop I had previously predicted. This came in February, 1921, and it precipitated a temporary industrywide crisis which only veteran oil men who had ridden through similar crises before could accept with the requisite equanimity.

As for myself, I considered my job to be the production of oil, not the operation of a kindergarten for starched-collared financiers harboring get-rich-quick hopes. In time, I bought up large blocks of the company's outstanding stock, and when, finally, I owned slightly more than 99 per cent of all shares issued and outstanding, I dissolved the company. I classify the venture as a business failure in that I failed to build the company into a thriving and prosperous concern. On the other hand, I was glad to wind up its affairs so that I could concentrate my efforts and energies on my other—and proliferating—business interests and enterprises.

From 1919 onwards, I was active in both Oklahoma and California, and I traveled extensively between the two states. Minnehoma Oil Company, of which I was, of course, still a director, continued its development and drilling operations in Oklahoma. On New Year's Eve, 1919, the Minnehoma drilling crew working on the company's Lookout Lease in Osage County brought in a spectacular gusher. It was one of Oklahoma's biggest-ever initial producers and gushed between twelve thousand and twenty thousand barrels of oil a day for two days until it was capped.

Unfortunately, the remainder of the story is not a very happy one. It provides a trenchant example of the many unforeseeable risks which every oil producer encounters during the course of his career. Excellent contemporary accounts of the episode appeared in the *Oil and Gas Journal* and Oklahoma daily newspapers in January, 1920. I can think of no better way to tell the story of the Lookout gusher than by quoting directly from them.

On January 2, 1920, the following account appeared in the *Oil and Gas Journal* under the byline of the publication's correspondent, J. L. Hunter:

> Pawhuska, Okla., Jan. 2, 1920—Muzzled by a two-ton, high pressure gate valve, the Minnehoma Oil Co.'s Osage gusher that for forty-seven hours had been deluging the surrounding prairie with oil was success-fully shut in by the drilling crew at 3:30 P.M. last Friday. As the crew left the derrick after completing their task, Harry Robinson, cos-tumed in a rubber suit from which oil was dripping, remarked, "I

have worked on a number of big wells in West Virginia and Oklahoma, but this is the humdinger of them all."

The oil-besmirched derrick stands on a high elevation overlooking miles of country. To the northwest, east and south, the ground falls away in a gentle slope to a slight depression in the prairie a quarter of a mile distant. West of south and probably forty rods from the well is a little frame dwelling house surrounded by a grove of spreading trees, with oil dripping from their branches. Forming a three-quarter circle around the well and covering in area not less than 75 acres, the prairie is a dirty brown in color caused by the oil mist, carried thither by the shifting wind. In the depression referred to, three gangs of men with teams, scrapers, and shovels were busily engaged in constructing dams to catch the oil that for hours had been running in streams down the incline. Such was the scene presented when our correspondent visited the well on the afternoon of January 2.

The correspondent then gives some of the background about Minnehoma Oil Company and describes how the lease was purchased and drilling begun. Then he continues:

The Mississippi lime was struck at a depth of 2,295 feet and was penetrated but a few feet when a good showing of oil was struck that increased with each screw. With the resumption of drilling after the Christmas shutdown, it became evident that the well was good for 200 bbls. a day if not more, but all bets as to its caliber were off when the sun disappeared behind the Osage hills on the evening of December 31. The log of the well showed 50 feet in the Mississippi lime. Robinson was letting out screw when he turned to his toolie, saying: "Throw on the tug ropes, Roy, something has broke loose down in this hole."

This was quickly done, the temper screw detached and the bull wheels set in motion. The engine played along so lightly that for a moment the driller thought the tools had become detached from the wire rope, but long years at drilling told him that a heavy gas pressure was behind it all. With the kinking of the rope, he kept opening the throttle until the engine was running at its best speed. When the tools were 500 feet from the top of the hole and, despite the fast revolving bull wheels, the wire rope began forming loops on the derrick floor,

Near Mont Blanc before
the First World War.
Adolphe Couttet, Chamonix

On the way to Amsterdam for the Olympic Games in 1927.

Gordon and George Getty.

Gloria and George Getty
at a ball at the Waldorf-
Astoria in April, 1958.

the driller and tool dresser realized that they were courting death by remaining longer. The rest is soon told. Impelled by a gas pressure of 800 pounds to the square inch, the heavy tools shot out of the hole, struck the crown block a glancing blow and in descending crashed through the derrick floor, severed a cross sill and penetrated the earth to a depth of 15 feet. With a roar that was almost deafening, a column of oil spouting like a huge geyser, now rising many feet above the derrick to fall and spread out until only the lower sections of the structure were faintly visible, soon saturated the ground for rods around the well. The oil found its way into depressions in the prairie, hundreds of barrels soaking into the soft earth, entailing a big loss to the company, that had made no preparations for taking care of the gusher that conservative oil men say was making anywhere from 8,000 to 10,000 bbls. a day before shut-in. . . .

A bulletin-item in the same edition of the *Oil and Gas Journal* amended correspondent Hunter's estimate, describing the well as a "20,000 barrel" gusher.

The well continued to flow wildly for nearly two days. It made headlines and drew thousands of people to the site.

There are more strangers seen on the streets of Pawhuska these days than ever in the town's history, the Oil and Gas Journal reported. *Automobiles flaunting pennants of far distant cities are seen on the streets. The hotels are unable to take care of increased patronage and sleeping quarters are at a premium. The Minnehoma Oil Company gusher is the one theme of conversation on the streets and in hotel lobbies.*

But the well was located on property under the jurisdiction of the Osage Indian Agency. The spouting oil was running down the hillside and polluting streams in the vicinity; thus, the Agency ordered the well shut down.

The gusher was finally capped, shut in, after forty-seven hours of running wild.

And then the oil, or the vast majority of it, seemed to disappear.

Correspondents of the Pawhuska *Daily Capital* and the Tulsa *Daily World* wrote that capping had "ruined" the well. Whatever had happened, post-capping swabbing operations proved disappointing. When the well was finally completed and put into production, it produced only some fifty barrels a day. From then on, its total cumulative production up to the time it was abandoned was only some thirty thousand barrels—about the same amount as it had gushed in its first two days of existence.

It was a great disappointment, but eternal hope and optimism are the strongest suits in any wildcatter's hand. Father and I figuratively shrugged the incident off and told each other there would be other big strikes in the future. As it happened, we were right. The biggest successes lay just ahead.

9

THE rule which holds that what goes up must eventually come down applies on occasion to crude oil prices with as much validity as it does to tennis balls and slingshot pellets.

By 1920, the posted price being paid for crude oil in Oklahoma had soared to a record $3.50 per barrel, plus additional premiums for especially high-grade crudes. In that year, the Minnehoma Oil Company was actually receiving as much as $5.25 per barrel for the top-quality crude oil produced by its wells in the Garber Field, this price representing a $1.75-per-barrel premium over the prevailing posted price.

Naturally, such high prices meant large profits for oil producers. Just as naturally, the prospects of earning big returns fast spurred oil exploration and drilling operations throughout the country. Frantic expansion roared ahead in the Ranger, Burkburnett, and Breckenridge fields of Texas and, in 1919, the great Desdemona and Mexia booms added their oceans of petroleum to Lone Star State production.

There were several sizable new strikes in Oklahoma. The Burbank, Tonkawa, Bristow, Lyons-Quinn, and Hewitt Fields all promised to give significant boosts to the state's petroleum production. By 1922, the output of the rich Burbank Field alone was to add more than twenty-four million barrels of crude oil to Oklahoma's annual total.

The year 1920 saw the rapid expansion of production in the giant Salt Creek, Wyoming, Field, and there were important developments at El Dorado and Smackover in Arkansas. In the meantime, the historic Los Angeles Basin booms, involving the fields at Santa Fe Springs, Signal Hill, Huntington Beach, and Long Beach, were gradually gathering steam in California.

All these developments were pouring enormous new rivers of oil into the world's petroleum markets or at least guaranteeing that vast new petroleum reserves would be tapped as soon as large-scale drilling got under way in the new fields. Snowballing oil production—and promise of more to come—was bound to result in surpluses and fears of surpluses. The fact and the fear could not help but have a marked effect on crude oil prices. The inevitable break came early in 1921, and its impact was felt by the Minnehoma Oil Company to no less a degree than it was felt by countless other independent oil-producing companies.

On January 24, 1921, the price that purchasing pipeline companies were paying for Oklahoma crude stood at $3.50 per barrel. Overnight and without warning, the price collapsed, plunging to $1.75 within ten days.

On February 10, 1921, the directors of Minnehoma Oil—my father, my mother, Mabel McCreery, and I—held what took on many characteristics of an emergency meeting. It was in a tense atmosphere that we studied the facts and acknowledged that we were facing a serious crisis.

Minnehoma's directors had little choice but to make a distasteful decision. To quote from the minutes of that meeting:

> The President and Treasurer reported that since our last meeting, the price of crude oil in the mid-continent field had been cut by the purchasing pipeline companies $1.75 per barrel or exactly 50 per cent of the price prevailing on January 24 of this year, and that it would appear inadvisable to declare the regular dividend to stockholders at the present time.

But there was worse to come. Another directors' meeting was held on March 21, 1921. The President reported a very small amount of cash available to meet the company's operating expenses.

Now, Minnehoma was not exactly what one would call a small or poor company. Its assets—leaseholds, producing wells, equipment, tools, accounts receivable, and so on—were valued at more than two million dollars at that time. However, the price break had left the company short of actual cash.

Minnehoma's immediate cash requirements were estimated at fifty thousand dollars. The sum would tide it over the next ninety days, during which time certain accounts receivable would be collected and emergency retrenchments would sharply reduce operating costs. In the meanwhile, the fifty thousand dollars had to be obtained—in cash. The only practical solution was to borrow the money from a bank. The directors consequently voted the necessary authority for the company to borrow fifty thousand dollars from the Security First National Bank on a ninety-day, 6½ per cent note. The loan was obtained—and, I might add, repaid promptly. Nonetheless, by June 9, 1921, when yet another director's meeting was held, it became obvious that additional drastic measures would have to be taken if Minnehoma was to ride out the price-break crisis. To quote once more from the minutes of the meeting:

> The meeting reported that the price of oil had again been reduced in the mid-continent field by twenty-five cents per barrel, making the base price $1.25 per barrel; that the price a few months ago was $3.50 per barrel and by successive cuts in the price, the base price has now reached $1.25.
>
> This price, considering the price of material and labor, is so low that we are having difficulty in keeping sufficient money in the bank to meet disbursements; that at the present time our lifting cost of oil on nine of our properties exceeds $1.25 per barrel and on fourteen of our properties, lifting cost exceeds $1.00 per barrel. In order, therefore, to continue in business, it is necessary for all officers and employees in the company to bear a portion of the burden.
>
> On motion duly seconded, it was unanimously ordered that the salaries of all officers and employees in the Los Angeles, California, and Tulsa, Oklahoma, offices be reduced 20 per cent, taking effect June 21st, 1921.

Such were the morale and loyalty of Minnehoma's employees that all accepted the 20-per-cent salary reductions without complaint. Some, I recall, even came to my father or me and offered to loan the company their personal savings to help tide it over the slump. A few months later, when the crisis had passed, the cuts were, of course, restored and year-end bonuses were given to employees. Also, by carefully managing Minnehoma's affairs during the remainder of the year, it was even possible to pay stockholders the dividends which had been deferred at the February 10, 1921 meeting.

In the meantime, trouble seemed to come in bunches, and Minnehoma Oil had an extra helping heaped on its already well-filled plate.

Back in May, 1914, Minnehoma Oil Company had purchased a five-eighth interest in a lease covering one-half of a property known as the Lete Kolvin Allotment, which lay at the north end of the rich Cushing Field in Oklahoma. Minnehoma subsequently sold one-eighth of this interest and then went on to drill several very productive wells on that portion of the property on which it retained its lease-rights.

Sinclair Oil and Gas, Gilliland Oil, and other producing companies owned what they thought were entirely valid leases on other portions of the property and they, too, drilled wells.

The Lete Kolvin Allotment proved to be a very valuable oil property. In time, Minnehoma alone would realize some $2,250,000 in clear profit from the oil its lease produced. Unfortunately, several individuals contested the rights of Minnehoma and the other companies, and they filed a total of seven lawsuits, one of them against Minnehoma. Although qualified legal counsel was convinced that these were nothing more than nuisance suits brought in an effort to get some share of the wealth being produced by the property, the suits dragged through the courts for years.

In January, 1921, the lawsuits were at last consolidated for a nonjury trial before Judge Lucien B. Wright of the District Court of Creek County, Oklahoma. The manner in which Judge Wright conducted the proceedings gave the defendants reason to doubt his impartiality from the very start. After the case had been heard for more than six weeks, the defendants obtained what seemed conclusive proof that the presiding judge was not only biased against them, but that he also had a personal interest in the outcome of the litigation.

At this point, the defendants, Minnehoma Oil Company among them, petitioned the Oklahoma Supreme Court to force Judge Wright to disqualify himself from hearing the case. The State Supreme Court then appointed one of its former justices, the Honorable Robert M. Rainey of Oklahoma City, to act as referee, take evidence, and report his findings and conclusions to the Court.

The involved Lete Kolvin Allotment affair made headlines in Oklahoma over a period of several months, mainly because it quickly degenerated into endless cross-barrages of lurid allegations. The story is best told by newspaper accounts of the time. I have the now-yellowed newspaper clippings in my possession, and they offer a rather sensational and sometimes very amusing commentary on the rough-and-ready frontier atmosphere that prevailed in the Oklahoma of the early 1920's.

A July, 1921, story in the Tulsa *Tribune* serves to set the scene:

JUDGE WRIGHT CHALLENGED BY OIL FIRMS

New Charge Demands He Disqualify Self

The Sinclair Oil & Gas Co., Minnehoma Oil Co., Gilliland Oil Co. and other large Tulsa oil interests late yesterday filed in the court of District Judge Lucien B. Wright at Sapulpa a formal request that he disqualify himself from further proceeding in the Lete Kolvin case, involving title to oil properties worth between $3,000,000 and $5,000,000.

The request was lodged on the ground that Judge Wright was recently informed against by Attorney General S. P. Freeling and is now under arrest charged with having solicited, accepted and received a bribe for deciding the $2,000,000 Tommy Atkins title case in favor of C. O. Lytle and others against the Charles Page interests.

The request for disqualification, on which Judge Wright is asked to disbar himself from finally deciding the Kolvin case, makes sensational allegations against the accused jurist.

In addition to reciting that he is now charged with a felony, it alleges that Wright acquired an interest in the Kolvin litigation adverse to the complaining oil companies while the case was before him for decision, that he was so under the influence of liquor while on the bench hearing the evidence that he could not make intelligent decisions and that C. O. Lytle, counsel and party in interest in the Tommy Atkins case, is both a party in interest in the Kolvin case and the attorney for Judge Wright in the bribery charge pending against him.

Officers now have in their possession for service upon Judge Wright a court writ notifying him that the matter will be carried to the supreme court in the event he does not disqualify voluntarily and the high tribunal will be asked to issue a writ of mandamus, compelling him to eliminate himself from the trial, and to grant an injunction prohibiting him from acting in its decision hereafter in any way.

The Lete Kolvin case is practically the same as the Tommy Atkins case, in which Judge Wright is charged with recently receiving a $10,000 bribe with the promise of $90,000 more. The Sinclair Oil Co. and other producers have had control of the title since 1916. In 1919 C. O. Lytle, a party to the Tommy Atkins case, and others filed suit attacking the Sinclair title on the ground that they had purchased the lease from other parties who were the rightful heirs of Lete Kolvin.

Since that time, the case has laid dormant in the Creek County district court until recently.

A few weeks ago Judge Lucien B. Wright tried the equitable issues and decided in favor of Lytle and his associates. An application for an accounting made by Lytle, et al., is set for hearing July 30.

Companies and individuals interested in the fabulously rich lease who are asking the disqualification of Judge Wright are the Minnehoma Oil Co.; Sinclair Oil and Gas Co.; Gilliland Oil & Gas Co.; John W. Gilliland, John D. Boxley, V. V. Harris, Robert Oglesby, William Buck, N. B. Freagin, H. B. Barnard, C. B. Hyde and Vera C. Gilliland.

The affidavit of W. H. Dill, made a part of the request for disqualification, charges Judge Wright with going out and purchasing an interest in the lawsuit while he was trying it. Attorneys say it is one of the most amazing charges of corruption ever made against any judge.

A few weeks later, when Supreme Court referee Robert M. Rainey was hearing testimony in the mandamus action that grew out of Judge Wright's refusal to disqualify himself, the Oklahoma City *Times* ran the following story:

IMPEACHMENT TESTIMONY IN WRIGHT CASE

Health Inspector's Accounts Padded, Lawyer Claims

Witnesses took the stand in the mandamus action before the supreme court against Judge Lucien B. Wright of the twenty-second judicial district in the courtroom of Judge George W. Clark Friday morning, to impeach the testimony of Mrs. T. H. Sturgeon, state health officer and one of the principal witnesses against Judge Wright.

The hearing in the district courtroom was before Robert M. Rainey, acting referee of the supreme court named to hear the testimony in the case. The mandamus action is seeking to disqualify Judge Wright from sitting in the $5,000,000 Lete Kolvin oil case.

Testimony of the morning was directed against Mrs. Sturgeon. Attorneys for Judge Wright sought to show that Mrs. Sturgeon had been padding her expense accounts while working for the state health department under Dr. A. R. Lewis, state health commissioner.

Judge Wright, coatless, sat in the courtroom. He is to take the stand Friday afternoon, his attorneys announced.

"I propose to offer this evidence to show that Mrs. Sturgeon had a habit for six months of committing forgery daily, perjury once a month and larceny once a month," C. O. Lytle, of Sapulpa, attorney for Judge Wright, stated as his reason for wanting to place impeaching witnesses on the stand.

Attorneys for Wright sought to show that from January until July this year Mrs. Sturgeon padded her expense at the Tulsa Hotel, Tulsa, to the extent of $328.

Frank C. Carter, state auditor, was placed on the stand to identify expense accounts of Mrs. Sturgeon which had passed through his office. He testified expense claims had been paid totalling $605. A. B. Kealing, assistant manager of the Tulsa Hotel, testified her total bill was $277. Ruth Zoller, auditor from the Tulsa Hotel, identified bills Mrs. Sturgeon paid for room rent.

The hearing here Friday is but one of a series of hearings which have been held in the case.

On July 21, the Sinclair Oil & Gas Co., the Minnehoma Oil Co., the Gilliland company and other Tulsa oil interests filed a formal request that Judge Wright disqualify himself from further proceeding in the Kolvin case.

On August 23, 1921, The Tulsa *Tribune* published the following dispatch:

BOOZE PLAYS A BIG PART IN WRIGHT TRIAL

Judge Accused by Witness Who Is Then Branded As An Habitual Liar.

"Judge Wright became so drunk in a drug store one night during the trial of the Lete Kolvin case at Sapulpa that the druggist asked me to get him out and I took him to his room at the France Hotel in a cab," testified Andy Higgins during the taking of depositions before Judge Robert M. Rainey, former supreme court justice, here late yesterday on the application of the Sinclair and other Tulsa oil companies to have Wright disqualified from sitting further in the Kolvin case.

W. H. Dill, who claims an interest in the Kolvin lease and who was the star witness yesterday against Judge Wright, testified that Higgins is an assistant of his whom he used at the trial to "look after witnesses." Character witnesses for Judge Wright called Higgins "a gambler and a bootlegger."

"I met Judge Wright in his room at the hotel the night before the trial started and gave him a bottle of whisky which he had requested," said Higgins. "About a week after the trial started I took another quart up to the France Hotel to him. I had to take him home in a cab that night," Higgins added.

"Why?" asked Judge Harve Maxey, representing the Minnehoma Oil Co.

"Because he was drunk," retorted Higgins.

"Higgins, what is your business?" asked Attorney Lytle, for the defense.

"Farming a little and handling a little stock," answered Higgins.

"You handle a little whisky, too, don't you?" persisted Lytle.

"Yes, I handle a little when I drink, like when me and you drank together yesterday morning," Higgins flashed back. Lytle quickly dismissed the witness from the stand.

J. E. Thompson, Clearview Negro, who with Dill owns a one-half interest in the William Barnett claim to the Kolvin lease, took the stand and told of purchasing the A. A. Hatch interest at the direction of Dill while the Kolvin case was being heard before Judge Wright at Sapulpa. Dill had previously testified that his interest in the big lawsuit was purchased by him for Judge Wright at the jurist's request.

Thompson's testimony indicated, according to the State, that Judge Wright had held up his final decision waiting for the Hatch deal to be closed.

Several hours were spent in hearing testimony relative to the character of W. H. Dill in and about Okemah, his home. Dill had been the star witness for the oil companies at the Okemah hearing, declaring Judge Wright was intoxicated many times during the Kolvin trial, was unduly friendly with a Mrs. T. T. Boarman at Oklahoma City, although he was a man with a family, and finally that the jurist had withheld decision of the Kolvin case after the testimony was in while he instructed Dill to acquire the Hatch interest in the suit for him.

Many witnesses were called by the defense who testified that Dill could not be believed under oath. Then the prosecution placed on the stand an even larger number who declared his reputation for truth and veracity was of the best. Judge Rainey finally stopped the character testimony, declaring it was leading nowhere.

The hearing is being continued at Okmulgee today, Sapulpa tomorrow and Tulsa Thursday.

And so the testimony went, day after day, as the case followed its tortuous course through endless barrages of charges and countercharges.

On October 9, 1921, Robert Rainey, the Supreme Court referee, finally made his report. He found nothing to sustain the charge that Judge Lucien Wright had used intoxicating liquors to an extent incapacitating him during the Lete Kolvin trial. It was also noted that since Judge Wright had been acquitted of the bribery charge growing out of the Tommy Atkins case, this charge had no bearing on the questions at hand. Referee Rainey did, however, find that Judge Wright had been biased in favor of C. O. Lytle. Six weeks after Rainey's report was issued, the Oklahoma Supreme Court approved his findings and ordered Judge Wright to disqualify himself from sitting further in the Lete Kolvin case.

Eventually, the rights of Minnehoma and the other oil companies involved in the litigation were vindicated, and they were shown to have valid and legitimate leases.

The cost of the legal fight was staggering. Minnehoma's own legal bill in the various Kolvin litigations totaled more than $123,000.

What with the drop in crude oil prices and the Lete Kolvin Allotment lawsuits, 1921 was not the best of years for the Minnehoma Oil Company and the Getty interests. Nonetheless, Minnehoma came through with flying colors, showed a profit for the year, and paid a fair dividend to its stockholders.

But my father and I had found the time and opportunity to embark on other ventures during the year. Among these were our first important investments in southern California oil properties.

10

PARADOXICALLY enough, although he had been a resident of Los Angeles since 1906, my father waited until 1921 to make his first investment in the oil business in California.

I had made an abortive assay into California oil in 1919, when I began drilling on the Didier Ranch near Puente, but the senior member of the Getty partnership had held off for fifteen years—and for at least two good reasons. First, the cost of drilling oil wells in California had always been much higher than in the midcontinent fields. Second, areas considered to be prospective oil lands during the period 1906–1920 appeared to be tightly controlled by a few large companies. Under such conditions, it was difficult to obtain leases save on highly doubtful properties located on the outer fringes of producing areas.

But times and situations change. By 1921, the gap between Oklahoma and California well-drilling costs had narrowed. In that year, the average cost of drilling a well in Oklahoma was around thirty-five thousand dollars, a 1,000 per cent increase over the 1912 average of about thirty-one hundred dollars.

Furthermore, the Oklahoma oil business was not what it had been even a few years before. An overly large element of speculation had entered into the over-all conduct of operations in the midcontinent. For example, the Oklahoma Corporation Commission, concerned over the emergence of hastily organized, fly-by-night oil stock companies in the state, issued an official estimate that only one dollar was being returned for every five hundred dollars invested in such stock companies. Plainly, individuals who knew little or nothing about the business were promoting oil ventures, an unhealthy situation which was at least partially reflected in the fact that in 1921, 4,149 producing oil wells—and 1,428 dry holes—were drilled in Oklahoma. This ratio of dry holes to producing wells was markedly higher than it would have been had all the drilling been conducted by experienced oil operators.

Insofar as the California oil business climate was concerned, this, too, was changing. As more and more producing areas were discovered and developed, the large oil companies lost their ability to maintain control over the land. Hence, all things considered, in 1921 Father and I agreed that the prospects for investment in California oil were good and getting better all the time.

On November 3, 1921, the Union Oil Company brought in its Bell No. 1 well at Santa Fe Springs, California, for an initial daily production of twenty-five hundred barrels. This started the Santa Fe Springs oil boom, and Father decided the moment had come to give serious consideration to starting operations in California.

Two days after the Union Oil Company well came in, my father and I drove out to Santa Fe Springs to look the ground over. Wanting to have the best of expert advice, we retained a highly regarded and high-priced geologist—who, for reasons which will soon be apparent, had best remain nameless—to accompany us.

I drove the car, and, when we reached Santa Fe Springs in the early afternoon, we rode around slowly, all three of us carefully studying the topography of the largely undeveloped land around us. The geologist declared that he thought the field opened by the Union Oil Company well was a rather limited one.

"In my opinion, the most promising oil land lies to the east of the well," he declared in a pedantic manner as I drove along Telegraph Avenue, which lay to the south of the Bell No. 1 well. "The land around here doesn't look as though it would produce very much oil. I'm sure the pool lies to the east."

"Shall we take another look in that direction?" I asked my father.

"Not yet," he replied. "As long as we're here, we might as well drive a little further. I'm not so sure that the best oil land isn't here in this section."

A few moments later, we saw a long, heavily loaded freight train straining and laboring across what appeared to be a level expanse until it reached the grade-crossing at Telegraph Avenue. After that, the locomotive's power obviously eased off, but the train nonetheless began to gather momentum and pick up speed.

This could mean only one thing. The terrain was not as flat as it seemed to be. Gradients, imperceptible to the naked eye, sloped away from a Telegraph Avenue summit.

The implication of what we had seen struck my father and me at almost the same instant.

"Did you notice that train, Paul?" he suddenly asked, a strong note of excitement in his voice.

"I'll say I did!" I exclaimed.

"The top of the structure—the dome—is right here, along Telegraph Avenue," Father declared. "Now I'm sure of it—the richest part of the pool extends here, to the south of Union Oil's well."

On November 9, Father bought the Nordstrom Lease in Santa Fe Springs. The property consisted of four 50-by-145-foot lots fronting on Telegraph Avenue and totaled only some two-thirds of an acre in area. Evidently, the consensus concurred with the opinion of our geologist for, while there was already a rush to buy leases covering properties lying to the east of the Bell No. 1 well, leases on land located to its south were still being sold for the proverbial song. Father paid only a minimal $693 for the Nordstrom Lease.

Having broken the ice, George F. Getty also bought leases on some properties in Huntington Beach and Long Beach, where other oil booms were even then getting under way.

Father's first California well—Synoground No. 1 at Long Beach—was spudded on February 16, 1922. On April 16, two months later to the day, the well was completed for 2,375 barrels initial daily production. It was only the beginning. From then on, the Getty name would be associated to an ever increasing extent with California petroleum production.

The first well to be drilled on the Nordstrom Lease was spudded on March 10, 1922, and completed on August 26 of that year for 2,300 barrels initial daily production.

The real value of the discovery we'd made while watching the freight train chuff its way past the Telegraph Avenue crossing at Santa Fe Springs became apparent soon enough. The Nordstrom Lease proved to be fabulously rich in oil, and it also proved to be one of the finest investments George F. Getty made during his entire career as an oil man.

Within the next seventeen years, the less-than-one-acre Nordstrom Lease property showed an excess recovery of $6,387,946.65—a clear-profit figure more than ninety-two hundred times the original $693 cost of the lease.

During 1922, ten wells were started on the Nordstrom and other Santa Fe Springs region leases. Five wells were spudded on Getty properties in Long Beach and one was started at Huntington Beach.

The following year, eight more wells were spudded at Santa Fe Springs, four at Long Beach, and two at Huntington Beach. In addition, a total of sixteen new wells were started on a Torrance property which had been acquired after the others. Most of these wells were completed successfully and proved to be fine producers.

The remarkable production of the Santa Fe Springs properties prompted my father to erect a gasoline plant there. In early December, 1922, he entered into an agreement with Ben Koehler, who was to build and operate the plant. Construction was begun on December 26, 1922, and under Koehler's efficient direction, it was completed the following March. The enterprise was a highly profitable one from the very beginning. Dividends totaling as much as $55,000 annually were paid on the overall initial investment of $200,000, which, incidentally, was the price received for the plant when it was sold a few years later.

The expansion and growth of my father's and my own business interests proved to be little short of explosively rapid during the years following 1919. By the beginning of 1923, my father was worth somewhere in the neighborhood of fifteen million dollars. My own fortune had grown to about three million, due to the success of ventures on which I had embarked on my own account as well as those in which I had engaged in association with my father.

However, let me make it quite clear that when I cite these figures, I do not mean to imply that either of us possessed anywhere near these respective amounts in ready, spendable cash.

Our fortunes, like those of all active businessmen, were mainly invested in the various companies and enterprises we had formed and were operating. The overwhelming majority of the money was invested in those enterprises—invested in such business assets as leases, machinery, equipment, producing oil wells, and the myriad other components of the business machine—and at work as operating capital.

I doubt if my father's personal cash balance in the bank exceeded $100,000. I know that mine certainly did not.

In Father's case, something like 90 per cent of all his rated wealth was invested in his own companies, which he personally managed and directed. Investments in the stocks of other companies, bonds, real estate, or such other assets as accounts personally receivable by him accounted for only about 10 per cent of his rated wealth.

Parenthetically, it might be pointed out that George F. Getty drew comparatively small salaries for his services as head of the companies he controlled. For example, in twenty years as President and General Manager of the Minnehoma Oil Company, he received an average salary of less than eight thousand dollars per year.

This was not due to any tax considerations, either. Income taxes in those days were far from being the overriding factor they are today.

My father's philosophy in regard to top-management personnel salaries marked him as a man whose thinking was far ahead of his times. He believed that upper-bracket management personnel deserved reasonable basic salaries for the services they rendered to a company. On the other hand, he felt that they should receive a large portion of their compensation in the form of dividends on the stock they owned in the company.

George F. Getty maintained that, in this manner, management personnel would have added reason and incentive to do their utmost for the benefit of the company and thus for the benefit of all the stockholders. He also held that a consequent desire to see the value of their stock grow would act as a sort of built-in safeguard. It would keep management alert for sound opportunities for expansion while deterring it from taking rash and irresponsible steps which might hinder or prevent such growth.

In 1923, because I was still in the process of building my business, the ratio of my other assets to my capital investments in my various enterprises was even lower than in my father's case. I regularly reinvested most of my profits in my business ventures. Considerably more than 95 per cent of my rated fortune was tied up in the form of capital investment.

All in all, 1923 was a very busy year and, in many ways, a crucial one. It was marked by several important developments which had deep and lasting effects on both the business and personal spheres of my life.

My father was sixty-seven in 1923. The sudden and tremendous growth of his business since his initial essays into the oil business in California in 1922 had greatly strained his health, taking a much heavier toll of his strength and energies than any of us imagined.

On the afternoon of March 23, while playing a leisurely round of golf at the Brentwood Country Club, Father suffered a paralytic stroke and had to be rushed to his home. I received the news of his collapse over the telephone and went immediately to his bedside, where his doctors grimly warned me that he was desperately ill.

King ibn-Saud, of Saudi Arabia, and J. Paul
Getty in 1954. *Studio Badran, Kuwait*

On board King ibn-Saud's yacht: Mr. MacPherson, Abdulla Mubarek, Abdulla Turiki, J. Paul Getty, King ibn-Saud, Abdulla Mulla Saleh. *Studio Badran, Kuwait*

I did what I could to comfort my mother, who, herself, was near collapse from shock and worry. Mother and I waited out the first crucial days together until Father's physicians reported that they believed the crisis had passed and that they would be able to save his life. But, they warned us again, his recovery would be a very slow one, and we had to reckon with the possibility that he would be permanently crippled.

George F. Getty had always managed the affairs of his companies himself. Now his illness made it impossible for him to do so. He was, in fact, so ill that his doctors would allow no one—not even Mother or me—to mention anything about business matters during the brief periods he was permitted visitors.

I found myself faced with a dilemma. It was impossible to forecast the duration of my father's illness. Doctors hinted that it might be many months before he recovered sufficiently to take any part in the management of his companies. During these months, the enterprises which he had so painstakingly built could well suffer serious damage for lack of leadership.

There was a great deal that needed doing, particularly in the relatively new Los Angeles Basin operations. Planned new wells had to be started on schedule; drilling operations on those which had already been spudded required supervision. Oil from completed wells had to be sold; an eye had to be kept on the gasoline plant which was even then nearing completion at Santa Fe Springs. A thousand and one details which Father normally supervised had to be looked after.

To my mind, the situation was further complicated by the fact that I did not share my father's confidence in some of his field management personnel. I had seen several examples of what I considered inefficiency and slipshod work on various drilling sites; but, even though these were located on leases in which I held a partnership interest, I'd said nothing to my father, out of deference for his judgment.

Now, however, I felt that lacking a firm hand to guide it from the top, his entire organization might suffer from the lacks and weaknesses I had previously noted. I felt that emergency measures were called for, and I took them. Without specific authorization from my father—this, of course, would have been impossible to obtain in view of the doctors' strict orders regarding any business discussions—I assumed direction of his business affairs.

As I had anticipated, I came into collision with certain members of the field management staff. Not wishing to usurp my father's authority,

I did nothing to eliminate these individuals from the payrolls. I did, however, firmly insist on a general tightening up of field operations. My instructions were followed with a degree of reluctance and resentment that I found personally galling, but which I accepted because I viewed my emergency stewardship as purely a temporary, stopgap expedient.

The management of my father's business affairs in addition to my own made it necessary for me to work virtually around the clock until, toward the end of May, Father recovered sufficiently to issue at least broad policy instructions regarding the operations of his companies.

Because of his still enfeebled condition—he remained partially paralyzed—I carefully avoided making an issue, or even mention, of the frictions and difficulties I had encountered with his field management personnel. These matters were, however, brought to his attention by others and presented in a light which was hardly favorable to me.

Father then directed that his affairs were to be conducted by his own organization. Once again, I remained silent, making no protest and advancing no arguments. Time, I felt, was needed—time for my father to regain his health and strength and time for him to view the situation in proper focus. The last was to take a year, but he finally recognized the unnecessary—and, indeed, unconscionable—expenses, delays, and losses caused by the less-than-efficient field management, and the individuals responsible were "allowed to resign."

Father's partial paralysis affected his speech and one side of his body. Nevertheless, he insisted on resuming active management of his companies. His shrewd, keen mind was completely unimpaired, and, despite his physical limitations, he was soon planning and implementing new programs and ventures. He steadfastly maintained that hard work would effect the quickest and most complete of cures, and he threw himself into his work in a manner that was at once the despair and the wonder of his doctors.

Great as my concern was for my father's health, I knew that he could not abide idleness, least of all in himself, and it was with overwhelming joy that I watched him improve slowly as the pressure of the work he took upon himself mounted.

Then, in October, 1923, two months before my thirty-first birthday, I took my first plunge into the troubled seas of matrimony.

11

LOVELY, dark-haired Jeanette Demont and I were married in Ventura, California, on October 1, 1923. It was, in effect, an elopement. Neither of our families and only a handful of our closest friends had any inkling of our intentions until after the ceremony had been performed and we returned to Los Angeles as Mr. and Mrs. J. Paul Getty.

At first, our marriage was a very happy one, and shortly after the beginning of 1924, Jeanette joyfully informed me that she was pregnant. The prospect of becoming a father delighted me, and I reacted instinctively, redoubling my efforts to build my business. I wanted a son, and I wanted him to grow up to be as proud of me as I was of my own father and his accomplishments.

Ten months after we were married, Jeanette gave birth to a boy—my first son, whom we named George Franklin Getty II after my father.

I was jubilant, but unfortunately, jarring notes of dissension and discord crept into the relationship between Jeanette and me soon after George was born. As is frequently the case with married couples, minor arguments and disagreements grew into serious quarrels.

Among the causes of the friction between us were my necessarily frequent and long absences from home. I traveled extensively, throughout California, to Oklahoma and other places, inspecting potential oil properties, buying and selling leases, and looking after operations on leases which I had bought and was developing. It was often necessary for me to remain on a site for several days and nights in a row when drilling operations reached crucial stages. It was not unusual for me to receive telephone calls at all hours and then to pack hurriedly in order to be at a certain place at a certain time to conduct important business.

In retrospect, I can readily see that most of the fault was mine. No wife, and especially not one with a bright, active mind and strong personality of her own, enjoys feeling that she is being neglected for an oil rig or that she is playing a minor supporting role to a corporate balance sheet.

This conflict between the demands of my burgeoning business activities and the responsibilities of married life is one that would make itself evident and strongly felt—and, I fear, would prove unfavorably decisive—in all my marriages. To my deep regret, it is a conflict I was never able to resolve satisfactorily.

In any event, as I look back, it seems that by the time either Jeanette or I realized what was happening to our marriage, it was too late. Irreparable damage had been done. We had passed the point where reconciliation was possible, and she filed suit for divorce.

But while my personal life was following an up-and-down course that finally led to this unhappy turn, there were many important and fast-moving developments on the business front.

The first directors' meeting of the Minnehoma Oil Company since my father's stroke was held in Los Angeles on December 13, 1923. As the charter of the Minnehoma Oil Company was about to expire, and it was not considered desirable to renew the charter, a new company named the Minnehoma Gas and Oil Company was formed. The other directors and I gave unanimous approval to the plan which called for share-for-share exchanges of stock and the transfer of assets to the new company from the old.

A month later, Father organized the George F. Getty, Inc., company, which would take over his California operations; theretofore, he had conducted these as an individual. I was one of the original incorporators and directors of George F. Getty, Inc., which started life in a suite of offices in the A. G. Bartlett Building in Los Angeles and had an initial permanent staff of twenty management and administrative employees.

George F. Getty, Inc., was capitalized at three million dollars, the capitalization consisting of thirty thousand shares of common stock with a par value of one hundred dollars per share. I would later purchase ten thousand shares for a million dollars.

Among the new company's assets were fifty-four oil and gas leases on California properties, of which no less than twenty-three were already producing oil. Included in these producing leases were some which I had purchased and developed and then sold to the pre-incorporation

George F. Getty organization, subject to interests of up to one-half, which I retained for myself.

By making such arrangements, always common in the petroleum industry and highly advantageous to all parties concerned, I retained the traditional wildcatter's freedom of operation. I could work independently, with very little overhead expense, seeking out promising leases, buying them, and drilling test-wells on the properties at comparatively low cost because I had no burdensome administrative tail to wag the production dog. Once I had completed a producing well, the routine day-to-day operations on the property could be better handled by an established organization. In the meanwhile, I was again free to go on to the next prospective venture.

The established organizations which were parties to these arrangements also gained. For their part, they were spared many of the problems and risks of wildcat prospecting and drilling. They were glad to acquire proven, producing properties, the output of which they could sell profitably through their regular and presumably well-organized and smoothly functioning channels.

But, as I have indicated from time to time, many of my ventures were made entirely on my own account. One of the more fortuitous of these during this period was my outright purchase, in May, 1924, of a property known as Lot 1, Block 19 in the Athens Township, about ten miles south of "downtown" Los Angeles.

I did not merely buy the lease on this property. I bought the property itself, obtaining title to it "in fee." The significance and implications of the difference to the oil producer might bear a few words of explanation.

Oil producers do not, as a rule, actually own the properties on which they drill their wells. In the majority of instances, they only acquire leases giving them certain rights to the crude oil or natural gas they find on the property. The reason for this is that the asking price for such leases, whatever that price may be, is always lower than the sale price of the properties themselves. No matter how wealthy he may be, it is not economically feasible for an oil producer to buy outright every property on which he intends to prospect for oil. Besides, he is in business to produce oil, not to encumber himself with ownership of vast tracts of real estate.

Now, the bonus price an oil man pays for an oil and gas lease depends largely on how promising the property appears or is believed to be by the owner of the property or the current owner of the lease. Obviously, the lease on a property that, even though undeveloped, lies in the middle of a producing field will be infinitely higher than the price of one covering a property located in an area where no oil has ever been found or indicated to exist.

Leases being generally transferable, it follows that they are very often bought and sold for speculation, with the original owners deriving no benefit from the staggering prices sometimes paid for leases after they pass through the hands of several speculators. For example, in the great Spindletop boom, original owners of properties located in what became the Spindletop Field sold oil and gas leases on their properties for as little as ten dollars an acre before the boom—and then saw the value of those leases skyrocket until, at the height of the speculative frenzy, some were selling for as much as $900,000 per acre.

However, all of this does not mean that the actual owner of the property received no further compensation. Customarily, leases are for specified periods and call for certain rentals. They provide that, if oil or gas is found on the property, the owner in fee of the property or his assigns shall be paid a royalty on the production. Normally, this royalty is set at one-eighth of the production. Sometimes, it is set at one-sixth or even higher. Furthermore, some leases provide that the owner in fee or his assigns shall receive the first few hundreds or even thousands of barrels of oil produced (or the value thereof).

Withal, when an oil producer does happen to buy a property outright and strikes oil on it, he is in seventh heaven, for all the oil produced is his. He has no royalties to pay to anyone.

I bought Lot 1, Block 19, in the Athens Township outright, giving the owners my personal check for twelve thousand dollars for the deed to the property. The property consisted of a corner lot on Hoover Street between 127th and 128th Streets. It measured 75 feet on 127th Street, 70 feet on 128th Street and 165 feet along Hoover.

I felt certain that I had made a wise investment. On May 6, just six days before I bought Lot 1, a well producing one thousand barrels a day of thirty-seven-gravity clean oil had been brought in by the Union Oil Company only thirteen hundred feet southwest of the property.

The consensus of opinion held that the oil structure being tapped by the new well extended to the southwest. I, on the contrary, felt that the structure extended in the opposite direction, to the northeast. Few, if any, shared my belief. That, of course, was the reason why I was able to buy Lot 1 for twelve thousand dollars when leases alone on properties to the southwest were already bringing more.

As I was then heavily engaged in drilling operations elsewhere, I did nothing further with the property until October, when I made a deal with a man named Roy Perkins to drill the first well on the site. As the Union Oil Co. well had come in at 4,938 feet, I contracted with Perkins to drill to 4,900. A derrick was erected, Perkins moved in a rotary rig and spudded in on November 1, 1924. He got down a few hundred feet—and stopped.

Drilling, not delays, is what produces oil. I was unwilling to wait further, particularly since the Athens boom was by then running full tilt. Several other wells were being drilled in the vicinity by various operators, including the Union Oil Company, which had brought in the first Athens well. I took over the drilling operation from Perkins on January 7, 1925, hired my own drilling crew, and, once more donning overalls and safety helmet, personally supervised work on the site.

By February 16, my men and I had gotten down to 4,350 feet, at which level, nearly six hundred feet above the first Union Oil Company well's pay zone, we struck oil. We thus discovered an entirely new and rich oil zone in the Athens Field, a fact of sufficient general interest for oil men to inspire the following account in the California State Mining Bureau Bulletin:

> The upper oil zone in the Athens area was discovered, by accident, early in 1925. A driller on Union Oil Company of California well No. "Howard Park" 9 noticed some oil sand on a bit drawn from the well at a depth of about 4,300 feet. Cores taken immediately below showed rich oil sand.
>
> At about the same time, J. Paul Getty noticed a rich oil showing while drilling just below 4,200 feet in his well No. 1. He also had cores taken which revealed good oil sands. A water string was set above the oil showings in each of these wells. The Union Oil Company of California well came in February 14, 1925, with an initial yield of 550 barrels per day of 37.7-degree gravity oil.
>
> The J. Paul Getty well was completed February 16, 1925, at a depth of 4,350 feet, with an initial yield of about 1,500 barrels per day of 36.5-degree gravity clean oil.
>
> The completion of these wells caused other operators drilling wells in this area to alter their programs, as it demonstrated that probably

greater production could be obtained at less expense from the upper zone than from the deep zone.

Important as the Athens well may have been, I could not share the elation of the men on my drilling crews at our success. On February 15, the day before the well came in, my wife, Jeanette, was granted her divorce petition by the courts.

I found it difficult to reconcile myself to the thought that my son, George, would not be growing up at my side. I also knew what effect the separation and divorce were having on my parents. I turned my energies to my Athens property, thinking that I could derive some solace from work, and stepped up the pace of my wildcatting operations.

On February 23, a well situated near my Athens No. 1 well blew out, and for a few days, the efforts of everyone working the field were concentrated on extinguishing the roaring blaze and preventing it from spreading to surrounding wells and storage tanks. Luckily, the wild well was brought under control before the fire spread to other properties.

I went ahead with my drilling program on Lot 1. My headquarters was a cubbyhole, desk-space office in a downtown Los Angeles building. My office staff consisted of a part-time combination bookkeeper-stenographer.

I spent most of my time in the field, acting as my own drilling superintendent. My only field employees were the men who worked directly under me on the drilling rigs and wells. It was almost like the early days in Oklahoma, save that instead of a battered Model T Ford, I now drove a long, gleaming Duesenberg.

Duesenberg or not, I still worked side by side with the top-notch men I had selected for my drilling crews. Among them were three of the finest drillers in the entire oil industry: Walter Phillips, Oscar Prowell, and "Spot" McMurdo. The team was a remarkably efficient one. It seemed that every task, whether it involved fishing for a twisted-off bit or an over-all drilling operation, was completed in record time.

This, of course, helped to keep costs down and contributed materially to the success of my Athens venture. Lot 1 proved to be highly profitable. My original $12,000 investment eventually produced a net profit of more than $438,000.

In March, 1926, after all drilling had been completed on the Athens site, I left Los Angeles for a motor tour of Mexico. I felt I needed a change of environment and a chance to get away by myself so that I could do a great deal of serious thinking about a great many things. The realization that my marriage had ended in divorce still depressed and discouraged me. I felt that I, not the marriage, had failed.

It was during this period and while I was in this frame of mind that I met Allene Ashby, the attractive and vivacious daughter of a Texas ranch-owner. We attended the National University in Mexico City, where we had both enrolled to take special summer courses in Mexican history and the Spanish language.

Perhaps I was on what is commonly called the rebound. Possibly, we were both influenced by the romantic atmosphere of Old Mexico, a country which has always enchanted me with its mellow beauty. Whatever the reasons, Allene and I imagined ourselves to be in love, and we were married in Cuernavaca that summer.

Almost immediately, we both realized that it was an ill-advised marriage, one into which we had entered precipitately, without knowing anything about each other or even about each other's personalities, likes, and dislikes.

We had made a great mistake, which we tried to rectify by separating very quickly. Allene would finally obtain a divorce two years later, in 1928.

But by September, 1926, I was back in Los Angeles—alone.

12

I TURNED from the ruins of my short-lived second marriage and again went to work.

In December, 1925, I had purchased a producing lease and two wells from the Hercules Gasoline Company in Los Angeles. At that time, the No. 1 well was making thirty barrels a day and the No. 2 three hundred barrels a day. I paid a total of $140,000 for the lease and equipment.

This proved to be a very poor investment. The No. 1 well played out after producing only one thousand barrels of oil in all. The No. 2 continued to produce, but the cost of working over the wells, the losses incurred in the abandonment of No. 1 and other expenses were staggering. Upon my return to Los Angeles in September, 1926, I found that losses on the Hercules Lease, which would eventually exceed $114,000, were mounting rapidly.

I naturally wanted to offset these spiraling losses as soon as possible and in September leased a promising Huntington Beach, California, property from the Superior Oil Company. Having several other irons in the fire, I did not want to devote as much time to this venture as I had to the Athens Lease. I consequently employed H. M. Macomber to supervise drilling on the property, paying him a well-deserved eight-hundred-dollar-per-month salary.

A highly efficient, seasoned drilling superintendent, Macomber wasted no time before or during drilling operations. Between October 10, 1926, when he spudded the No. 1 well on the property, and mid-February, 1927, he completed a total of five wells. All were producers, with combined initial daily production in excess of 4,450 barrels.

Notwithstanding this, the history of the Superior Lease clearly demonstrates that not all producing oil properties return profits as great as, for example, the Athens Lease. It shows, in fact, that the profits on some producing properties are far below the absolute minimums which, say, a corner haberdashery would require to stay in business.

The proof lies in the simple arithmetic of the Superior Lease payout statement. (I've taken the liberty of rounding the figures off to the nearest thousand.)

I originally paid $13,000 for the lease.

During the eight years that I owned the lease, additional direct costs such as the cost of equipment, production, and development expenses, etc., amounted to $442,000.

This makes a cost total of $455,000.

In eight years, the property produced an income of $492,000.

I received $9,000 for the lease when I sold it in 1934.

Thus, the total on the plus side of the sheet is $501,000.

Deducting from this the $455,000 spent on the property, it is plain to see that my total profit over a period of eight years was only $46,000.

In other words, the return on my nearly half-million-dollar investment worked out to an imperceptible shade more than 1¼ per cent per year!

Needless to say, I could not have long survived in the oil business if very many of my ventures had resulted in losses like those incurred on the Hercules Lease or had produced only microscopic profits such as those earned by the Superior property. Fortunately, there were brighter sides to the picture.

In mid-October, 1926, even while H. M. Macomber was spudding in Superior No. 1, I met C. R. Houser, a lease broker who had purchased the Cleaver Lease at Alamitos Heights, California, a few days previously. In the course of our ensuing conversation, Houser hinted broadly that he might be persuaded to part with the lease.

It so happened that I knew the property in question. It was unproven, but I also knew that the Petroleum Securities Company was drilling a well only four hundred feet away from it. Considering how close this was to the Cleaver property, it was tantamount to having someone drill a test well free of charge for whoever owned the Cleaver Lease. The opportunity was too good to miss.

"How much do you want for the lease?" I asked Houser.

"I'm a great believer in doubling my money," he replied. "I paid four thousand dollars for it, and I'll take eight thousand."

"You've just made yourself a deal," I grinned, taking my personal checkbook and a pen from my pocket. I scrawled a check for the specified amount, gave it to Houser, shook hands with him, and I owned the Cleaver Lease.

After that, I bided my time, waiting to see what results would be obtained by the test well which, in a manner of speaking, the Petroleum Securities Company was so kindly drilling for me, gratis.

On February 20, 1927, the PSC well found oil at 4,757 feet.

That was all I needed to know.

On the next day, my best drillers and I spudded in Cleaver No. 1.

Our operation proceeded at a much faster pace than had the one conducted by the neighboring PSC crew. Our first well was completed within forty days, and three more were in various stages of drilling.

All four wells proved to be exceptional producers. Between 1927 and 1939, the excess recovery on the Cleaver Lease would be nearly $800,000.

Yet, within a few weeks after the first well came in, I was very close not only to losing a fortune, but also to losing the lease itself. Behind this apparent paradox lie two stories. One illustrates what the average wildcatter faced when he jousted with certain major oil firms. The other proves that while some large companies had no compunctions about trying to strangle an independent operator, others were ready and willing to give him a helping hand when he needed it most desperately.

As soon as I'd brought in Cleaver Well No. 1, which produced an impressive fifty-one hundred barrels a day initially, I cast about to find a buyer for my crude production. To my dismay, the major companies I approached refused to deal with me. None would buy so much as a drop of crude from independents operating in the Alamitos Heights area.

This posed a serious problem which threatened to become critical in very short order. Development costs on the Cleaver, Superior, and other leases on which I was then drilling had run high and my cash resources were strained. If I could not sell my production, I would have no immediate income with which to meet current operating expenses.

The motives behind the apparent boycott of independently produced Alamitos Heights crude soon became infuriatingly clear. In the space of only a few days, I received several telephone calls from lease brokers who grandiosely offered to buy the Cleaver Lease from me at a ridiculously low price. Without exception, they refused to name the principals for whom they were acting.

"Just some people who'd like to buy the lease," was the answer with which they evaded my questions about whom they were representing.

By then, I was an old hand in the oil business. I recognized all the classic signs which indicated a well-organized squeeze-play. Certain interests wanted my lease, and doubtless the leases held by other independents in the Alamitos Heights area. Either I sold out at an arbitrarily set and disastrously low price, or I would be left without any market for the oil the property produced.

Unable to sell my oil, I had to find some way to store it. There was no adequate tankage anywhere near the property. In fact, there were no large tanks available anywhere in the Los Angeles Basin. After some days of increasingly frantic searching, I finally found a defunct refinery which had two storage tanks with a total 135,000-barrel capacity. The refinery was located in Watson, about ten miles from the property, but the tanks were empty and in good condition. The trustees of the bankrupt refinery wanted $675 a month rental for the tanks, an amount I paid gladly under the circumstances.

In the meantime, even while I was vainly seeking a buyer for the crude my Cleaver No. 1 well was producing, No. 2 came in for five thousand barrels daily production. This was followed by No. 3, which had an initial daily production of fifty-one hundred barrels, and then by No. 4, the runt of the litter, which came in for twenty-one hundred barrels a day.

This production rate began to fill the two storage tanks I had leased at a very rapid clip, and I was still unable to find a buyer for my oil. I was grimly aware that when the tanks were topped off, I would have no choice but to shut down production completely on the Cleaver Lease property.

Obviously, I was receiving no income from the four highly productive wells. My cash resources, already stretched transparently thin, dwindled further at a dizzying rate. The situation could have easily turned into financial disaster for me. With my leased tanks almost entirely filled, I remembered an old oil field adage.

"When in doubt, go right to the top. The 'No' you get there can't be any louder than the one you get at the bottom."

Desperate, I decided to make a frontal attack on one of the biggest of all the major oil companies—Shell Oil. By a fortunate coincidence, Sir George Legh-Jones, then the president of the Shell Company, happened to be visiting Los Angeles at the time. Despite the trepidation I felt about approaching one of the top men in the entire world petroleum industry, I asked for a personal interview with Sir George. To my surprise, I was informed that he would be happy to see me.

The expression "every inch a gentleman" might well have originated with someone who knew Sir George Legh-Jones and sought to describe him. A warm, friendly man, he listened attentively to what I had to say. The deepening scowl that etched across his face as he heard me out was all the proof I needed that his company was not a party to the boycott and that he heartily disapproved of such tactics.

When I finished speaking, he smiled his reassurance.

"You may stop worrying, Mr. Getty," he told me. "We'll be glad to help you out."

With that, he glanced at his wristwatch, noted that it was four o'clock in the afternoon, and invited me to join him in the hearty English-style tea he had served every afternoon at that hour. I thanked him and accepted his gracious offer. When we had finished our tea, he turned again to business and rapidly outlined precisely what the Shell Company would do to help me out. I could hardly believe my ears.

As a starter, Sir George declared, Shell would contract to purchase the next 1,750,000 barrels of crude oil produced by my Alamitos Heights wells. Then, he said, Shell would begin immediate construction of a pipeline to link my lease to the company's own pipeline network. As for the oil I had in my by then brimful leased storage tanks, I was free to sell it myself; there would be no boycott when word got around that the giant Shell Company had come to my assistance. And sell the storage oil I did, not long thereafter; I sold all 135,000 barrels of it at the posted price of ninety-two cents per barrel.

Sir George Legh-Jones and the Shell Company were as good as their word. Shell work-crews descended on my Cleaver Lease site bright and early on the morning after my conference with Sir George and started to lay the promised pipeline while my astonished drillers watched with popping eyes.

My immediate problems were solved, and the Cleaver Lease was safely and profitably mine.

I might add that I have never forgotten this nor the many other kindnesses and courtesies the Shell Company and its people have shown me on various occasions during my business career.

In May, 1927, my mother and father expressed a longing to see Europe again and asked me to go there with them for a summer holiday. I agreed eagerly, though not without a strong pang of sadness. My parents were both over seventy. Father had never fully recovered from the effects of his stroke in 1923; his right hand was partially paralyzed, and he had to walk with a cane.

I delighted at the thought of spending the summer in Europe with my mother and father, but I realized that at each stage of our travels nostalgic memories of other trips and earlier days would assail me when we saw remembered scenes and places. I also had to face up to the possibility that, considering my parents' ages, the trip might well prove to be the last one the three of us would take abroad together.

It is unfashionable in this glib and brittle age to speak with tender emotion about one's parents and about the love and devotion one feels toward them. I have often had occasion to marvel at the casual, almost callous, manner in which many younger men and women of today dismiss the debts they owe to their parents and how they wilfully disregard and even sneer at family ties and traditions.

Perhaps it is because I belong to an entirely different generation that I feel no twinges of self-consciousness when I say that I loved my mother and father dearly. We enjoyed a close and loving relationship in which they were not only my parents, but also my mentors, friends, and companions. A glance at the pages of my diaries shows that even after I had reached middle age, I unembarrassedly continued to refer to them as my "darling mother" and "dearest father." And they were darling and dear— and much more—to me. It is without any hint of self-reproach or self-abnegation that I say they made me their debtor in countless ways, and I could never hope fully to repay them or their memories.

I hurried to get my business affairs in order during the last two weeks of May, organizing them so they would move along smoothly during my absence. In early June, Mother, Father, and I left Los Angeles for New York. We went by train and were accompanied by Frank Komai who, for more than twenty years, had been my father's trusted and devoted Japanese valet. Like most Japanese people, Frank had trouble pronouncing the letter "L," and as far back as I could remember, I had always been "Mista Pawr" to him.

Mother, Father, and I spent much of the trip from Los Angeles to Chicago looking out of our Pullman window and commenting on the tremendous changes that had taken place everywhere since we made our first trip from Minneapolis to Oklahoma Territory more than twenty-three years before.

"Do you remember how much you hoped to see wild Indians on that trip to Bartlesville?" my mother asked me with a gentle, faraway smile as our train rolled across a stretch of Middle Western prairie.

"Yes, I do, Mama," I replied—and turned my head away. I did not want my parents to see the tears which for no reason that I could explain had suddenly come to my eyes.

We sailed from New York aboard the S.S. *Resolute* on June 7. The weather was fine and the eight-day ocean voyage to Southampton seemed to do my parents a great deal of good. By the time we landed in England, they both seemed rested, relaxed, and several years younger. I determined that I would do everything I possibly could to make their European vacation a pleasant and memorable one.

13

MY PARENTS and I spent two weeks in London and another in Paris, from where we went by rail to Strasbourg, spending a day there and then going on to Baden-Baden. After a few days at the Stephanie Hotel in Baden-Baden, we hired a comfortable Horch limousine for a leisurely drive to Venice, Italy, with stopovers in Augsburg, Munich, Innsbruck, and Cortina d'Ampezzo.

Arriving in Venice, we took a gondola to our hotel, the Royal Danieli. Up to this point in our tour Father's valet, Frank Komai, had maintained an inscrutably noncommittal silence about the sights and scenery. Now, however, as our gondola proceeded along the Grand Canal toward the Danieli, his moon face assumed a half-baffled, half-awe-struck expression, and he made his first and only comment on anything he had seen in Europe.

"I thinking this very funny place. Nothing like same in Japan!" he exclaimed, shaking his head, and rendering his "L's" as "R's."

Several days in Venice, several more at the beachfront Excelsior Hotel on the Lido, and we went on to Rome, then Naples, from where we returned to Paris and later London.

It was a wonderful holiday for all of us. My mother and father were sun-bronzed, greatly refreshed and revitalized. The time we spent together served to dispel their last, lingering irritation and exasperation over my marital misadventures. They decided to return to America in late August but urged me to stay on in Europe if I wished to do so—which I did. I saw them off on the S.S. *Olympic* without qualms, for I knew that the faithful and ubiquitous Frank Komai would see to their every need on the voyage home.

I remained in London until September, then went to Paris, where I rented a *petit meublé* at 12 rue St. Didier for six weeks. I left Europe in late October and arrived back in Los Angeles early the following month. Finding that my business affairs were in good order, I cast about for fresh opportunities. I learned there was a great deal of new activity in the Long Beach, California, area. Although the region had been thoroughly worked over, operators there had started drilling much deeper than before on the theory that rich, untapped pay zones lay below the levels reached by existing wells. Early results achieved by some of these operators were extremely encouraging, and I felt a venture into deeper drilling around Long Beach was a worthwhile gamble.

But leases located anywhere near producing areas in Long Beach were very difficult to obtain. Almost all promising properties had been snapped up long since, during earlier Long Beach booms. Undaunted by this knowledge, I determined to make an old school try.

I made my initial inquiries close to home, checking with the field management personnel of George F. Getty, Inc., my father's firm, but this led me nowhere. The men with whom I spoke informed me that they had made several attempts to secure additional Long Beach leases without success.

"There isn't much chance of finding a lease that's any good down there," they shrugged, adding that they didn't have very much faith in the outcome of deeper drilling in Long Beach anyway.

I had long ago learned never to rely too heavily on anyone's unsupported opinion and felt that the best and most reliable information was always that which one gathered for oneself at first hand. I therefore spent several days in and around Long Beach, making good use of my friendships among lease brokers, drilling superintendents, and drillers working in the area. From information and leads they provided me and data gathered at the county clerk's office, I soon compiled an impressive list of properties in or near producing fields on which the leases were still available.

I inspected each of these properties personally without further delay and narrowed the list down to about a dozen promising ones. All but five of these were either greatly overpriced, or titles to the leases on them were clouded or appeared undesirable for other reasons. I thereupon bought the remaining five leases, known as the Carson, Fidelity, Industrial Fuel, Whittier, and Wyatt leases.

I later transferred these to George F. Getty, Inc., under the arrangement which, as I explained in a previous chapter, left me with a participating interest in the leases. In these instances, as in some others, I retained a 50-per-cent interest.

The wells drilled on these properties were excellent producers. My half-share of the subsequent excess recovery totaled considerably more than $2,000,000. In fact, as I later had occasion to point out to certain George F. Getty, Inc., management personnel, had it not been for the nearly $5,000,000 in excess recovery—profit—produced by these and other leases I transferred to the company, it would have shown a net loss of some $400,000 over a ten-year period!

However, I did not feel justified in resting on the laurels of the Long Beach leases. There were other leases to be acquired and other wells to be drilled. By now, I had splurged on a one-room office of my own in the Bartlett Building and had even hired a full-time secretary. My fear of getting bogged down in administrative detail and paper work being all but phobic, I stayed out in the field as much as possible. At first a bit bewildered by it all, Lillian Marvin, my secretary, finally got accustomed to the idea of not seeing her employer for weeks on end and talking to him only occasionally on the telephone.

I think that three of my experiences during this stage of my business career illustrate the extent of the need for flexibility, adaptability, improvisation, and informality in the wildcatter's operations.

In the 1920's, a rotary drilling bit that broke or twisted off in a hole usually meant that the drillers had a serious problem on their hands. Days, even weeks, could be spent "fishing" for the broken bit. There could be no further drilling until the bit was recovered and pulled out of the hole. Such delays were, needless to say, costly to the operator, who had to keep on paying regular wages and meeting most other expenses even though the drilling operation had stopped dead.

Fishing—grappling blindly for a piece of metal that might be as much as a mile below the ground in the drill-hole—was the only answer, and the tools used for fishing were far from perfect.

Then, in 1927, one of my drilling crews had a twist-off on a Santa Fe Springs site. Weeks during which the well might have been completed were wasted while the crew fished vainly for the broken bit that was somewhere three or four thousand feet below them. Costs mounted steadily and it began to appear that the men would never be able to locate the bit and bring it to the surface.

I racked my brains in an effort to contrive some alternative way of solving the problem. At last, I had what seemed a far-out but nevertheless theoretically feasible idea. One afternoon, I drove my Duesenberg to a stoneyard that adjoined a Los Angeles cemetery. I parked in front, got out, and searched among the various sample grave-markers on display until I found what I wanted—a six-foot-long marble shaft. I told the stonecutter I would buy it, but that I wanted him to cut it to taper at one end.

"And the inscription?" he asked.

I rather imagine he thought me slightly mad when I said no inscription was needed, that I'd just take the shaft with me in my car after he'd cut it to taper. The exasperated drillers who were still hard at work fishing also must have harbored doubts about my sanity when I drove onto the drilling site with a Duesenberg load of marble grave-marker shaft.

"Get your fishing tools clear and then throw this down the hole," I told them. They stared at me, shrugged, and did as I instructed.

The improvised expedient worked. The heavy granite shaft permitted the driller to sidetrack the fish and continue drilling without further hindrance. Granite whipstocks have been used successfully in similar situations ever since. They're called "Paul Getty Specials" in the oil business.

The great California oil booms of the Roaring Twenties created a chronic shortage of experienced oil-field workers. With hundreds of new wells being drilled constantly throughout the state, there were more jobs than qualified men to fill them. The personnel managers of most large oil companies were generally engaged in wild scrambles to find the necessary manpower to carry out their respective companies' drilling programs. They bid frantically against each other in the labor market, offering special inducements and fringe benefits to rig builders, drillers, roustabouts—to anyone who'd had any actual experience working on an oil rig.

Characteristically, most veteran oil-field workers resented the implication that they had to be bribed with frills in order to do a day's work. Hard-bitten rugged individualists, they preferred to sign on with up-from-the-ranks wildcatters who offered no fancy extras but spoke their language and worked along with them on the job.

I'll never forget one occasion when I began drilling operations on a property not far from the site on which a major oil company was drilling a well—and what a well. Carrying its "employee relations program" to ludicrous extremes, the company had designed and built what its press agents glowingly described as the last word in drilling rigs. "The finest structure of its kind in the world," they called it.

The entire rig was steam-heated, all the way up to the crown block.

A neatly raked white-gravel drive led from the nearest road to the site. There were hot showers for the men and even a laundry to wash their work-clothes while they waited. Rest rooms that would have done credit to a first-class hotel had been built a discreet distance from the elaborately lit derrick.

One afternoon, about a week after I had spudded my well, a sun-baked, leathery roustabout appeared on the site. He announced that he wanted to see "whoever was boss." As I was acting as my own drilling super-intendent, one of my men sent him over to me. The roustabout wasted no time asking me if I would give him a job.

"You working now?" I inquired.

"Yeah," came the sour reply.

"Where?"

"Over there," the job-hunting roustabout replied, inclining his head toward the de luxe drilling rig that stood only a few hundred feet from my property.

Now there were no home comforts available for my crew, and I told the man as much. And, I added, I couldn't understand why he would dream of leaving a job that offered such luxuries to come over and work on my comparatively primitive operation.

"I've been on that damned rig for four months," the roustabout rasped angrily. "We've only gotten down to four thousand feet."

I laughed. Four thousand feet in four months was a ridiculously slow rate for drilling a well through the type of formations that were encoun-tered in that particular field.

"How long do you think it's going to take me to get down that far?" I asked out of curiosity.

"From the looks of you—about ten days!" came the reply. "That's why I'd rather work for you than for that creampuff outfit over there!"

Needless to say, he got the job, and he stayed on my payrolls until his retirement many years later.

As a footnote, I might add that my well was drilled in record time and proved a fine producer. The last word in drilling rigs brought in a dry hole and was finally abandoned.

A good example of what close teamwork and mutual confidence be-tween a wildcatting working boss and his crew could accomplish can be found in the story of how my men and I licked the "insoluble" problem posed by an "impossible" lease.

The lease was on a tiny piece of property set in the midst of a forest of oil wells in the rich Seal Beach, California, Field. By some fluke, the lease had been overlooked by the firms which were operating in the field. A company in which I held a substantial interest acquired the lease but was about to write it off as a dead loss. Everyone agreed that nothing could ever be done with the property—certainly no oil well could ever be drilled on it.

In the first place, it was a plot barely larger than the floor area of a small house. In the second place, the only right-of-way providing access to a road was over a strip of ground several hundred feet long but less than four feet wide. It was impossible to bring supplies and equipment to the property over this constricted path. Even if it had been possible, the postage-stamp-size plot would not have accommodated a standard-sized derrick and drilling rig. The companies holding leases on adjacent properties refused to grant any easement of right-of-way over their sites, for if a producing well was brought in, it would only diminish the production of their own wells, since it would unquestionably be pumping oil from the same pool.

"Forget that lease," associates with whom I discussed the matter advised me. "You'll never get a well drilled there—not in a million years."

Stubbornly, I insisted that there must be a way. I put the problem before the men in whom I had the greatest confidence, the members of one of my drilling crews. They listened to me, and their reaction was identical to mine. They considered the problem an irresistible challenge, and they refused to accept the "impossibility" of the situation.

"Hell, boss, let's all just mosey out to the property and take a good look at things," one of my drillers drawled. "We'll find some way—I'll bet on it."

The members of the crew and I drove out to survey the situation for ourselves. I had to park my car on the road—not even a passenger automobile could go over the right-of-way to the property without encroaching on the properties which bordered on it. Things did look quite hopeless. Reaching the property on foot, we stood around for several minutes without saying anything. Then the driller who had suggested that we come out there in the first place hunkered down on his haunches and scratched thoughtfully at the soil with a stick.

"I guess we could drill the well with an undersized rig," he mused after some long seconds of deep thought. "If you could find someone to design and build it, we could sure set it up and get it operating, but I can't figure how we're going to bring everything we need in from the road."

The obstacle provided by the limited access right-of-way seemed insuperable until my mind began to turn over the driller's suggestion about a miniature drilling rig. If we could drill with a miniature rig, why couldn't we solve our transportation problem with a miniature railway?

It was a perfect solution: a narrow-gauge track and a car or two on which the disassembled "baby" derrick and supplies could be manhandled from the road to the drilling site.

Mulish obstinacy? A compulsion to prove that we could accomplish what everyone said was impossible? Possibly—even probably. But both the miniature rig and the miniature railway were procured. The former was moved in sections over the latter—mine-sized flatcars pushed by hand from the road to the drilling site. The rig was assembled by hand on the microscopic plot and placed in operation.

Drilling proceeded satisfactorily and soon the well was near completion. Unfortunately, I had to leave Los Angeles on business for several weeks. During my absence, the drillers had a bit twist off, and a long, arduous fishing job followed. The well was finally abandoned.

I've always regretted that we gave up after having worked so hard to get a rig in place, and when we were only a few hundred feet from pay sand. The story, however, has a happy ending. The lease was sold at a profit not long thereafter to a company which owned and operated adjoining drilling sites.

14

ONE cannot look back on 1928, the year in which the Roaring Twenties moved into their final and most hectic stage, without remembering its countless contradictions and, in retrospect, recalling the unreal, Alice in Wonderland atmosphere that prevailed.

In 1928, the federal budget totaled some $4,250,000,000; the United States national debt stood at $17,500,000,000. Round steak was priced around 40 cents per pound, and milk was delivered to the door for 14 cents per quart. Prohibition was still the law of the land, but floods of bootleg liquor inundated the nation, speak-easies flourished, and gangland murders made daily headlines.

Business appeared to be booming, at least in some sectors. Sales of radio sets alone totaled over $650,000,000 that year. Automobile output was rising, and streams of Model A Fords, first introduced in December, 1927, were pouring off assembly lines, adding their numbers to the more than 20,000,000 automobiles already on United States highways. In September, 1927, 104,943 people paid a total of $2,658,660 to see Gene Tunney win a ten-round decision over Jack Dempsey. In 1928, more than 437,000 people had enough spare cash to take trips and tours abroad. Prosperity, everyone seemed to agree, would continue forever.

Below this bright and glittering surface, there were indications that everything wasn't as good as it appeared. Farm prices were down, and general employment was sagging. Credit was overextended, and production in many industries was dropping off. Nearly 60 per cent of the country's families received incomes of less than two thousand dollars per year.

The majority ignored the warning signals. People continued to pour more and more of their own money—and money they had borrowed—into the stock market. On March 3, 1928, the great bull market entered into its most frenzied phase. Although many stocks were already fantastically overpriced in relation to earnings and dividends, their prices soared even higher as speculators and self-styled "investors" started a new orgy of buying.

Sharp market breaks in July and December should have been sufficient to sound the alarm, but people refused to recognize their significance. The market recovered each time, and stock prices rocketed even higher than their previous peaks until, just before the final 1929 crash, some issues were selling for seventy-five and more times their earnings.

Nor was the American petroleum industry without its problems in 1928. Continuing expansion and steadily mounting production were gradually threatening to glut petroleum markets once again. Crude oil production not only exceeded consumption but even refining capacity. Increasing quantities of crude were being moved from wells to storage rather than to refineries. While crude prices held fairly steady, posted at around 90 cents per barrel on the West Coast and in the neighborhood of $1.40 in the midcontinent, there were many people in the industry who felt that "something" would have to be done to regulate production. Otherwise, they predicted, the entire petroleum price-structure, and a goodly portion of the industry itself, would collapse. What exactly that "something" that needed to be done was, few could agree.

Some favored proration—the limitation of the quantity of oil a well in a flush field could produce per day or over a given period. Others plumped for unitization—the development of an oil field as a unit, with producers being limited to drilling only so many wells or only so many wells per acre or per a given number of acres. Proponents of both methods split over whether regulation should be voluntary or compulsory and, if compulsory, then whether the federal, state, or local governments should do the regulating.

Oklahoma had passed a trial proration law in 1915, and Texas had done the same in 1919. These had been steps forward at the time, but the failure of other oil-producing states to follow suit and other factors had rendered the laws largely ineffective.

As far back as 1923, Henry L. Doherty, head of the Cities Services Companies, had urged passage of a federal unit-operation—unitization—law. The prospect of federal regulation being no less repugnant then than now to many people, the proposal found few supporters. In 1927, the first voluntary proration agreement was entered into by producers operating in the Yates Field in Texas. This was followed by some scattered similar agreements elsewhere, but these took only drops from the overflowing petroleum bucket.

The layman may be excused for wondering why, if production was again beginning to outstrip demand, oil men continued to prospect and drill new wells and open new fields.

The reasons for this in 1928 were no different than they have always been in the history of the petroleum industry.

Although there may be too much oil aboveground at any given time, there is no way of determining what the situation might be a few years or even a few months later. Oil wells—indeed, entire fields and even whole producing areas—have a disconcerting habit of playing out unexpectedly and rapidly, as may be seen in the following few random examples taken from among the many hundreds that are available to anyone who cares to check the facts and figures.

The great Texas Spindletop Field, discovered in 1901, produced 17,-400,000 barrels of oil in 1902; output skidded to around 1,000,000 barrels in 1906 and fell well below the million mark five years after that.

Oklahoma's Glenn Pool produced more than 20,000,000 barrels in 1908. By 1912, production had been halved, and in 1919 the field's output had dropped to 5,000,000 barrels.

In 1925, the state of Arkansas produced nearly 78,000,000 barrels of petroleum. Four years later, production had skidded to less than 24,000,-000 barrels.

In short, there is only so much oil at the bottom of any hole—assuming, of course, that there is any at all—and it's difficult to tell when the reservoir will be exhausted. Nor is there any reliable means for gauging future demand. That the demand for petroleum products can rise very suddenly and sharply is due to causes as diverse as exceptionally cold winters, which raise the demand for heating oil, early springs, which cause millions of motorists to take to the highways a month or two ahead of normal schedule, prolonged labor-stoppages in coal mines, or declarations of war.

In recent years, a graphic example of the kind of situation which might develop at any time was provided by the 1956–57 blocking of the Suez Canal. This had the effect of virtually cutting the Western world off from its vital Middle Eastern crude oil sources. During the months that the Canal was being cleared to permit passage of ship traffic once more, available aboveground oil supplies in the West were rapidly drained off. For a time, it appeared that a serious oil shortage would develop.

Opposed economic forces have always pulled the oil producer in two directions simultaneously. On the one hand, he is more aware than anyone else that overproduction can drive prices down to levels at which it is economically impossible for him to remain in business. On the other hand, he must maintain production to obtain income, meet competition, and survive in business. He must continue to prospect and drill for oil, for he must continually seek new sources against the day when the production of his existing wells drops off or ceases altogether. He cannot keep his discoveries secret nor monopolize the production of a new field. A single new producing well in a previously unproved field is sufficient to bring a rush of other producers to the area, and they will buy up leases and drill additional wells on surrounding properties.

It cannot be emphasized enough that the financial risks the oil producer takes are often enormous and the costs of his operations are even more often staggering. It is not unusual for a producer to spend a million dollars or more on a single prospecting and drilling operation today—and to have nothing to show for his money and efforts but a worthless duster. In fact, up to one-third of all drilling operations nowadays result in dry holes.

After World War II, the Pacific Western Oil Corporation, which I controlled, and which has since been renamed the Getty Oil Company, spent over $18,500,000 in payments to the Saudi Arabian government and on prospecting and drilling for oil in the Middle East before bringing in a single producing well.

By 1928 some definite steps were already being taken to prevent runaway overproduction in at least some American oil fields. The effects of this were felt by George F. Getty, Inc., in connection with its Armstrong Lease in Kern County, California. On April 28, the company had acquired the lease, which applied to a property in a region known as the Kettleman Hills, almost by accident and for a price that could be said to have been only a few bars of the proverbial song. The Kettleman Hills area would subsequently prove to be one of the richest oil-producing areas ever developed in the state of California. George F. Getty, Inc., would finally reap a profit of over four million dollars when it sold the lease a few years later. However, in 1928, drilling on the property had to be suspended pending the outcome of complex negotiations between Kettleman Hills producers who wanted to establish a unit-operation plan.

Withal, 1928 was a fairly prosperous and satisfactory year. My own ventures were profitable. The Athens, Cleaver, and Superior properties, which I operated on my own account, were producing at a good rate and, since the Shell Oil Company had helped break the boycott on my Alamitos Heights crude, I was having no great difficulty disposing of my crude production at the prevailing prices.

On December 31, 1927, George F. Getty, Inc., had assets of some $3,-700,000. The company showed a profit during 1928, largely as a result of the income produced by the Santa Fe Springs and Long Beach leases I had bought, then sold to the company while retaining a participating interest in them. One huge cost-item during the year was the disastrous blowout of well No. 17 on the Nordstrom Lease in Santa Fe Springs. The well blew out in September and burned for six weeks. The fire was only extinguished after a long, laborious tunneling job that tapped the well-casing below the surface.

The blowout and the battle to conquer the blaze cost the company more than $300,000 in direct expenses and an incalculable sum in lost oil.

As for the Minnehoma Oil and Gas Company, successor to Minnehoma Oil Company, its 1928 dividends were the highest in six years. In 1927, my father had incorporated the George F. Getty Oil Company and began operations in New Mexico, where he opened up a new producing area known as the Getty Pool in 1928, bringing in five producing wells between February and September of that year.

Despite the apparent success of Father's companies, it did not seem to me that they were being managed and operated altogether as he would have wanted, or as he would have managed and operated them personally. I recognized areas of activity in which I felt that economies could be achieved, and I believed that greater production and profits could be obtained through more energetic efforts in certain other areas of activity.

I was aware that my father had been unable to devote the necessary time and energy to his companies since suffering a stroke in 1923. Although he was still mentally alert and remained a keenly enterprising businessman, he never managed to recover the strength and energy he had possessed prior to his illness.

I brought these matters to my father's attention as circumspectly as I could. I did not want to worry or upset him, but at the same time I realized that the worry would be infinitely greater if things began to slide, and he suddenly realized that his business affairs were not as he would want them to be.

I pointed out the things I thought were wrong and presented the facts and figures to sustain my contentions. Obviously, Father recognized that the situation was not all that it should have been. He offered me ten thousand shares of stock in George F. Getty, Inc., at one hundred dollars a share. This would give me a 30-per-cent interest in the company itself—and, even more importantly, would give me a considerable voice in the management of its affairs.

I accepted the offer immediately, paying my father one million dollars for the stock. I soon began to wonder if I hadn't bitten off a great deal more than I could comfortably chew.

15

Cornelius VANDERBILT, JR., who has been married six times, not long ago wrote: *In my view, we much-married people are the idealists, the romantics, the searchers for an ideal of happiness that seems to elude us in this life.*

I am not certain that I would endorse Mr. Vanderbilt's views one hundred per cent, but I would be the first to admit that a rich man, just like a poor one, does seek personal happiness in life. He does want to love and be loved—and to have a wife, children, and a happy home.

The rich man learns that not only is it impossible to buy these things with money, but that his wealth is, in itself, often a bar preventing him from having and holding them. Nonetheless, he continues to seek—and to hope.

While in Vienna during my 1927 European tour, I had met tall, blonde, and lovely Adolphine Helmle. The daughter of a well-to-do German engineer and businessman, she was visiting Vienna with her parents, and we saw each other several times. Romance blossomed despite the strictly chaperoned climate in which it was nurtured.

Adolphine—"Fini"—and I corresponded regularly after my return to the United States. In December, 1928, after my second wife finally obtained a divorce decree, Fini met me in Havana, Cuba, where we were married. We honeymooned in Florida and then drove cross-country from Palm Beach to Los Angeles.

As I have already indicated, my mother and father had been deeply hurt by the fact that two of my marriages had ended in divorce. In 1928, I was older and a bit more mature than I had been before. I sought to avoid causing my parents any further emotional upset or pain and discussed my plans to marry Fini with them beforehand. I wanted to bring my wife home to them and to have them accept her in their home. Mother and Father gave their approval to my marriage, and they received Fini as warmly and affectionately as if she had been their own daughter when we arrived in Los Angeles after our honeymoon.

Unfortunately for the future of my third marriage, I had neither time nor opportunity for further honeymooning after I returned to southern California. I had purchased a 30-per-cent interest in George F. Getty, Inc., the year before. On March 11, 1929, just a few days after Fini and I arrived in Los Angeles, I was elected a director of the company and began to take an active part in its management even while I continued to manage my own ventures and enterprises.

While my father seldom failed to appear at his office daily whenever he was in Los Angeles, he could remain at his desk for only an hour or two at a time. He was also away quite frequently. In 1926, he had spent about three months in Boston, where he studied Christian Science. In 1927, he had, of course, toured Europe with Mother and me. The following year, he and Mother had gone to Hawaii. Christian Science, the sea voyages, and the rest and relaxation he obtained during his holidays appeared to help him, and if they did not markedly improve his physical condition, at least they seemed to keep it from deteriorating any further.

In view of these circumstances, I found it advisable to devote an increasing amount of attention to the affairs of George F. Getty, Inc., during the weeks that followed my election to the company's Board of Directors.

The balance sheet of George F. Getty, Inc., showed that on December 31, 1928, the company had assets of more than $5,280,000. The firm's profit and loss statement showed a 1928 total gross income of over $3,600,000 and a net profit of some $350,000.

Back in 1923, as I have said, friction developed between the company's field management and myself. The bone of contention then had been the manner in which operations were being conducted on the partnership leases which I had sold to George F. Getty, Inc., but in which I retained a working interest. In 1924, the field management team had been replaced and the frictions ceased. However, in 1929, history seemed to be repeating itself with a vengeance. Once again, I found that my views and opinions were at wide variance with the incumbent field management. The differences were over questions of policy and operation. Now I owned 30 per cent of the company's stock. My interest in the manner in which the company's affairs were conducted was no longer limited solely to certain leases; it extended to the over-all operation, for I now had a one-million-dollar investment-stake in George F. Getty, Inc.

It soon became obvious that the conflict of views could not be readily resolved. The situation was complicated by the fact that the company was even then in the midst of a heavy—and costly—drilling program. The solution to the growing dilemma came on July 1, 1929, when the field superintendent and his assistant tendered their resignations. Their resignations were accepted, and Clayton Hall, a thoroughly experienced man who had been with the company for years and had worked his way up from tool-pusher to drilling superintendent, was then appointed field superintendent. Aggressive, farsighted, and imaginative, Hall had a knack for keeping production up even while he held costs down.

This and certain other changes had highly beneficial effects. In 1929, the company drilled a total of seventeen new wells to completion and started nine others in the Santa Fe Springs field alone. That year, the excess recovery—profit—from the Santa Fe Springs Field reached a record $2,400,000, while the excess recovery from Long Beach leases came close to $1,000,000. All other fields showed increased production, and the company purchased 114 new leases during 1929. Altogether, 1929 would prove to be a fine year for George F. Getty, Inc. The company's daily production of crude oil reached 30,000 barrels, and profit for the year exceeded $1,600,000, or nearly five times the profit earned in 1928.

On August 1, 1929, Board of Directors' meetings were held by both George F. Getty, Inc., and Minnehoma Oil and Gas Company. At the former meeting, my father resigned as General Manager of George F. Getty, Inc., and I was elected Vice-President and General Manager. C. C. Beem, a friend of mine, was elected Assistant General Manager of George F. Getty, Inc. I was also elected a director, Vice-President and General Manager of Minnehoma Oil and Gas Company.

These new responsibilities made enormous additional demands on my time and energies.

George F. Getty, Inc., was conducting extensive drilling operations in various fields throughout southern California. Minnehoma Oil and Gas was simultaneously in the process of developing four leases covering 310 acres in Oklahoma. These and other equally important business matters required much attention and close supervision. Having accepted the position of General Manager of both companies, I was determined to do a good job and increase the efficiency and profits of both. For the next three months I worked almost literally around the clock to achieve the aims and goals I had set.

No matter how worthwhile I may have considered my efforts in these directions, the pressures and demands of business were again to take their toll in my personal life.

In late spring, 1929, my wife, Fini, told me that she was pregnant and expected the baby to be born sometime in December. I was thrilled and extremely happy, but I could spare scant time to spend with her during the early months of her pregnancy.

I probably should have taken into consideration such things as Fini's then-sketchy knowledge of English and her natural and understandable feelings of unease and insecurity at being in a strange country. Even more, I should have realized that she knew very little about business or how men in the oil business had to operate. But I was busy, extremely busy, and, although she lived with my parents in our family home on Wilshire Boulevard, Fini viewed my inability to give her constant attention as neglect and my preoccupation with business as lack of interest in her and the child she was expecting.

Fini expressed a desire to return to Germany. She wanted to be near her own family when she had the baby. I could not accompany her and reluctantly sent her back with the promise that I would follow as soon as it was humanly possible.

That was in late summer. I continued doing what I felt I had to do if I were to discharge my obligations to my father and the stockholders and employees of his companies. By mid-October, I felt that I had accomplished a goodly portion of what I'd set out to do. Both George F. Getty, Inc., and Minnehoma Oil and Gas were functioning smoothly. Accountants' reports already indicated that the former company would end the year with record earnings, and Minnehoma's drilling operations in Oklahoma were proceeding in an entirely satisfactory manner. It appeared that I could safely take several weeks off and go to Germany to be with Fini.

Then, just as I had completed my plans and preparations for a trip to Europe, the "Black Thursday" panic struck Wall Street.

On Wednesday, October 23, 1929, the nervousness the stock market had been exhibiting since early the previous September jelled into a large-scale selling wave that sent *The New York Times* averages for fifty leading stocks tumbling more than eighteen points.

A sell-off by skittish small investors . . .

A minor readjustment . . .

Wall Street experts predict an immediate rebound . . .

Such were the reassuring statements that appeared on Wednesday afternoon in an American press that had become accustomed to reporting nothing but steadily rising stock prices through the booming years of the big bull market.

The "immediate rebound" which had been so confidently prophesied by the Wall Street experts on Wednesday failed to materialize when the New York Stock Exchange opened the next morning—on Thursday, October 24, 1929. On the contrary, the previous day's selling wave surged up again and almost immediately assumed the proportions of a disastrous flood that swept away stock prices and brought panic in its wake.

Early-morning "sell" orders caused prices to drop below their Wednesday closing levels. As the prices fell, more "sell" orders poured in from countless thousands of people who had bought shares on slender margins and were unwilling or unable to increase those margins when prices plunged down to levels below those at which they had originally purchased their stocks.

The Stock Exchange was in a turmoil as prices tumbled ten, twenty, thirty, and even more points. The ticker lagged far behind, and the lack of up-to-the-minute information caused worried individuals to dump even more shares on the market.

Bankers representing six of the largest financial institutions in the United States held an emergency meeting and pledged a fund totaling nearly a quarter of a billion dollars in a desperate effort to stabilize the stock market long enough for trading to resume an orderly course. These men, the real financial experts, sought to avert the financial chaos that they knew would inevitably follow a sustained panic. For a short time, it seemed as though they would succeed in holding the dike. When the trading day ended on Thursday with a record volume of nearly thirteen million shares, the panic had been halted—temporarily. Many shares had made fairly good last-minute recoveries, and there were even a few that had regained or surpassed their opening-gong levels.

Wall Street and much of the nation watched and waited with bated breath. For the moment, it appeared as though the stock market had managed to ride out the crisis and avoid calamity.

Then, on Monday, October 28, the full fury of the temporarily suspended panic selling struck again, once more carrying prices to dismal lows. The next day was even worse. *The New York Times* averages of fifty leading stocks took a staggering nose dive, falling almost forty points in the day's trading.

The panic spread to the grain and commodities markets and to foreign and smaller American stock exchanges. Prices, many of which had been bid far too high during the bright boom years of the Roaring Twenties, collapsed everywhere. And, as one price fell, it dragged another with it.

People who had bought stock on margin and could not provide more margin—and by then there were very few who could—were sold out and, in many cases, completely ruined financially. Banks and other lending institutions began calling their loans, while borrowers, wiped out overnight by the Wall Street collapse, were numbly realizing that they could not pay their debts.

Wall Street staged an almost miraculous recovery on Wednesday and Thursday, but uncountable billions had already been lost by investors and speculators, both large and small. The upward jog of prices was shortlived. The stock market trend was definitely established as "down," and prices continued to drift and stagger lower until the year's low was reached on November 13, when the *Times* averages of fifty leading stocks stood at nearly half what they had been at their September high.

The news of the initial October 29 "Black Thursday" price collapse caused me to cancel my immediate arrangements for traveling to Europe. I decided to postpone my European trip and to go instead to New York City. At first glance, it might well seem to have been a foolish—or at best, unnecessary—change in plans.

My father and I owned comparatively few stocks outside those of our own companies. And, at that time, no Getty companies were public-stock companies. Thus it would appear that I had no overriding reasons for being on the scene.

But I felt that what was happening on Wall Street would have extremely far-reaching effects. I sensed that the stock market collapse and its ramifications would set the course of the nation's over-all economy for several years to come. I thought it important to be on the spot—to look and listen and, above all, to learn.

I made regular visits to the New York Stock Exchange during the hectic, chaotic days that had their gloomy climax on November 13, 1929. I watched the debacle at first hand and talked to brokers and bankers, businessmen and financiers, investors and speculators. What I saw and heard and learned during the fortnight I remained in New York would prove invaluable to me in the years that followed.

I learned much about the stock market, stocks, investment, and the perils and pitfalls of speculation. Throughout it all, I was conscious of the awful drama that was being played around me. I realized that I was an eyewitness to the violent death of an era.

16

LIKE almost all veteran businessmen, I have been asked frequently for my interpretation of the 1929 stock market crash, its causes and implications.

I doubt seriously that there is much, if anything, I can add to what has already been said and written about the crash and the great economic slump which followed. Both crash and Depression have been cursed, discoursed upon, analyzed, and dissected by unnumbered experts and authorities, historians, and economists for more than three decades.

The basic, underlying causes of the boom and bust of the twenties are fairly easy to identify, at least in retrospect. There was overproduction in industry. Credit was overextended. Overoptimistic investors and speculators overbought stocks which were overpriced.

Many people today tend to forget the fact that the big bull market of the late 1920's climbed to its most dizzying heights during a period when the general state of American business was anything but good.

By the beginning of 1929, there had already been sizable cutbacks in iron, steel, and automobile production. The building industry was in the doldrums. The nation had a gnawing and growing unemployment problem, and consumer goods were piling up in warehouses and on dealers' shelves.

In short, the nation's economy was already limping. But stock prices continued to soar, driven ever higher by an irrational speculative buying-fever that had become nothing short of a national mass hysteria and that completely ignored the most fundamental economic home truths. To make matters worse, much stock buying was on margin, and this served to further strain the country's already thinly stretched credit resources.

There were many warnings. Hard-headed bankers and financiers tried to convince people that stock prices were at dangerously high levels, but no one listened. Federal Reserve System officials warned against the ever-increasing perils of wild speculation, and the System itself used what means were at its disposal to restrict loans and fight the insane inflation of stock prices, but none of these things helped.

The day of reckoning had to come—and it did. True that it might have come in a more orderly fashion. Tragically, at the first signs of a serious stock market price break, what had been speculative buying fever turned into an even more virulent and panic-inducing fever to dump out, to sell at any price.

The stock market crash did not alone and in itself cause the Depression. The causative structural flaws and weaknesses were present in the American economy long before the price break that began on October 23, 1929.

The explosion that brought down the entire sagging framework could have come from almost any business quarter. A slump was just around the corner anyway. Only the most drastic measures—or a miracle—could have averted it. It could have been triggered by a sudden spate of bank failures, big price breaks on the commodities markets, or by any of a dozen other events and factors.

It just so happened that it was the stock market which gave first. The reverberations of its crash blasted the props out from the entire tottering structure.

As for the stock market per se, the seeds of its October 23 bust were inherent in the big bull market boom which had long before outstripped the rate of American business and economic expansion. That the stock market was the first to go is due in large degree to the fact the most people who were buying stocks during the boom were not really investors. They were speculators who knew very little about the stock market, the theory or practice of sound stock-investment, or even about the companies issuing the stocks that they so avidly purchased in the totally illogical and unreasonable belief that Wall Street prices would continue to spiral upward indefinitely. The abysmal lack of knowledge displayed by many stock-buyers of the 1920's is graphically exemplified by Frederick Lewis Allen's true anecdote about the people who rushed to buy Seaboard Air Line (Railway) shares in the belief that they were buying an aviation stock.

People did not invest. They "played the market," obviously viewing stock certificates as betting slips in some mammoth and, as they seemingly believed, foolproof gambling venture rather than as deeds of ownership in business enterprises.

The majority of stock-buying in the late 1920's was emotionally inspired. Self-styled "investors" hoped—and, indeed, expected—to reap huge profits fast, even overnight.

From the over-all standpoint, it was tragic that many did just that, at least temporarily and on paper. Each report or rumor that someone had "made a killing," even though the profits were purely paper ones, was enough to impel more emotional speculators to "take a flyer" and "get in on a good thing."

Prices went higher and higher, bid up by irrational buyers who apparently gave no thought whatsoever to real values or, for that matter, to any realities at all. Speculators paid no attention to the earnings of the companies whose stocks they were buying or to the dividends that were or were not being paid on the shares. They knew or cared nothing about what the companies did or sold, what their assets or potentials were, or how good or bad were the companies' policies, management, and financial positions.

Stock prices soared into a never-never land stratosphere. Calm, seasoned financiers and brokers and level-headed investors warned that prices would eventually have to come plunging down, but their warnings went unheeded and they were labeled doom-mongers and worse.

The long-delayed awakening came at last. Doubts about the true worth of insanely inflated stocks were raised in many minds. Confidence was lost. The great wave of selling began, and prices plunged down.

The 1929 crash taught—or should have taught—all investors and would-be investors several harsh and painful, but invaluable, lessons. Among these are three which can be considered and stated as axiomatic rules for investment in common stocks. They are, incidentally, as valid and valuable today as they ever were or ever will be:

One: While sound, selected common stocks are likely to be fine investments, they are just as likely to prove risky when purchased purely for speculation.

To put it another way, investors are individuals who bank on the climate, while speculators bet on the weather. The climate follows an established and predictable pattern year after year and decade after decade. The weather is notoriously temperamental and changeable.

The investor buys for the long pull and reaps his profits from dividends and through the gradual growth of his capital. He banks on the historical fact that the over-all trend of stock prices, like the over-all trends of living costs, wages, and almost everything else, is *up*. He calmly waits out the dips, slumps, and recessions, and even depressions, and holds on to his stocks.

The speculator buys in the hopes that he can make big, short-term profits and is blind to the fact that short-term developments are highly unpredictable and are generally governed by countless variable and imponderable elements, factors, and forces.

Two: Common stocks should be purchased when their prices are low, not after they have risen to high levels during soaring bull market spirals. It is illogical to buy when stock or any other prices are at or near their peaks.

Three: An investor should know as much as he possibly can about the companies which issue the stock in which he invests his money. Among the questions that every prospective investor should ask and to which he should obtain clear and satisfactory answers before buying *any* stock are these ten:

1. What is the history of the company which issues the stock—is it a solid and reputable firm with a good reputation and seasoned, efficient management?

2. Is the company producing or dealing in goods or services for which there will be a continuing demand in the foreseeable future?

3. Is the company operating in a field which is not overcrowded, and is it in a satisfactory competitive position within that field?

4. Are company policies and operations far-sighted and aggressive without calling for or involving unjustified or unreasonably hazardous expansion?

5. Will the corporate balance sheet stand up under close scrutiny by a critical and impartial accountant?

6. Does the company have a satisfactory earnings record, and does the price of its stock bear a reasonable relationship to those earnings?

7. Have reasonable dividends been paid regularly, and, if not, were there good and sufficient reasons and explanations for not paying them?

8. Is the company well within "safe" limits insofar as both long- and short-term borrowing are concerned?

9. Has the course followed by the price of the company's stock over

the last several years been fairly regular, without any violent, wide, and apparently inexplicable swings?

10. Does the per-share value of the company's net realizable assets bear a favorable relationship to the per-share value of its common stock?

Far too many people disregarded these basic investment rules during the stock-buying spree of the Roaring Twenties. It can only be hoped that present-day investors will take example from their mistake and apply the rules in their own stock-buying operations.

In one, purely business, sense, I consider myself very fortunate to have been an eyewitness to much of the October–November, 1929 debacle on Wall Street. The experience impressed upon me the utter folly of irrational speculation and the need to proceed with caution and care when and if I ever found it advisable to buy shares on the stock market. I say "when and if" because in November, 1929, I had no reason to even guess that within less than a year I would find it absolutely essential to begin buying huge blocks of stock costing millions.

On November 18, I boarded the liner *Berengaria* and sailed for Europe. I wanted to join my wife, Fini, in Germany and to be with her when our child was born.

17

MY second son, Jean Ronald, was born on December 19, 1929, in a Berlin hospital. Fini, my wife, was reluctant to return to the United States, and I decided to remain awhile with her and the baby in Europe.

The stock market slump had not directly affected the companies I owned or in which I held an interest. The impact of the spreading general economic recession had not yet been felt in the petroleum industry. I'd left my stateside business affairs in fairly good order, and I felt confident that I could exercise the necessary degree of supervision over them by mail, cable, and transatlantic telephone.

The interval lasted almost exactly four months from the day that Ronnie was born. On April 22, 1930, while I was in Montreux, Switzerland, I received a grim cable from Rush Blodget, my father's personal attorney and close friend.

My father, then in his seventy-fifth year, had suffered another stroke. His condition was grave, and this time, his physician could offer no optimistic reassurances. They held little hope for his recovery, and Rush urged me to come at once.

I left Montreux within an hour after receiving the cable. There were no transatlantic flights in 1930, and I went to France, where I booked passage on the first available ship for the United States. From New York, I continued on to Los Angeles by the first fast train.

The entire voyage was an ordeal of fearful suspense. Cables, radiograms, and telegrams reaching me en route kept me informed of my father's condition, which was worsening steadily. My greatest fear was that I would arrive too late to see him before he died.

I reached Los Angeles nine days after leaving Montreux. Father was still alive, but it was clear to all that the end was only a matter of time.

Again, I did what I could to comfort my mother during the agonizing days that passed while Father stubbornly fought his battle for life. Together, Mother and I maintained a vigil outside his bedroom. Periodically, I would argue and beg until she would go to her own room to obtain the rest and sleep she so desperately needed.

Father hung on gallantly until May 31, when he lost the long, tortured battle to live. The three decades and more that have passed since my father's death have not dimmed my memories of him or lessened the anguish and sense of helplessness I felt at his loss. Not long after his passing, I had occasion to write the following words:

> His loving kindness and great heart, combined with a charming simplicity of manner, made him the idol of all who knew him. His mental ability was outstanding to the last. I, his son and successor, can only strive to carry on to the best of my ability the life work of an abler man. This is said in no sense as eulogy, but as an impartial appraisal of the facts.

On July 3, 1930, at the first meeting of the directors of George F. Getty, Inc., after Father's death, the directors adopted the following resolution:

> WHEREAS, George Franklin Getty, Founder and President of this Corporation, departed this life at his home in Los Angeles, California, on the 31st day of May in the year of our Lord nineteen hundred thirty: and
>
> WHEREAS, the Board of Directors of George F. Getty, Incorporated, in meeting assembled, desire to record upon the minutes of the Company a tribute to his memory, that all who may later benefit from the industry so ably founded and builded by him may pause in later years and learn a lesson from his life: and
>
> WHEREAS, George Franklin Getty was born in Grantsville, Maryland, in 1855, and commenced the battle of life in comparative poverty, armed only with his honest heart, his keen mind and his willing hands:
>
> He was self educated, paying his own way through college, later generously rewarding that college for its gifts to him from the bounty of his own success:

He was devout, always acknowledging his debt to his Saviour, and always walking in the paths of rectitude:

He was industrious, toiling ceaselessly that his industries might succeed and bring prosperity to all who labored with him and for him:

He was honest, always paying his just obligations, not only in money when money was due, but in kindly appreciation when others had done him a service:

He was loyal, always adhering faithfully to his friends and employees through the vicissitudes of life:

NOW THEREFORE BE IT RESOLVED: That the members of this Board of Directors, on behalf of the stockholders and employees of this Company, hereby record their tribute to the character and attainments of George Franklin Getty, and their sorrow at his demise; and extend to his bereaved family their heartfelt sympathy.

My father left an estate valued at more than fifteen million dollars. Ten years after his death, I was to write as follows about his career and wealth:

George F. Getty's fortune in 1930 was a matter of public record, appraised by the State of California $15,478,137. When he started his career as a lawyer he had no capital except for a few hundred dollars which he had saved. Many young men of his acquaintance could easily have saved more money than he did, had they not preferred the enjoyment of spending their money as fast as it came into their possession.

If a young man has a capital of even a few hundred dollars, it sets him apart from many of his fellows, and enables him to take advantage of business opportunities that always exist.

It is impossible to create capital without saving. The start of Mr. Getty's successful career was partly due to his ability to balance his personal budget and to leave a small surplus available for investment. Moreover, he had equipped himself with the tools of success, for he had secured a college education in spite of his poverty and then studied law and passed the bar examination so that he was entitled to practice an honorable and sometimes lucrative profession.

The essentials of success are no different today than they were in the 1880's, when my father began his career. One must take an interest in his work, be thrifty, save a little money, and be equipped to render service to his fellows. When George F. Getty practiced law he had great interest in his clients and great concern for their welfare. When he entered the oil business he was enthusiastic about it, and he never lost his enthusiasm. He delighted in business, not for the purpose of piling up dollars, but for the satisfaction of accomplishing something tangible, worthwhile, and lasting.

My father never owned country estates or yachts, although in his later years he was financially able to do so. He lived in an unpretentious manner for a man of his means although he never stinted himself or his family. His personal expenditures and those of his family varied with the years but never exceeded $30,000 annually.

The inheritance tax laws of today make it doubtful if such moderation in expenditure is advisable. Had my father cared to spend more money, he might well have done so, because the estate tax of $1,300,000 which his executors paid was probably a larger sum of money than the total living expenses and personal expenditures of my father during his entire lifetime.

It might be of interest to trace the growth of George F. Getty's fortune through the years.

I would guess that he was worth less than $5,000 in 1884, the year he arrived in Minneapolis from Caro, Michigan, where he had practiced law and served as Circuit Court Commissioner for two years. By 1892, his fortune had grown to $150,000. Four years later, it had increased to $250,000.

A severe attack of typhoid fever forced my father's temporary semi-retirement from business in 1896. As a consequence, he was not able to increase his wealth much for several years, and it remained in the neighborhood of $250,000 until 1903, when he first went into the oil business.

George F. Getty's success in the Oklahoma oil fields made him a millionaire in 1916. One of my father's old balance sheets, which is still in my possession, is dated January 1, 1917, and shows that his total personal net worth was then $1,062,590.14. Of the total, only $28,518.15, or well under 3 per cent, was in cash. The rest was invested capital. George F. Getty practiced his preachment that a wealthy man's money should "work" as invested capital to produce goods and services for the benefit of all.

Father's fortune grew rapidly in the years that followed. By 1923, his energy, ability, and his courage in risking his capital had led to the development of new production in California and Oklahoma. The success of his prospecting and drilling ventures in these states increased his personal wealth to $15,000,000.

Extremely hard work and great nervous strain were the factors which caused his first stroke in March, 1923. From then on, the growth of his personal fortune was greatly slowed. The economic slump of 1929–30 served to reduce his fortune, and though its true value at the time of his death was difficult to determine due to the uncertainty of the economic situation, which made estimates of the value of certain assets little more than educated guesses, the California state appraisal of his estate shows that it was about the same as it had been in 1923.

During his entire business career, my father scrupulously avoided debt wherever it was humanly possible to do so. In later years, he was wont to express his philosophy regarding debt in the following typical oil man's terms:

"I would much rather have five thousand barrels a day settled production and no debts than to have twenty thousand barrels a day settled production and owe ten million dollars."

Assuming the value of settled production to be one thousand dollars per barrel—the figure generally accepted at the time—he was, in effect, saying that he preferred to have five million dollars in assets and no liabilities to having assets of twenty million dollars with ten million dollars in liabilities. He frequently pointed out that he had seen many brilliant businessmen ruined by overconfidence and debt.

"It's best not to carry too much sail," Father often advised. "One never knows when a sudden storm might strike."

I believe that my father's over-all business philosophy may be accurately summed up in the tenets he frequently quoted to me when I was young and which were the principles by which he lived and worked.

"Moral responsibility can never be avoided."

"The last thing you should ever do is borrow. The first thing you must always do is repay your debts."

"If you can trust a man, a written contract is a waste of paper. If you can't trust him, a written contract is still a waste of paper."

"The man who works for you is entitled to decent wages, decent working conditions—and your respect."

"Money is only as good as what you do with it. The best thing you can do with your money is to keep it working to produce more and better goods and services for more people at lower prices."

It is never easy for the son of a successful businessman to step into his father's shoes. In my own case, it was made doubly difficult due to the provisions of my father's will.

Father had changed his will in 1926, at a time when he was hurt and angry that my marriage to Jeanette Demont, my first wife, had ended in the divorce courts. Under the terms of the "new" will, I received $500,000, and my first son, George F. Getty, II, received $300,000. But I had no real need for more money; I had several millions of my own. The difficulty lay in the fact that the bulk of Father's estate, including the controlling stock in his companies, was left to my mother. To further complicate matters, Father had carefully chosen and named the executors who were to administer the provisions of his will; I was not named among them.

I had been elected Vice-President and General Manager of George F. Getty, Inc., and the Minnehoma Oil and Gas Company in 1929 and had actively managed both enterprises. I had also made heavy investments of time, money, and energy in his companies, at the expense of my own personal business enterprises, as a result, and on the understanding that I would be his successor.

On July 3, 1930, I was elected President of George F. Getty, Inc., and continued as its General Manager. I was, however, greatly handicapped because I did not have clear-cut control over the companies; final authority rested elsewhere, with the majority stockholder, who, of course, was my mother, counseled and supported by the executors.

My mother admitted that she was very much surprised that Father had not again revised his will in my favor. She told me that she had long felt that he had forgiven and forgotten my 1926 divorce and had, in the years that followed it, many times stated that he realized the divorce had not been my fault.

Mother pointed out that Father had gratefully relinquished his position and responsibilities as General Manager of both George F. Getty, Inc., and Minnehoma Oil and Gas to me the year before. And, she added, he had seemed eminently satisfied with the manner in which I had managed and supervised the affairs and operations of the two companies. She hazarded the theory that he had simply forgotten to make the necessary changes in his will or that, perhaps, it was something he intended to do but somehow had never quite gotten around to doing it. In support of her theory that Father had allowed the 1926 will to stand through forgetfulness or oversight, she noted that he had made no provisions for his second grandson—my second son, Jean Ronald, who had been born in Berlin on December 19, 1929.

Whatever the reasons—or, possibly, the lack of them—behind my father's failure to change his 1926 will, it was still a completely legal document signifying his last wishes and binding upon all concerned. It would, of course, stand and be honored. However, with long-drawn-out appraisals and negotiations with federal and state governments over inheritance taxes and other hitches which are the inevitable adjuncts of any sizable bequest, it would probably take a year or two or even more to finally settle the estate.

Clearly, the companies had to continue operation, and it was my job to manage them. Under these circumstances, I did not feel that I could leave California. My wife, Fini, refused to leave Germany and come to the United States. Thus, I had to remain away from my wife and child.

I continued to actively manage the affairs of George F. Getty, Inc., but it soon became evident that the business philosophies shared by my mother, the executors, and the majority of the directors were at wide variance with my own.

It must be remembered that my mother was seventy-seven. Grief-stricken by the loss of the husband to whom she had been married for over fifty years, she wanted only to live quietly and tranquilly and to preserve intact the business he had so painstakingly built up. She was also alarmed by the economic recession, confused by the ambiguous and conflicting statements of pundits and politicians, and she wanted to follow the most conservative course possible.

The men my father had named as his executors were also extremely conservative in their views. He had selected them carefully, in "normal" times, and, through no conscious fault of their own, their views and attitudes were still geared to "normal" conditions. They, too, greatly feared the consequences of the stock market collapse and the business slump. Intelligent, conscientious men of integrity, they were at the same time staid and solid individuals who believed the wisest course was to maintain the company's status quo and to avoid taking any steps which might involve any degree of risk. Expansion, they felt, was obviously completely out of the question under the uncertain business conditions which prevailed in mid-1930.

I, on the other hand, argued vehemently that such stand-still policies could only lead to stagnation, and that stagnation would be followed by decay and finally destruction. I felt that the greatest risks and dangers lay in marking time. Although I sensed that the business recession would get considerably worse before things started to get better, I could not bring myself to believe that the nation's economy would ever reach the point where it collapsed completely, and this gloomy eventuality was being prophesied by far too many individuals who should have known better. I had faith and confidence that the nation and the nation's business would ride out the crisis and that the economic picture would begin to improve within a very few years.

It was my contention that the foundations of the American economy were entirely sound. Once the tangled wreckage of boom-and-bust had been cleared away, a new, far stronger and more enduring structure would be built on those foundations. I also felt that it was a good time to start buying stocks for investment. The prices of shares in entirely sound and healthy companies had skidded to bargain-basement lows. I could see promising opportunities for expansion through large-scale stock-purchases. The prices then prevailing were only a fraction of what they no doubt would be four, five, or six years later; of this I was certain.

But even beyond all this, I foresaw a danger which would threaten the very existence of George F. Getty, Inc., if the company did not begin to buy certain stocks immediately. To stave off the threat, I needed the authority to spend millions.

18

GEORGE F. GETTY, INC., had acquired the Armstrong Lease in the fabulously rich Kings County, California, Kettleman Hills Field in April, 1928. The drilling of two test wells on the property had been suspended pending negotiation of a unit-operation agreement among the producers owning leases in the area.

Most of the producing companies involved were much larger and more powerful than George F. Getty, Inc., and at least one among them—Standard Oil—was a giant that made the Getty company shrink to Lilliputian size by comparison. Obviously, when formulating any unit-operation agreement, the major oil companies would do everything possible to safeguard their own interests and assure that they would obtain the greatest possible return on their investments.

The heart of the unit plan then in the process of negotiation would be a line drawn on a map and enclosing the participating acreage. Producers with all or a considerable portion of their leased acreage inside the line would fare well; those who had only scant acreage inside it would not be so fortunate.

It was hardly unreasonable to assume that not overly much consideration would be given to such a relatively small and insignificant company as George F. Getty, Inc., when the line was drawn and participating acreages were designated. It was even entirely conceivable that George F. Getty, Inc., might be entirely "frozen out" in a unit-operation agreement dominated by major oil companies.

I knew that the steadily worsening business recession would mean some difficult days for the oil industry in the future. George F. Getty, Inc., would need all the crude production and revenue it could obtain if it were to survive in the highly competitive period that lay ahead. The company certainly could not afford the loss of production and revenue which would result if it were shut out by the Kettleman Hills unit-operation agreement.

I saw only one way to protect George F. Getty, Inc., interests in the negotiations. The company would have to buy appreciable blocks of stock in some of the larger producing companies operating in the Kettleman Hills Field.

As a minority stockholder in the larger companies, George F. Getty, Inc., could bring to bear the necessary influence and pressure to gain the support of those companies in insuring that it received a fair acreage allotment "inside the line."

By September, 1930, it became evident that quick decisions and action would have to be taken. After a thorough study of the situation, I determined that the Mexican Seaboard and Pacific Western oil companies, both large operators in the Kettleman Hills Field, were the most logical choices.

Early in September, I went before the directors of George F. Getty, Inc., and strove to impress upon them the urgent need for swift action if the highly promising potentials of the Armstrong Lease were not to be lost to the company. After several—and for me, nerve-racking—days of deliberation, the directors, among whom were the executors of my father's will, reluctantly agreed that I could begin buying stocks in the two companies for the account of George F. Getty, Inc.

A trading account was opened with E. F. Hutton & Company and, in little more than two weeks, George F. Getty, Inc., had acquired some three million dollars' worth of stock in the Pacific Western Oil Corporation and the Mexican Seaboard Oil Company.

When, in October, the Kettleman Hills operators met in the San Francisco offices of the President of the Standard Oil Company, I was able to face all of them with comparative assurance and equanimity. George F. Getty, Inc., was no longer a pint-sized independent producing company standing alone. As a minority stockholder in Pacific Western and Mexican Seaboard, it could count on support from those two larger companies when the time came to thrash out the details of acreage participation under the unit operation plan.

The maneuver accomplished its purpose. There was no shut-out of George F. Getty, Inc. When the unit plan was finally completed, George F. Getty had a total of 1,080 acres of its Armstrong Lease inside the determining lines that were drawn with and by the agreement of the Kettleman Hills operators. The amount of participating acreage allotted to the company was entirely fair and just. Without any doubt, George F. Getty, Inc.'s participating acreage was far greater than it would have been if the company's representatives had gone to the San Francisco meeting without the support of Pacific Western and Mexican Seaboard.

Confident that the company's Kettleman Hills interests were now adequately safeguarded and that my other business affairs were fairly well in hand, I felt that I could afford to leave Los Angeles and join my wife, Fini, and my little son, Jean Ronald, in Germany. I went to New York in November and, on the 28th of that month, sailed for Europe aboard the S. S. *Homeric*.

The trip was not an auspicious one from either a business or personal standpoint. First of all, the stock market turned very weak even while I was at sea and continued a steady downward movement during December. This had the effect of reducing the value of the Pacific Western and Mexican Seaboard shares I had purchased for George F. Getty, Inc., in September.

Admittedly, I had not foreseen this development, but I was not unduly worried about it. I was sure that both the companies were entirely sound, and I was equally sure that the prices of their stocks and the stock market itself would eventually take a strong upward turn. In my view, it was all merely a matter of holding on to the shares calmly and waiting out the recession. Not so in the view of the directors and executors. They—and my mother—became extremely worried when the paper losses on the company's Pacific Western and Mexican Seaboard holdings reached the neighborhood of one million dollars.

I kept in close touch with the Los Angeles office and argued that the drop in stock prices could be turned to good advantage by buying even more Pacific Western and Mexican Seaboard stock. Purchases at the current prices, which were considerably lower than those I had paid for the original blocks of shares, would serve to average down the per-share cost. This would result in just that much more profit when the stock market turned strong again, as I was certain that it would. In fact, I thought that George F. Getty, Inc., could make the very best out of what seemed on the surface to be a rather bad situation by buying very heavily in both companies and thus gaining control of them at bargain prices. As I received no support for these suggested plans of action, I reluctantly shelved them, at least for the time being.

Penelope Kitson and J. Paul Getty at his desk. Robina Lund and Jack Forrester in the foreground. *Geoffrey Sawyer Studios Ltd., London*

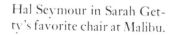

Hal Seymour in Sarah Getty's favorite chair at Malibu.

View from the highway from Acapulco to Puerto Marques.
The arrow points to the Hotel Pierre Marques. *L. J. Urbanek*

Sutton Place. *Associated Newspapers Ltd., London*

In the meanwhile, I was facing serious personal problems. My preoccupation with business during Fini's stay in America and my protracted separation from her in 1929 and again in 1930 had made my wife angry and resentful. No sooner had I arrived in Germany than I realized that our marriage had deteriorated. It could hardly be called a marriage any longer. Attempts at reconciliation and compromise of our differences led nowhere. Once more, the insoluble conflicts that have plagued all my matrimonial ventures presented themselves. It became painfully apparent that divorce was the only way out of the impasse.

Dr. Otto Helmle, Fini's father, seemed to feel that the outlook for American business was at best highly doubtful. He adamantly declared that he wanted to be absolutely certain his daughter and grandson would be financially secure no matter what happened in the United States. When he presented me with an outline of the financial settlement he wanted me to make with Fini prior to any divorce, I was forced to admit ruefully to myself that, in Dr. Helmle, I had encountered a businessman who was most certainly my equal.

The months wore on, and I continued to keep close tab on the general economic situation in the United States and particularly on the fortunes of the Getty companies.

Despite the effects of the worsening recession, George F. Getty, Inc., had ended the year 1930 with a $693,000 profit. But in the eyes of the directors and executors, my stewardship seemed to have been something less than an overwhelming success. There was the large paper loss on Pacific Western and Mexican Seaboard stocks to be considered, as well as a $400,000 expenditure on the drilling of a dry hole in the Lost Hills area.

The entire United States petroleum industry was having problems and troubles in 1931. The great East Texas Field, the largest oil field ever discovered on the North American continent, began producing tremendous quantities of "new" oil that year. With neither proration nor any unit operation plan to govern their production, East Texas operators were allowing their wells to run full blast. Their enormous added output poured oceans of petroleum into markets which had already shrunk considerably as a result of the depression and caused sharp price breaks in crude oil prices everywhere.

East Texas crude sold for 10 cents—and, in some instances, even less—per barrel. In March, 1931, the price of California crude oil was cut from $1.34 to 78 cents per barrel. The crude price in Oklahoma, where, of course, the Minnehoma Oil and Gas Company operated, dropped from

$1.29 per barrel in 1930 to 66 cents per barrel in 1931. In New Mexico, where the George F. Getty Oil Company had its wells, the price followed the East Texas nose dive and plunged to the sub-basement level of 10 cents per barrel.

Such low prices could only mean lean times and low profits ahead. Leaving my personal affairs unsettled, I left Europe and returned to the United States in the summer of 1931.

After spending a few days in New York on business, I went on to Los Angeles. Upon my arrival there, I found that the attitude of the George F. Getty, Inc., directors toward me was one best described as chilly to much colder, due to reasons I have already described.

I did not bother pointing out to the directors that a very large portion of the profits earned by the company since my father's first stroke in 1923 had come from leases originally secured by me and then transferred to the company on a participating partnership basis. Nor did I bother remind-ing them that I had used several hundred thousand dollars of my own money to purchase Pacific Western and Mexican Seaboard stock for the benefit of George F. Getty, Inc. I did not wish to harp on the past or waste time and words in efforts to justify actions which I was entirely certain had been wise and correct.

Instead, I proposed to sell the Armstrong Lease in the Kettleman Hills Field. I knew the sale would produce a very large profit which would more than offset the company's paper losses on Pacific Western and Mexican Seaboard stocks. I therefore employed E. A. Parkford, a highly competent and reliable lease broker and friend of mine, to find a buyer. By January, 1932, Parkford had gotten a buyer for the Armstrong Lease. It was the Shell Oil Company, and the price offered was $4,500,000. The offer was accepted, and the deal was closed.

In 1931, George F. Getty, Inc., had shown a slender profit of only some $148,000. In 1932, the company's profits were to rise above $3,000,000, largely because of the proceeds received from the sale of the Armstrong Lease. At the time the lease was sold, impartial observers in the petroleum industry agreed that no buyer would have paid such a high price had it not been for the liberal "inside-the-line" acreage George F. Getty, Inc., had been allowed when the Kettleman Hills producers made their unit operation agreement. And, George F. Getty, Inc., would not have been allowed so much participating acreage without the support of Pacific Western and Mexican Seaboard—support which it received solely because it was a minority stockholder in both those companies.

Thus, the stock purchases were clearly justified. But, beyond this, George F. Getty, Inc., still owned a big block of shares in Pacific Western, which was one of the ten largest oil companies operating in the state of California. The George F. Getty, Inc., interest in Pacific Western was almost large enough to constitute working control.

In January, 1932, at about the same time that E. A. Parkford began negotiating the sale of the Armstrong Lease to Shell, I received a visit from Charles Blyth, who owned 160,000 shares of Pacific Western stock.

"I'd like to sell," he announced.

I immediately recognized a golden opportunity. Purchase of Charles Blyth's 160,000 shares by George F. Getty, Inc., would mean that the company had gained working control of the Pacific Western Oil Corporation.

My confidence in the future of the nation's economy remained unshaken. I was convinced the general business outlook would soon begin to improve. Beyond these things, I knew that even at the depressed valuations then prevailing, Pacific Western's net realizable assets were worth as much or more than the market value of its common stock. At the first sign of business recovery, the value of those assets would soar and George F. Getty, Inc., would be in a very advantageous position if it controlled Pacific Western. Hence, although accepting it would entail a huge capital outlay at a time when ready cash was scarce everywhere, Blyth's offer to sell his Pacific Western stock seemed to be the chance of a lifetime.

Blyth and I dickered amiably over the price of his stock for several days. At last, we agreed on a figure of $7.00 per share. As the directors of George F. Getty, Inc., were not then ready to supply the funds needed for the purchase, I used my own money and bought the shares for $1,120,000.

Notwithstanding that it would mean that I was "carrying" George F. Getty, Inc., for more than a million dollars, when the directors finally gave a somewhat tentative indication they would reimburse me at some future date, I turned the shares over to the company. On May 1, 1932, the operations of George F. Getty, Inc., and the Pacific Western Oil Corporation were consolidated.

I had begun buying Pacific Western stock in 1930 to safeguard the interests of George F. Getty, Inc., in the Kettleman Hills Field. In less than a year and a half, these initial purchases had led to George F. Getty, Inc., gaining working control in Pacific Western, one of the ten largest oil-producing companies in California. It was a giant step forward in the expansion of the Getty interests. Time would prove its tremendous value;

future developments would show that it had been taken at an astoundingly low cost.

I could not spare much time for celebration or rejoicing over this success; other pressing problems were heaped on my plate.

The executors of my father's will had retained a tax attorney to prepare an appraisal of his estate for the federal tax authorities. In a rare burst of hopeful optimism, the attorney had produced an extremely low appraisal, estimating the total value of the estate at $3,800,000. The federal authorities, doubtless viewing this with raised eyebrows, had countered with their own appraisal, which set the value of the estate at over $20,000,000.

Obviously, the former figure was too low, and the latter was far too high. Like the earlier-mentioned California state appraisal, the federal estimate was evidently based on engineering rather than market values. At 1932 value-levels, it was completely out of proportion to the facts. The estate would have been hard put, indeed, to realize anywhere near that amount through even the most fortuitous liquidation of its assets.

Negotiations between the executors and the federal tax authorities over setting a more realistic value on the estate had reached the log-jam stage. The threat of lengthy and extremely costly litigation was present. In April, I proposed to make a personal effort at adjusting the differences. The executors consented—not without relief, I thought—and I went to Washington.

I had a long series of conferences with the federal valuation expert. I presented him with all the facts and figures and, after another trip to Washington in November, we succeeded in hammering out a compromise which set the net federal tax valuation of the estate at a more realistic figure. The way was now cleared for final settlement of my father's estate.

But 1932 was not a year of unbroken successes. As a matter of fact, I would later discover that I had made one of the worst and costliest mistakes of my entire business career in 1932.

I had been thinking seriously for some time about obtaining an oil concession in what was then called Mesopotamia and is now known as Iraq. Geological surveys, exploration operations, and test drilling by European and British oil companies indicated the presence of vast petroleum deposits beneath the hell-hot sands of the Mesopotamian desert. In 1927, a well was completed for ninety thousand barrels daily production in Iraq and this, of course, had served greatly to increase interest and activity in the area.

The entire Middle East appeared to offer fabulous opportunities and potentials, and enterprising European and British companies were expanding their prospecting and drilling operations throughout the region. I thought it would be an excellent idea to get in on the ground floor. I had appointed a representative to negotiate an exploration and drilling concession for me with Iraqi officials in Bagdad. In 1932, my Bagdad agent reported that a tempting concession was available at a price that could be tallied in a few tens of thousands of dollars.

I should have jumped at the chance and grabbed the concession—but I didn't. East Texas crude was selling for ten cents a barrel. The American oil industry was in one of its bleakest periods. Much of my capital was tied up in Pacific Western stock and in other ventures. I hesitated to risk large capital outlays on operations in the Middle East; I was afraid that I would be spreading my available resources too far and too thin. After debating the question with myself for several weeks, I decided against the Middle Eastern venture and instructed my agent in Bagdad to cancel the negotiations.

My decision was a classic boner, one that I would rue and regret in the years that followed. I had allowed a fantastically valuable concession to slip out of my hands even though it was being offered at a comparatively negligible price. The next time I was offered a Middle Eastern oil concession, I seized it unhesitatingly. But that wasn't until 1949. Conditions then were far different than they had been in 1932. In 1949, Pacific Western Oil Corporation, of which I was President, had to pay $12,500,000 in cash upon signing the concession agreement and would spend nearly $8,000,000 more before completing its first producing well.

Even though I missed the Middle Eastern bus in 1932, I did at least recognize and seize another opportunity which grew out of my purchases of Pacific Western stock in that year.

In March, 1932, I bought my first shares of stock in the Tide Water Associated Oil Company—and thus commenced the toughest battle of my entire business career.

19

IN 1932, many oil stocks were selling at all-time lows. They were spectacular bargains. Having obtained working control of the Pacific Western Oil Corporation for George F. Getty, Inc., I cast about for additional opportunities to strengthen the position and expand the operations of the Getty companies.

The more I thought about the matter, the more convinced I became of the feasibility of putting together a completely integrated and self-contained oil business, one which engaged not only in oil exploration and production, but also transportation, refining, and even retail marketing.

The companies I controlled or in which I held substantial interests were engaged exclusively in finding oil and bringing it up out of the ground. The basis for building a self-contained oil business was to obtain a substantial interest in a company which had good refining and marketing facilities but did not produce all the crude it needed for its operations.

There were only seven such companies operating in the state of California; all were "majors."

The list was headed by the giant Standard Oil Company of California, which was obviously far too big a chunk for any independent operator to bite off and digest. The same held true for the Shell Oil Company. The next possibility was the Union Oil Company, but Union had its own crude petroleum sources. So did the General Petroleum Company which, in any event, was owned by Socony-Vacuum and was virtually a closed corporation since its stock was not available for purchase.

That left three firms: Richfield Oil, then in receivership and consequently not a very tempting prospect; the Texas Oil Company, which was amply supplied with crude oil from its own sources; and, lastly, the Tide Water Associated Oil Company.

Tide Water Associated seemed the likely choice. The company met less than half its refineries' crude requirements from its own resources, buying the remainder from other producers. Tide Water also had a good marketing organization and its products enjoyed a good reputation with the consuming public.

I saw great potential advantages in linking the Getty companies up with Tide Water Associated. The Getty companies would have outlets for their crude production, and they could guarantee that Tide Water would have ample crude supplies. Furthermore, with the companies working interdependently, large-scale economies could be effected and all-around efficiency could be improved. Savings and economies could be passed on to the consuming public in the form of lower gasoline and oil prices. Increased profits could be shared not only by Getty company stockholders, but also by the more than three thousand individual common and preferred shareholders of the Tide Water Associated Oil Company.

I started buying Tide Water Associated Oil Company stock in March. My initial purchase of 1,200 shares at $2.50 per share was modest enough, but within the next six weeks, I had increased my holdings to 41,100 shares. It was only the beginning; the buying campaign which would result in my gaining control of Tide Water was to last nearly twenty years!

In business, as in politics, it is never easy to go against the beliefs and attitudes held by the majority. The businessman who moves counter to the tide of prevailing opinion must expect to be obstructed, derided, and damned. So it was with me. My associates and friends, to say nothing of my competitors, felt my buying spree would prove to be a financially fatal mistake. There were many who were inclined to believe that I had lost all sense of perspective and proportion—and, perhaps, even my senses.

Major oil companies could, and often did, buy out independent operator's companies. But for an independent operator to try and buy a major oil company? That was heresy—an attempt to turn the established order upside down!

My first attempt to obtain a voice in Tide Water Associated's management—my initial step toward meshing the operations of Tide Water and the Getty companies—was made in May, 1932. I went to the Tide Water Associated Oil Company's annual stockholders' meeting armed with my own 41,100 shares plus proxies for 126,000 additional shares. At the last moment, the proxies for 126,000 shares were revoked. My efforts ended in failure.

I went ahead and bought more stock and tried to sell my ideas to Tide Water's directors. They, however, did not see things my way and dug in for a long, hard fight. Why? Well, I suppose there were several reasons. First of all, I was an outsider. I'd had little or no experience in the heady atmosphere of board rooms.

"Paul Getty should stay where he belongs—on a drilling rig!" one Tide Water director supposedly exclaimed disdainfully when informed that I was buying the company's stock right and left. I fear there were others on the board who were even less kindly disposed toward me and my ambitions.

I had studied Tide Water's organization and operations with meticulous care, and, as a minority stockholder, I recommended that the company make certain changes and practice certain economies to reduce its overhead and administrative costs. These recommendations, apparently too radical to suit the conservative directors, were rejected and, I might add, caused considerable resentment in certain Tide Water management quarters.

I'd also concluded that much of Tide Water Associated's refining plant was obsolescent and would soon be obsolete. I believed the company should make immediate provisions for modernization and replacement, but the incumbent Tide Water management was reluctant to make capital expenditures during the period of the business slump. I argued, without avail, that since the company had the necessary funds available, this was precisely the time to do these things, for construction costs and material and equipment prices were at record lows. The directors did not agree. They characterized their attitude as one of "due and necessary caution." I regarded it as shortsighted and dangerous penny-pinching.

Then, I strongly objected to the payment of large preferred stock dividends at the expense of common stockholders. The record showed that Tide Water Associated had earned some $14,000,000 in 1929, paid over $4,000,000 in preferred stock dividends and nothing in common stock dividends. In 1930, preferred stock dividends again topped $4,000,000, while common stock dividends were less than $3,500,000. Tide Water lost money in 1931, but earned $4,718,000 in 1932. Of this sum, more than $4,000,000 again went to preferred stockholders, while common stockholders received nothing. My contention was that Tide Water should buy up as much of its preferred stock as possible so that it could use a much

The Great Hall at Sutton Place before the redecoration. Left to right: J. Paul Getty, Penelope Kitson, Dudley Delavigne, and Carl Farbach.

A party for orphans at Sutton Place. Daily Sketch

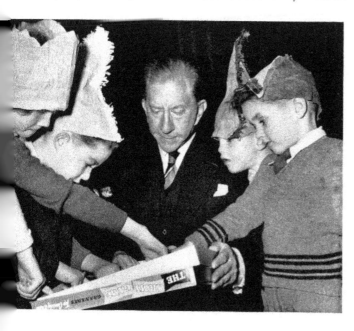

J. Paul Getty, 1957. *Jean Marquis, for* Time

larger percentage of its profits for paying dividends to common stockholders. I made little headway in these directions.

Broadly speaking, this was the situation and atmosphere in which the Getty interests began making heavy purchases of Tide Water Associated common stock.

Date	Number of Shares Purchased by Me	Price Paid per Share
March, 1932		
15	1,200	$2.50
16	2,500	2.50
	800	2.625
17	2,500	2.50
21	300	2.25
	2,200	2.375
22	1,700	2.25
23	3,900	2.25
Total for March	15,100	
April, 1932		
1	1,000	2.25
4	100	2.25
5	1,800	2.125
6	3,200	2.125
7	2,900	2.125
8	1,800	2.125
11	4,600	2.125
12	200	2.125
13	2,200	2.125
14	2,300	2.125
15	1,300	2.125
18	300	2.125
20	200	2.125
22	1,900	2.125
26	100	2.125
27	1,100	2.125
28	1,000	2.125
Total for April	26,000	
Total to Date: 41,100		

DATE	NUMBER OF SHARES PURCHASED BY ME	PRICE PAID PER SHARE
May, 1932		
3	100	2.125
4	1,800	2.125
5	900	2.125
6	1,100	2.125
9	1,200	2.25
20	1,300	2.25
23	2,500	2.25
24	5,400	2.25
26	900	2.25
27	3,000	2.25
31	1,300	2.25
TOTAL FOR MAY	19,500	
TOTAL TO DATE: 60,600		

DATE	NUMBER OF SHARES PURCHASED BY ME	PRICE PAID PER SHARE
June, 1932		
1	3,400	2.25
3	400	2.125
6	200	2.125
8	400	2.125
9	900	2.125
10	100	2.125
13	300	2.125
17	100	2.125
20	100	2.125
21	2,100	2.125
22	100	2.125
23	200	2.125
24	800	2.125
28	1,400	2.125
TOTAL FOR JUNE	10,500	
TOTAL TO DATE: 71,100		

Date	Number of Shares Purchased by Me	Price Paid per Share
July, 1932		
1	200	2.125
6	700	2.25
7	900	2.25
12	300	2.25
Total for July	2,100	
Total to Date: 73,200		
August, 1932		
18	10,000	5.00
29	3,400	5.00
	6,800	5.125
30	4,800	5.125
Total for August	25,000	
Total to Date: 98,200		
September, 1932		
7	10,000	5.125
9	4,200	5.125
12	100	5.125
13	4,800	5.125
14	5,900	5.125
16	7,200	5.00
	2,800	4.875
19	700	4.75
20	100	4.75
23	400	4.75
	500	4.375
	500	4.50
26	1,100	4.25
28	900	4.25
Total for September	39,200	
Total to Date: 137,400		

Date	Number of Shares Purchased by Me	Price Paid per Share
October, 1932		
5	200	3.875
6	800	3.875
	800	3.75
7	200	3.75
	400	3.125
	1,000	3.375
	1,000	3.50
	1,000	3.25
	1,000	3.625
10	2,500	3.25
	1,500	3.125
11	2,200	3.125
Total for October	12,600	
Total to Date: 150,000		
December, 1932		
20	500	3.50
21	6,300	3.50
Total for December	6,800	
Total to Date: 156,800		
January, 1933		
18	9,400	3.25
19	400	3.25
20	400	3.25
23	200	3.25
24	600	3.25
25	6,100	3.25
26	300	3.25
27	1,100	3.25
30	1,100	3.252
31	400	3.25
Total for January	20,000	
Total to Date: 176,800		

Date	Number of Shares Purchased by Me	Price Paid per Share
February, 1933		
1	800	3.25
2	2,500	3.25
3	8,700	3.25
6	700	3.25
7	700	3.25
	300	3.125
8	500	3.25
9	400	3.25
14	1,500	3.25
17	300	3.375
20	700	3.375
21	200	3.375
23	200	3.375
24	2,900	3.375
27	3,500	3.375
28	4,600	3.375
Total for February	28,500	
Total to Date: 205,300		
March, 1933		
1	400	3.375
	100	3.25
2	4,800	3.375
3	1,000	3.375
7	4	3.75
15	1,800	3.375
16	35,000	3.75
	200	3.375
17	1,200	3.75
18	200	3.625
20	100	3.625
21	4,400	3.625
22	500	3.625
24	200	3.625
27	1,800	3.625
28	1,000	3.625
Total for March	52,704	
Total to Date: 285,004		

My judgment in commencing the campaign when the stock market was at its rock-bottom low was soon vindicated at least in part by the performance of Tide Water Associated stock. A day-by-day list of my Tide Water purchases between March, 1932, and March, 1933, shows the steady rise of Tide Water stock prices. True that there were some dips and setbacks along the way, but the stock appreciated in value almost 50 per cent during the twelve-month period. Perhaps it might be of interest to go back in time and figuratively watch the ticker over my shoulder as I started to "buy into" the Tide Water Associated Oil Company, one of the nation's major oil companies.

For these 285,004 shares, I paid a total of $923,285.30, including commissions.

The average price paid per share to the last date shown above was $3.59.

One year after the last date shown on the foregoing list—on May 31, 1934—Tide Water Associated Oil Company stock was selling for $11.25 per share.

By 1936, the price of the stock had risen to over $19.00 per share.

The investments I was making in Tide Water Associated Oil Company stock during 1932–33 were sound ones. But I was not able to buy as much stock as I could and should have bought and wanted to buy. Nor could I devote as much time and energy as I would have liked to the rapidly developing Tide Water campaign.

Trouble, they say, always comes in bunches. Certainly my experiences in 1932 and 1933 would seem to bear this out. Problems and complications, both business and personal, piled up on me during those years.

20

I HAVE referred to my father as a "self-made man." And so he was. But it would be no reflection on his record of achievements or his memory to say that no inconsiderable part of his success was due to the deep love and unswerving loyalty of his wife and my mother, Sarah Catherine McPherson Risher, whom he married in 1879.

At the time of their marriage, my father owed one hundred dollars—money that he had borrowed while putting himself through college. His bride paid the amount so that they could start their married life free of debt, using some of the money she had painstakingly saved from her meager salary as a schoolteacher. Throughout the more than fifty years of their married life, my mother and father were partners in all things, sharing whatever life and fate brought them.

Theirs was, indeed, a perfect union. I recall the pride and joy with which my father gave my mother a diamond ring for Christmas in 1904, shortly after the fourth producing well was brought in on his first lease, Lot 50, in Oklahoma. I also remember the infinite pleasure with which he gave Mother the house he had built for her on Wilshire Boulevard. Certainly, my memories of life at home and our experiences together on our trips in the United States and abroad are replete with instances and examples of the great love and respect my mother and father had for each other.

My mother and I were always very close. A great bond of love and affection existed between us. My father's death served to draw us even closer together insofar as our personal relationship was concerned. However, when it came to business, our opinions sometimes differed greatly.

Mother and I did not allow our business differences to affect our personal relationship in the slightest degree. On the other hand, we did not let the fact that we were mother and son prevent us from having and expressing our respective, independent—and, on occasion, vigorously opposed—views regarding business matters.

Needless to say, this relationship, to the casual observer an ambivalent one, gave rise to many paradoxical and often delightfully amusing incidents. "Mama"—as I called her from the time I was a child—and I often chuckled over the astonishment registered by some who saw and heard us arguing vehemently over business affairs one moment and then switching abruptly to an affectionate mother-and-son conversation the next.

I had a tremendous amount of respect for my mother's business judgment. Extremely intelligent, coolly logical, and capable of swiftly grasping and understanding the most complex problems, she had always been Father's closest friend and confidante, the person with whom he discussed all his business affairs.

Nonetheless, when Mother learned that Father had left her the controlling stock interests in his companies, she was surprised.

"I believe he made a mistake leaving the responsibility to me rather than to you," she often told me.

But, having the responsibility, she was determined to discharge it to the best of her considerable ability, and in the manner in which she felt that Father would have wanted her to do it. By then elderly and inclined to be quite conservative, Mother viewed many of my plans and programs as being too aggressive and risky. Her outlook was supported—and, perhaps, in part inspired—by the even more cautious and conservative men who had been appointed executors of my father's will.

I wanted to build and expand the Getty companies by taking full advantage of the opportunities offered by the decline in stock market prices. As I have already begun to outline in previous chapters, I reasoned that the bargain levels that had been reached by stock prices provided a once-only chance to put together a completely integrated oil business.

Mother inclined toward the opinion of the executors, who held that the dangers of large-scale stock-buying during a recession outweighed whatever potentials it offered. She—and they—argued that cash surpluses or money invested in government bonds offered far more safety and security than any equities purchased in a depressed market during a business slump. I countered by pointing out that a "do-nothing" policy could lead only to the eventual liquidation of the Getty companies, and that an aggressive program would, on the other hand, expand those companies into an organization that would be a powerful factor in the oil industry.

I had obtained all-around consent to my first stock-buying campaign—the one launched in September, 1930, to obtain sizable blocks of Pacific Western and Mexican Seaboard shares for the purpose of protecting George F. Getty, Inc., interests in the Kettleman Hills Field. When the stock market took another sudden dip in November–December of that same year, causing the value of the stocks I had purchased for the company to fall more than a million dollars, Mother and the executors felt their viewpoint had been vindicated, their contentions proved. The profitable sale of the Armstrong Lease, which provided George F. Getty, Inc., with a comfortably large amount of cash, and my additional stock purchases which gave the company control of Pacific Western eased the tensions somewhat and stilled the most strident criticisms.

The respite was a short one. The pendulum took a violent swing back to what, from my standpoint, was the extreme negative position when I announced my intention of buying into the Tide Water Associated Oil Company and began purchasing its stock. The executors of Father's will and many of the other directors on the boards of the Getty companies were convinced that I was going too far. They held many lengthy conferences with my mother, who came away from them at least partially convinced that my policies could lead only to the wrack and ruin of the companies George F. Getty had built during his lifetime.

Mother urged me to stop buying stocks. She particularly objected to any buying of stock on margin and to the borrowing of money from banks for the purpose of purchasing shares.

"Your father hated debt," she told me. "He would never have borrowed the sums you propose to borrow."

I disagreed. While I was well aware that my father had always abhorred and avoided debt as such wherever possible, I was also aware that he had not hesitated to use his credit when it was necessary in order to take advantage of opportunities which presented themselves. I was certain that if he had lived to see the remarkable stock bargains that became available in 1932, he would have done just as I was doing and intended to do.

"Father never missed a chance to expand his business enterprises," I argued. "And there will never again be opportunities such as there are today."

Besides, I pointed out, whatever loans I had obtained or proposed to obtain from banks were loans that were or would be fully secured by ample collateral. Cash was in short supply throughout the business world because of the Depression. The Getty companies had large, valuable assets which, in a manner of speaking, had been temporarily "frozen" by the chill of the recession. These assets were not producing the income or the profit they should have been producing and would have been producing if business conditions were anywhere near normal. But they were of a nature to make the companies prime credit risks. The only way to "un-freeze" them and make them productive of income and profit under the conditions that prevailed was to convert them temporarily into fluid cash through the use of credit. The cash could then be used to buy stocks which I, for one, was convinced would soon increase greatly in value.

I seemed to be making headway with my arguments in early 1932. My mother, the executors, and the other directors appeared to be at least partially convinced. They did not want to use any of George F. Getty, Inc.'s resources as yet, pending the settlement of inheritance tax questions. They assured me, however, that I could go ahead and use my personal funds and credit. As soon as the inheritance tax was settled, the company would take over whatever stock I bought at my cost.

Armed with this assurance, I began to buy. The volume of my purchasing can be seen in the table shown in the previous chapter. But even this was only part of the story. Between March, 1932, and March, 1933, I would use more than two million dollars of my own money to buy stock for George F. Getty, Inc. But it would not be until April, 1933, that the directors would fulfill any part of their promise to pick up the shares I bought.

And, I might add, the two-million figure includes only Tide Water Associated stock and stock of the Petroleum Corporation of America, which I purchased because it had tremendous strategic value in the Tide Water campaign. The sum does not include the amounts paid for large blocks of Pacific Western stock purchased by me in order to give George F. Getty, Inc., numerical as well as working control of the Pacific Western Oil Corporation.

I was rich, but there were limits to my personal resources. I stretched them to the breaking point, but when the directors continued to vacillate about picking up the stock I had bought I was forced to put the brakes on my purchasing.

Let me make it quite clear that I felt no anger and harbored no resentment against the directors then, and I have no such feelings against them now. They were honest, conscientious men who acted as they thought best for the company. Their opposition to my programs was not intended as opposition to me, but stemmed from their earnest desire to steer an entirely safe course. That they did not recognize the opportunities which were present may well have been due to the fact that they were of another, older generation than my own and thus not as readily able to adjust to the confused and unprecedented business conditions which obtained in the early 1930's.

The consequences of my slowing the buying campaign were serious and long-lasting. The bargain days of 1932 and early 1933 were not exploited to the full. Had they been, George F. Getty, Inc., could have snapped up a third or more of Tide Water Associated's common stock during that period. If that had been done, the Tide Water campaign would have been won many years earlier and at much lower cost than was finally the case.

The disagreements between the directors of George F. Getty, Inc., and me over my stock-buying continued throughout 1932. My mother sided more and more consistently with the directors. As she held 66⅔ per cent of George F. Getty, Inc., stock against my 33⅓ per cent, I found that I was often being outvoted.

It was, I will admit, an odd situation. I had invested more than a million dollars of my own money in George F. Getty, Inc., in 1928. More than this, I had, between 1924 and 1929, turned extremely valuable leases over to the company, retaining only participating interest in them. These leases had provided a very sizable portion of the company's income during that period. In fact, if the income produced by those leases was deducted from the company's gross income for the period, George F. Getty, Inc., would have shown a small loss rather than a healthy profit for its operations during those years. The leases were continuing to produce income—in fact, they were the most profitable of any owned by the company.

Yet, even though I was President and General Manager of the company, I was being hamstrung by the directors and by the voting power held by my mother. Perhaps I should have made an issue of the matter with Mother much earlier. But I did not wish to worry or upset her. I preferred to argue my case with the directors and to try to convince her that I was right in the gentlest and least disagreeable manner possible.

I suppose I could have obtained her support much sooner than I finally did by pressing the matter, by being insistent and demanding her help. I did none of these things in 1932. Instead, I saw her as usual, regularly several times each week when I was in Los Angeles. We had lunch or dinner together or went riding in my car—or we engaged in one of her favorite pastimes, going to the beach at Santa Monica and feeding the sea lions, which used to amuse visitors with their antics there.

It was thus that matters stood in mid-1932, when my personal affairs took precedence over business for a short period. It had been impossible to save my marriage to Fini. She had filed suit for divorce and, in August, 1932, obtained her final decree.

Still chasing what for me has always been the elusive will-o'-the-wisp of marital happiness. I embarked on yet another matrimonial venture. I married Ann Rork, the beautiful and vivacious daughter of Sam Rork, the Hollywood motion picture producer and manager of Clara Bow, the famous "It Girl" of the silent films. Ann would bear me two fine sons— Eugene Paul and Gordon Peter—before this marriage, too, ended in the divorce courts.

Returning to Los Angeles after the wedding ceremony and the briefest of honeymoons, I once more turned my attention to my business affairs. I resumed my one-man campaign to buy enough stock to obtain a voice in the management of the Tide Water Associated Oil Company.

As far back as May, 1932, I had begun buying stock in the Petroleum Corporation of America, a company which was one of the principal stock-holders in Tide Water Associated. My intent, of course, was to obtain a strategically advantageous position in P.C.A. and, through it, to increase my holdings or at least influence in Tide Water.

Again, a list of my stock purchases—this time in Petroleum Corporation —might prove of interest, if for no other reason than it shows the steady rise in prices occasioned by the strong stock market upturn which commenced in the spring of 1933:

Date	Number of Shares Purchased by Me	Average Price per Share	Total Cost
1932			
May	10,000	$ 3.45	$ 34,500.00
June	17,000	3.532	60,050.00
July	6,600	4.041	26,670.00
August	6,400	6.638	42,480.00
September	34,700	6.580	228,340.00
October	10,700	5.644	60,390.00
November	7,300	5.195	37,922.50
December	20,000	4.774	95,475.00

DATE	NUMBER OF SHARES PURCHASED BY ME	AVERAGE PRICE PER SHARE	TOTAL COST
1933			
January	21,200	5.149	109,165.00
February	5,900	5.533	32,642.50
March	4,100	5.200	21,320.00
April	6,100	6.909	42,145.00
May	11,400	7.973	90,892.50
July	8,700	9.975	86,790.00
August:			
8	300	9.575	2,872.50
16	1,000	10.250	10,250.00
17	2,000	10.125	20,250.00
September:			
7	8,500	14.422	122,587.50
8	5,500	14.454	79,500.00
12	200	14.625	2,925.00
13	200	14.625	2,925.00
14	2,200	14.864	32,700.00
GRAND TOTALS	190,000	$ 6.537	$1,242,792.50

During the same period, George F. Getty, Inc., also purchased Petroleum Corporation of America stock in the amounts shown below:

DATE	NUMBER OF SHARES	AVERAGE PRICE	COST
April, 1933	4,700	$ 6.005	$ 28,227.50
August, 1933	5,300	10.082	53,435.00
TOTALS	10,000	$ 8.166	$ 81,662.50

It can be seen from these figures that the purchases of Petroleum Corporation stock proved highly profitable in a comparatively short space of time. The stock market took a very strong upward turn in May, 1933; the general rise is reflected in the steadily increasing value of the P.C.A. shares.

As indicated by the figures for September 14, 1933, the price of Petroleum Corporation stock had by then risen to a per-share average of $14.864.

But the over-all average price I had paid for the 190,000 shares I purchased was only $6.537 per share.

The per-share paper profit was thus $8.327.

On paper, the total profit on the 190,000 shares I had bought up to September 14, 1933, was consequently $1,582,130.00.

It can also be seen from the figures given in the table that the purchases of Petroleum Corporation stock made by George F. Getty, Inc., represented only a fraction of the total bought by me; *viz.:* 10,000 shares bought by the company versus 190,000 purchased by me.

No attempt was made to realize the paper profit. This was not the reason for which the P.C.A. stocks had been bought. In September, the combined holdings of 200,000 shares of Petroleum Corporation stock were traded for 300,000 shares of Tide Water Associated common.

But much of vital importance to the future of the Getty companies was to transpire between the time I purchased my first shares of P.C.A. stock and the time they were traded for Tide Water shares.

21

The failure of George F. Getty, Inc., to pick up the stocks I had purchased for the company in 1932 made it necessary for me to abandon one of my own highly promising ventures, and I thereby lost at least a million dollars.

I had been buying large amounts of stock in the Mexican Seaboard Oil Company on my own account—and, of course, using my own funds to do so. I believed the value of the shares would increase, and I fully expected to make a tidy profit for myself. But this would have been a purely personal profit, and my primary goal was to expand the Getty companies.

It was to this end that I had begun buying Pacific Western, Tide Water Associated, and Petroleum Corporation stocks, and it was for this reason that I continued to buy them after the directors of George F. Getty, Inc., had promised to take the shares over at my cost. The promise was not kept during 1932. However, being committed to the campaign, I had to continue it with all the resources at my disposal. Then, as volume buying of the stocks I was purchasing for George F. Getty, Inc., strained those resources to the breaking point, I found it necessary to abandon my pet personal project and halt the buying of Mexican Seaboard shares for my account.

When, as weeks and months passed and George F. Getty, Inc., still withheld its promised support, I had no choice but to liquidate my previously purchased holdings in Mexican Seaboard in order to obtain additional funds with which to continue the Tide Water campaign.

The net result was that I was forced to dump a total of 58,000 shares of Mexican Seaboard stock at an average price of $10.25 per share. It was a painful but unavoidable expedient. I knew the stock was easily worth

$20.00 per share and fully anticipated that its price would rise to that level before very much longer. Nonetheless, there was no alternative to dumping the shares if the Getty companies were to obtain the Tide Water Associated stock required for building the integrated oil company I envisioned. And this was the goal which loomed most valuable and important.

As I had foreseen, the price of Mexican Seaboard began to rise sharply, but only after I had sold my shares in the company. Had I been able to hold on to them, I would have realized a half-million-dollar profit within a few months. Furthermore, if it had not been necessary to divert my available personal capital from Mexican Seaboard purchases to the buying of Tide Water and related stocks, I would have continued buying Mexican Seaboard throughout 1932 and the early part of 1933. Had I been able to do this, I would have acquired, by the most conservative reckoning, sufficient Mexican Seaboard stock to have realized a profit of well over a million dollars by the spring of 1933.

It was then, in the spring of 1933, that stock prices surged upward. Perhaps encouraged by this, the directors of George F. Getty, Inc., belatedly began to take over some of my Tide Water and related shares, reimbursing me for them at the prices I had paid.

I could not refrain from somewhat sourly pointing out to the directors that they were arriving at the party rather late, after all the door-prizes had been given out and most of the buffet supper had been eaten.

Along with the prices of most other sound issues traded on the New York Stock Exchange, the price of Tide Water Associated shares had by then risen far above their 1932 bargain-levels. The money that George F. Getty, Inc., was beginning to repay me for a portion of the stocks I had purchased on the company's behalf months before was, I will admit, welcome. However, the actual value of the money as working capital had depreciated considerably in the interim. I was being reimbursed at my cost-prices, and these sums bought far less stock than they would have purchased a short time earlier.

Had the directors made good on their promises and picked up all the stock earlier, I could have used the personal capital thus returned to me in buying even more Tide Water shares. As it was, Tide Water Associated stock, of which I had bought 258,004 shares at an average per-share price of $3.59 between March, 1932, and March, 1933, was selling for almost $9.00 per share by May, 1933. And, as has been seen, the rise in the price of Petroleum Corporation stock had been even more spectacular.

There was one major consolation, though. By May, 1933, when Tide Water Associated held its annual stockholders' meeting, the Getty interests owned a total of 258,004 shares of Tide Water common and approximately 160,000 shares of Petroleum Corporation, which latter company, of course, held a substantial block of stock in Tide Water. This represented a far more important and impressive interest than the 41,100 shares with which I, representing the Getty companies, had gone to the Tide Water stockholders' meeting the year before.

In May, 1933, the incumbent management of the Tide Water Associated Oil Company could no longer ignore or brush off the "upstart" Getty interests. A minority stockholder owning 258,004 shares of the company's stock outright could not be denied some recognition.

Armed with their now-substantial holdings, the Getty interests sought to obtain representation on the Tide Water board of directors. Hunter S. Marston, an experienced and highly regarded businessman associated with the Getty companies, was proposed for membership on the board. In a surprise move, the Tide Water Associated management rejected Marston and proposed instead that I serve on the company's board. I had not previously given any thought to becoming a director; nonetheless, I accepted the offer and was duly elected a director of the Tide Water Associated Oil Company. It was a comparatively minor victory in the campaign, but it had the effect of establishing a Getty beachhead on a shore which, if not exactly hostile, was a step or two removed from being warmly hospitable.

No sooner had I been elected than I proposed that Tide Water, which had ample surplus cash available for the purpose, buy up its own outstanding preferred stock, which carried cumulative 6 per cent dividends and was then selling for about thirty-five cents on the dollar. By buying up its preferred stock, the company would eliminate the need for paying the compulsory 6 per cent annual dividend on it. Thus, more of its profits would be available for distribution in dividends to its some seventeen thousand common stockholders.

The proposal was turned down. One of the major reasons put forward for the rejection was that the business outlook was still uncertain, and that it was consequently "smarter and safer" to maintain a large cash surplus than to buy up equities. Viewed from one angle, this was tantamount to saying that the majority of Tide Water's directors did not have too much faith in the future of their own company. Although I was only a director representing a minority stockholder, I had ample faith in the company's future and believed that the price of Tide Water preferred would rise—and quite soon at that. Events were to prove that I was correct in this belief.

George F. Getty, Inc., bought a total of 18,600 shares of Tide Water Associated preferred stock between April and early December, 1933, paying a total of $732,000 for them. In late December, Tide Water's management apparently reconsidered my earlier suggestion, and Tide Water began buying up some of its outstanding preferred stock. But by that time, the market value of the preferred shares had soared far above their May, 1933, prices. By selling most of its preferred holdings in Tide Water back to Tide Water, George F. Getty, Inc., realized a tidy profit of no less than $428,000.

On March 31, 1933, I had resigned as president and general manager of George F. Getty, Inc. Various factors contributed to my decision to resign. I was frequently absent from Los Angeles. The increasing tempo of the Tide Water campaign was requiring more and more of my time. I was wearing too many hats, trying to hold down too many different jobs at a critical period. All in all, I was not able to devote the necessary attention to the affairs of George F. Getty, Inc., to justify my holding the titles and positions. But, although I resigned these, I continued to work with and for the company, in which I still retained my 30 per cent stock interest.

In August, George F. Getty, Inc., resumed its stock-buying through E. F. Hutton & Company. In the corporate resolution authorizing the establishment of an account with the brokerage house, I was named as the company's agent, with authority to purchase for the company's account. The resolution set a $300,000 maximum on the amount for which the company could be obligated to Hutton & Company at any one time. This was a very low ceiling, and I went to great lengths to persuade the company's directors and my mother to raise it. On August 28, the limit was increased to $650,000.

For some time I had seen the need for forming a new company of my own to manage and safeguard the securities I had bought and was buying. Among these were not only shares I had purchased for my own account, but also some sizable blocks which I had bought for George F. Getty, Inc., and for which the directors of that company had still not reimbursed me.

Getty, Inc., was incorporated on September 8, 1933. Among the stocks I transferred to Getty, Inc., were the 190,000 shares of Petroleum Corporation of America common which I had purchased since April and which had not been picked up and paid for by George F. Getty, Inc.

Not long after Getty, Inc., was organized, E. F. Hutton & Company transmitted an offer it had received from Harry Sinclair. The multimillionaire veteran oil man proposed to trade the Getty companies 300,000 shares of Tide Water Associated common stock for their combined holdings of 200,000 shares of Petroleum Corporation common. The offer was accepted before the end of September. As a result of the transaction, the holdings of the Getty companies in Tide Water Associated Oil were doubled.

In October, I made an exhaustive inspection tour of Tide Water properties in Texas and Oklahoma. I was accompanied by William Humphrey, soon to become the president of Tide Water, and two of the company's other directors. Oddly enough, none of the other directors had showed any interest in making the tour. My curiosity aroused, I did some checking. I found that although the company's large refinery at Bayonne, New Jersey, was only a twenty-minute ride from its New York offices, few of the directors had ever even bothered going there.

In all, there were twelve board members. Seven were outsiders, not otherwise connected with the company and not even oil men. Admittedly, I was just a wildcatter at heart and not accustomed to the rarefied atmosphere of paneled board rooms, but I thought this was a hell of a way to run a railroad, much less an oil company. Unaccustomed as I was to keeping quiet about matters that bothered me, I did not hesitate to say as much, which did nothing to improve my standing on the popularity polls in some quarters.

My enthusiasm for the Tide Water campaign had not flagged during the year, and I had even managed to infect the directors of the various Getty companies with it. Toward the close of 1933, the Getty companies held a total of 743,154 shares of Tide Water Associated common stock. At then-current market prices, this represented an investment of considerably more than seven million dollars. The shares were held as follows:

George F. Getty, Inc.	340,000 shares
Pacific Western	218,700 shares
Getty, Inc.	184,454 shares

Returning to Los Angeles from a New York business trip in December, I realized that I could no longer delay finding a solution to the problems created by the differences in business philosophy that existed between my mother and myself. She still tended to be very conservative in her outlook.

I explained the entire situation to Mother in great detail, and she understood and agreed with my viewpoint. Having signed over her stock interests in George F. Getty, Inc., to me, on January 2, 1934, Mother resigned—"gratefully," as she herself said—from the company's board of directors. It was clear to all who knew her that she was greatly relieved and very happy to be out of the company's active management, able to devote her time once more to her home, relatives, friends, and charities.

"I'm sure that Father would have approved," she declared simply when I drove her home from the directors' meeting at which her resignation was formally accepted. To me, her words constituted a vote of confidence, and I silently vowed to prove that it was not misplaced.

As for myself, as the now sole stockholder in George F. Getty, Inc., I could at last put the Tide Water campaign into high gear. Or so I thought, never dreaming that I was about to receive a highly unpleasant and shocking surprise.

Within a few months, I was to discover that the Tide Water Associated Oil Company, in which I thought the Getty companies had obtained an influential minority interest, was really controlled by the gargantuan Standard Oil Company of New Jersey. By mid-1934, I would learn that I would have to do battle with the Standard giant—and win—if I hoped to accomplish any of my aims.

In the meantime, nothwithstanding the continuing adversity of general business conditions and the tremendous overproduction of oil in 1933, the Getty companies could report fair success for the year.

On December 31, 1933, the balance sheet of George F. Getty, Inc., showed that the company had assets of nearly $8,000,000. Although no new wells had been drilled and only five leases purchased for a total of $2,148, the company's profits for the year stood at around $1,000,000.

In Oklahoma, the Minnehoma Oil and Gas Company embarked on no new drilling, but nonetheless managed to pay a ten-cent-per-share dividend. Crude oil prices remained very low in New Mexico; George F. Getty Oil Co. did no additional drilling there, but still managed to show a small profit for 1933.

In May, 1934, Tide Water Associated held its regular annual stockholders' meeting. H. P. Grimm, a Getty executive, was elected to the board of directors. With that, the Getty interests had two members on the twelve-man board. Mr. Axtell Byles, president of the company, retired a few days later, and William "Billy" Humphrey was elected president in his place. Although Bill Humphrey and I were soon to square off for a major business battle that would last for years, I liked him personally and had a very high regard for his keen intelligence and ability.

Broadly speaking, I had no reason to be dissatisfied with the outcome of the stockholders' meeting. I could see that we—the Getty interests—had made some progress; not much, but enough to be encouraged by it. The rude awakening came the next month, in June, 1934.

Prior to starting the Tide Water campaign, I had investigated the composition of the stockholders. I knew that Standard Oil Company (New Jersey) had once controlled the company, but I learned that Standard had rid itself of its working control of Tide Water in 1930, selling its 1,078,000 shares of Tide Water to Mission Securities, Ltd. Thus, in 1932, I felt assured that Standard had no further interest in Tide Water save for a small 50,000-share block it had picked up on the open market after selling its million-plus-share interest to Mission Securities.

It would hardly seem necessary for me to point out that I would never have begun buying into Tide Water if I felt that Tide Water was still dominated by the behemoth of Standard Oil of New Jersey. What I did not and could not know was that Standard had sold its Tide Water shares to Mission Securities on a time-payment plan, that Mission Securities, Ltd., would fail to make its payments through the years, and that Standard would consequently take back the shares.

In June, 1934, Standard Oil declared the purchase forfeited. In September, Standard transferred the 1,078,000 shares back into its own name. With this move, Tide Water Associated became a company dominated by the Standard Oil Company of New Jersey. Standard now had effective working control of Tide Water. The comparatively lilliputian Getty interests found themselves in the position of being very-much-in-the-minority stockholders, to all intents and purposes completely at the mercy of Standard.

Backed to the hilt by Standard Oil and all the influence and power it could muster, the incumbent management of Tide Water Associated dug in to prevent the Getty interests from enlarging their now suddenly precarious toehold in the company. I found myself faced with two alternative courses of action I could follow. Simply stated, I could on the one hand admit that I was outnumbered and outgunned and pull out, or, on the other hand, I could stand and fight.

I had been forced to make similar choices many times on payday nights in the Oklahoma oil fields. I'd learned then that the bigger the bully, the better the brawl was likely to be, that no matter how tough the opponent who backed you into a corner, there was always a good chance of out-slugging, outboxing, or outlasting him in the in-fighting.

I decided to fight; my associates agreed that it was the right decision. Only Mother appeared hesitant. When I talked the matter over with her, she indicated that she feared the consequences of a protracted battle for control of Tide Water. There would be endless legal skirmishes and proxy-battles which she was afraid might easily degenerate into noisy exchanges of mud-slinging and name-calling. Woman-like, she naturally wanted to avoid any and all possible unpleasantness. I assured her that if there was anything of this nature, it would come from the opposition, and that no matter what means it would use, the Getty interests were on solid ground with nothing to fear. Our companies had excellent reputations; there were no skeletons in any of their closets. As for our aims and motives in seeking a larger voice in the management of Tide Water, these were open and honest. We wanted to build a bigger, better, and more efficient company which would produce more at lower cost, provide more and higher-paying jobs for its employees, and pay bigger dividends to its thousands of individual stockholders.

"I doubt if anyone will be able to sling much mud over that," I assured Mother.

I made my first move in October, 1934, by seeking an interview with the top officers of Standard. I thought it would be wise to discuss the entire matter with them and, perhaps, arrive at some mutually satisfactory solution to what would almost certainly grow into a major problem. Standard's officials refused to see me. This convinced me that the only hope of Tide Water's seventeen thousand independent common stock-holders, the Getty interests among them, was to force Standard to divest itself of control over Tide Water by selling its stock in that company or by distributing it on a pro rata basis to its own stockholders.

My contention was that a large corporation such as Standard should not have a controlling interest in a smaller competing company such as Tide Water. My view was brought to Standard's attention in an attorney's letter written on December 19, 1934. In it, the attorney, who represented the Getty interests, stated:

> My clients have no desire for the sake of Tide Water Associated Oil Company and their interest therein to engage in controversy with Standard Oil Company either in the courts or elsewhere, but the

matter is of sufficient importance to the independent stockholders in that company to justify recourse to the courts should Standard Oil Company decline to relinquish the voting rights afforded by its stock ownership or to distribute these shares to its own stockholders or to make a bona fide sale or other disposition thereof. It is hoped that Standard Oil Company will give this matter its careful consideration.

Standard did not reply to this letter. However, on December 31, 1934, after the letter had been received and, it may be presumed, read carefully, the Mission Corporation was organized in Reno, Nevada, and Standard's 1,128,123 shares of Tide Water Associated Oil Company stock were transferred to the new company. On the face of things, Standard had relinquished its stock. Actually, it had merely transferred it to a company which was controlled by Bill Humphrey and other executives of the incumbent Tide Water management.

This had the effect of a declaration of open hostilities between the incumbent management of Tide Water and Standard Oil ranged on one side and the Getty group of independent stockholders on the other.

Even before Standard transferred its Tide Water stocks to Mission Corporation, I had realized that I would have to oppose the Tide Water management-Standard Oil combination with every weapon the Getty interests could marshal. A major obstacle preventing me from bringing all the financial resources of the Getty interests to bear was the debt, represented by interest-bearing notes, which George F. Getty, Inc., owed to my mother. The existence of this debt effectively limited—in fact, virtually eliminated—the company's borrowing power.

I went to Mother and explained the situation to her. She understood only too clearly the problems we faced. But, at heart, she was still a mother—and the grandmother of my four sons. Characteristically, the first and greatest concern was for their and my future financial welfare.

"I want to be certain that you and your sons are financially secure and protected against the possible catastrophe which may result from speculation," she declared. "It would be best all around if I established a trust for you and your children."

Mother used the notes she held to establish a "spendthrift trust" for my sons and me. I took it as a special mark of her trust and confidence in my judgment that she had me appointed as sole trustee. She turned her more than two million dollars' worth of George F. Getty, Inc., notes over to the trust on December 31, 1934, the same day that the Mission Corporation was organized in Nevada.

In April, 1935, the "spendthrift trust" sold the notes back to George F. Getty, Inc., for ten thousand shares of George F. Getty, Inc., stock, 1,800 shares of stock in the George F. Getty Petroleum Corporation, and an option to buy 300,000 shares of Tide Water common from George F. Getty, Inc., at $11.00 per share. The creation of the trust and the exchange of the notes for stock and options restored the company's borrowing power. And this was to be sorely needed in the months which followed.

22

During the first week in January, 1935, I was a house guest of Mr. William Randolph Hearst at his home in San Simeon, California. I might here add that, although I am aware of the many derogatory things that have been written and said about the late newspaper magnate, I found him to be a dynamic and highly personable individual.

Whatever may or may not have been wrong with his business philosophies and practices (and, never having done any business with him, I would have little knowledge of these), William Randolph Hearst was extremely charming and hospitable to his friends and acquaintances. I must say that, basing my opinion on a very brief acquaintance, I liked him —and *honi soit qui mal y pense*.

Actually, Hearst and I were neighbors, at least in a manner of speaking. He had a beach house in Santa Monica, and it was next door to the beach house I owned and in which I lived whenever I was in Southern California. Even so, we had never met. It was through a friend, an executive of one of the Hearst chain's newspapers, that I received an invitation to attend the New Year's house party at San Simeon.

I doubt if the world will ever again see a private individual living in a style and on a scale equal to those which prevailed at the fabulously splendid castle at San Simeon. I would be inclined to doubt if the world had seen any private individual live so lavishly since the days of Cardinal Wolsey at Hampton Court.

William Randolph Hearst spent a staggering fortune on building, furnishing, and running San Simeon. Famed as a collector of many things, Hearst had acquired a vast collection of Renaissance paintings, furniture, tapestries, ceilings, *boiseries*, and art objects of all kinds. A large part of this collection was housed and displayed at San Simeon. The furnishings in almost any room in the enormous castle were worth a king's ransom.

The guests at the New Year's house party—there were over a hundred of us—took their meals in the celebrated Refectory, with its huge, sixty-five-foot table and the famous collection of Siena banners hanging high overhead. The long side tables were laden with what I estimated to be a half-million-dollar collection of Georgian silverware. On the walls were two Gothic tapestries. Magnificent things, each of them was worth no less than $125,000, even at depressed 1934 prices.

Such were the surroundings and environment in which W. R. Hearst's house guests ate their meals. In its own way, each of the scores of rooms in the castle was equally spectacular and luxurious.

I was introduced to Hearst and to Marion Davies upon my arrival and found them both to be very gracious and charming. Their hospitality was unstinting, and they appeared to derive no small degree of pleasure from giving it and from seeing that their guests enjoyed themselves.

I, like anyone else who ever visited the fairyland castle, was awed and even overwhelmed by the magnificence and munificence of San Simeon. At one point, I got into a friendly conversation with one of Hearst's business associates, and I rather timidly asked him if he knew how much San Simeon had cost the publisher.

"It's doubtful if anyone could give an accurate estimate," came the reply. "But the cost is certainly over the thirty-million-dollar figure—and San Simeon isn't yet completed!"

Much work was still being done at San Simeon. In fact, the great indoor swimming pool had just been finished, after a year and a half of work and an expenditure of more than $1,500,000.

Even more timidly, I asked whether anyone knew how much it cost the newspaper tycoon to run his castle. The answer was that no one had any figures, but that operating expenses totaled several thousand dollars *per day*—something I could well believe after having spent my first day there.

Rulers of nations aside, "The Chief," as Hearst was known to his associates and employees, was probably the last human being who actually lived without ever giving a thought to cost or expense. Whether one approves or condemns this, or the man himself, is not the question. One cannot help but marvel at the flair—and the air—with which William Randolph Hearst ruled as lord of his private fief at San Simeon.

Although I made only this one visit to San Simeon, I recall my stay with great clarity, if for no other reason than because of a highly fortuitous incident which occurred while I was there.

On the morning of New Year's Day, one of the countless servants at San Simeon informed me that I had a long distance call from New York City. Slightly surprised, I went to the nearest telephone extension and took the call. It turned out to be from a good friend, Jay Hopkins, who, incidentally, would one day become the founder of the General Dynamics Corporation.

"Happy New Year, Paul," Jay said when we were connected. Then he went on to impart some news that would prove of vital importance to me in my campaign to obtain control of the Tide Water Associated Oil Company.

Hopkins told me that, on the previous day—December 31, 1934— a holding company, the Mission Corporation, had been formed in Reno, Nevada. The company had been formed to hold the large block of Tide Water common stock that was owned by Standard Oil of New Jersey. Instead of distributing its Tide Water stock holdings to its own stockholders, Jersey Standard would distribute the stock of the holding company to its shareholders on a pro rata basis. Thus, Jersey Standard's stockholders, by controlling Mission Corporation, would retain control over the Tide Water block.

This was anything but heartening news. Jersey Standard's opposition to the Getty interests was hardly a secret. The formation of the holding company and consequent retention of control over the large block of Tide Water stock by Jersey Standard stockholders made it that much more difficult, if not impossible, for the Getty interests ever to obtain a controlling interest in Tide Water.

But, Hopkins continued, he hadn't called merely to tell me that. His real reason for telephoning was to inform me that he had managed to pull a giant-sized rabbit out of his hat. Among the important stockholders in Jersey Standard was John D. Rockefeller, Jr. Mr. Rockefeller, he said, was traveling at the time, and Jersey Standard executives did not know his whereabouts. Hopkins, however, had learned where John D., Jr., was staying. Stealing a march on Jersey Standard executives, who would doubtless have advised Rockefeller against any such course, my friend had contacted John D., Jr., and asked him if he would be willing to sell his rights to Mission Corporation stock.

Apparently unaware that Jersey Standard hoped that none of the Mission stock would get out of its own stockholders' hands, John D., Jr., informed Hopkins that he would be willing to sell his rights to his share of the Mission stock at a price of 10⅛ per share. As he owned about 10 per cent of Jersey Standard's issued stock, his pro rata rights entitled him to an equal percentage of Mission stock, or about 116,000 shares.

Such a block would be of great strategic value to the Getty companies in their fight to obtain control of Tide Water, and Hopkins wanted to know if I would be interested in buying the Mission Corporation stock rights owned by John D. Rockefeller, Jr.

"Would I?" I repeated exultantly. "Of course I would!"

I authorized Jay Hopkins to close the deal, which involved more than $1,200,000, for me on the spot. I don't think the entire telephone conversation lasted more than five or six minutes. As I hung up the receiver, I thought that I had ample reason to feel that the business year of 1935 had begun most auspiciously.

There is an interesting and rather amusing sequel to the story.

I later saw Jay Hopkins in New York. He had heard from a good source that when Mr. Rockefeller returned from his trip, he was approached by some Jersey Standard executives. During the course of their conversation, they brought up the subject of Mission Corporation stock rights. John D., Jr., declared that he had already sold his.

"To—to whom?" one of the execs asked in the sudden hush that followed.

Mr. Rockefeller admitted that he couldn't remember the name of the "young man" whose representative had made the purchase.

"I understand that he's a very nice young man, though," John D., Jr., is said to have added innocently. "I think he's out in California, and he was apparently very eager to buy the rights."

It was the reference to California and to the eagerness to buy, rather than the adjective "nice," that made one Jersey Standard executive flinch as though expecting a blow.

"It—it couldn't have been someone by the name of J. Paul Getty, could it, Mr. Rockefeller?" he asked.

"Why, yes, I believe that was his name," John D., Jr., replied.

The reaction of the Jersey Standard executives can be better imagined than described!

I soon learned the magical influence of the Rockefeller name. I approached several others among Jersey Standard's minority stockholders with a view to purchasing their Mission Corporation stock-rights. Almost without exception, they flatly refused to sell, at least at first. When I told these stockholders, as I usually did, that I had already bought Mr. Rockefeller's rights, they were visibly affected. In many cases, they soon thereafter changed their minds, and I succeeded in acquiring nearly 40 per cent of the Mission Corporation's stock.

Some years later, I had the pleasure of meeting John D. Rockefeller, Jr.'s eldest son, John D., III; he and his charming wife, Blanchette, have become my friends.

At this point, I would like to say a few words about the Rockefellers, whose name, familiar to all Americans, was not infrequently maligned a few decades back. The history of the Rockefeller fortune is one of the great sagas of American industry, and certainly the story of the great Rockefeller philanthropies is one of the most inspiring of its kind in the nation's entire history. Few families have contributed as much in all fields —from industry through philanthropy to politics—as the Rockefellers. Certainly the example and leadership of John D., III, are worthy of note; he has proven himself a worthy successor to his grandfather and father.

That said—and from the heart—I shall once more pick up the thread of my narrative.

Unfortunately for our side, the controlling group of Tide Water directors learned of our purchases of Mission stock-rights all too soon. They moved swiftly and efficiently to block any further incursions into their preserves by the Getty interests.

At the annual Tide Water meeting held in March, 1935, the company's management proposed a resolution providing that directors be elected for three-year terms instead of the usual one-year terms. This, obviously, would entrench the incumbent management for three years. The controlling directors would be in and would stay in for three years, regardless of the outcome of any stock-buying campaign conducted by the Getty companies. Adoption of the resolution would make it virtually impossible to effect any changes in company control or policies for three years. It was entirely within the realm of possibility that the controlling directors could sell whatever holdings they had in the company and still continue to run it until their long terms ended.

I countered that the issue of directors' terms should be submitted to the stockholders for vote. It was a futile move. Tide Water management agreed, but in such a manner that the Getty interests had no time to organize anything resembling a proxy campaign that would acquaint the stockholders with their side of the argument. Incumbent management carried the day.

The Getty interests riposted by continuing to buy stock in Tide Water and Mission Corporation. At the end of 1935, the Getty group held 474,-155 shares of Mission and 836,254 shares of Tide Water.

In 1936, before the annual meeting of Tide Water stockholders, the Getty interests mailed proxies to all the company's stockholders. We did not expect to win—and we did not—but we felt that we had done what we could to bring our side of the story to the attention of the company's common stockholders.

In 1936, Tide Water management increased the amount of common stock issued and introduced a voting preferred. This served to reduce the proportionate influence of Tide Water stock held by the Getty interests and to reduce the voting power of the block held by Mission Corporation, control of which was gradually moving into the hands of the Getty group.

In the meantime, many other maneuvers were being employed in an effort to disrupt and demoralize the Getty group's campaign. Among these was a lawsuit brought by certain Pacific Western minority stockholders and aimed at enjoining Pacific Western from participating in the campaign to buy Tide Water and Mission Corporation stocks. The suit was finally dismissed by the courts as having no basis.

As 1937 opened, it was quite plain that the Tide Water campaign now centered on the fight to gain control of Mission Corporation. And that fight soon turned into a no-holds-barred last-ditch struggle.

On Thursday, March 15, 1937, the directors of Mission Corporation suddenly scheduled a directors' meeting to be held in Reno, Nevada, only four days later. The purpose of the meeting was to write up Mission's assets so that its Tide Water stock could be distributed to Standard Oil stockholders. The motive behind this was to break up the block and thus nullify the control the Getty interests were gaining in Mission Corporation through purchases of Mission's stock and through assurances of proxy support from other Mission stockholders.

I did not hear of the proposed meeting until late on the evening of March 15. The news was alarming, particularly since a weekend intervened between then and March 19, when the meeting was to be held. This left almost no time or opportunity to make plans or to take any legal action to counter the move which I thought would not only be harmful and costly to all Mission and Tide Water stockholders, but would also do great damage to the Getty group's Tide Water campaign.

The account of what transpired next rivals the scenario of any motion picture thriller for excitement and suspense.

My first move was to have a hurried consultation with David Hecht, of the law firm of Chadbourne, Stanchfield & Levy, who had been the New York counsel for the Getty companies since July, 1936. Dave spent the night and the next day working around the clock, conferring with the officials of Getty companies and gathering the necessary facts, figures, and documents which could be used in a legal move to delay the "surprise" meeting called for March 19 by the Mission directors.

Sleepless, haggard, Dave Hecht and Harold Rowland, who was an officer of the Getty companies, boarded an airplane in New York City on the evening of March 16. The weather was foul, and, in those days, airlines and aircraft did not have the navigational aids they now possess. Blizzards and squalls grounded the plane several times en route to Reno.

Time was of the essence, for Hecht would have to prepare voluminous briefs and documents upon his arrival in Nevada if he was to have any hopes of obtaining a restraining order from the courts on Monday morning. I followed Hecht's and Rowland's progress nervously as they reported by telegram and telephone from along the way.

Grounded Chicago. Hope to take off again in few hours.

Weather forced us to land in St. Louis.

So it went. Luck, however, seemed to be with the Getty group, at least to the extent that the weather cleared enough each time to permit their plane to fly another leg. Late Saturday afternoon, nearly twenty-four hours after their departure from New York, Hecht and Rowland arrived in Reno. They disembarked weary and disheveled and immediately set to work. The entire office force of the Reno law firm of Hawkins, Mayotte and Hawkins was dragooned into working straight through Saturday night and all day Sunday. It wasn't until late Sunday evening that the papers needed to apply for a restraining order and injunction were ready.

David Hecht was waiting at the judge's chambers well before eight-thirty on Monday morning. The jurist carefully examined the petition for a restraining order and signed the order at 9:23 A.M., only seven minutes before the Mission directors' meeting was to begin. The restraining order called for a hearing later that week to determine whether a preliminary injunction should be issued.

The restraining order was promptly served upon all the directors at the meeting. The Getty interests, and all the independent stockholders in Tide

Water Associated, had secured a vitally important breathing spell with only moments to spare.

The next step was to obtain subpoenas requiring all the Mission directors who had come to Reno to attend the meeting to remain there until the hearing and to produce their books and records. The subpoenas were obtained and duly served on the individuals concerned.

The legal skirmishing occasioned a wild flurry of activity. Huge amounts of documents and data had to be obtained, assembled, and collated so that the Getty group's counsel might establish the facts in the case and obtain the preliminary injunction. Dave Hecht and Harold Rowland sent representatives rushing by airplane to Los Angeles, San Francisco, New York, and other places to obtain the needed information and material. They rounded up expert witnesses, including professors of business administration and economics, and prepared them.

Naturally, the Mission directors were engaged in similar activities and were making similar preparations to prove their side of the case. All this took time, and an adjournment was requested and granted by the court.

Then, on the night before the hearing was to be finally held, Dave Hecht decided to have a midnight nightcap. And thereby hangs a rare tale.

23

ĪT IS said that President Abraham Lincoln, when informed that his victorious general, Ulysses S. Grant, "drank," observed that someone should find out what brand the General drank and send a barrel of it to every other Union Army commander.

Now, I would hardly compare myself to Lincoln or Dave Hecht to U. S. Grant. Nor did anyone ever take it upon himself to tell me that my brilliant attorney and friend "drank." However, like Lincoln basing my judgment on results obtained, I would never hesitate recommending that attornies engaged in tough legal battles indulge in the same kind of nightcap that Dave Hecht had on the eve of the Mission Corporation hearings in Reno.

By the most fortuitous of coincidences, Dave went into the same Reno bar in which the high-powered New York attorney representing the opposing forces was even then having a drink. The two men saw each other and, as even the most bitterly opposed lawyers will, entered into a friendly conversation.

Hecht, a suave, keen-witted individual with a fine, wry sense of humor, good-naturedly chevied the opposing counsel and, with bland self-assurance, asserted that the Mission directors—who, of course, were also the controlling directors of Tide Water—"would never get away with it." Blithely sipping his drink, Dave cheerfully added that he was entirely willing to keep all of the directors who had been subpoenaed on the witness stand until after mid-May. If that happened, he smiled confidently, the entire question would have to be submitted to the stockholders.

"And that is precisely what Pacific Western and the Getty companies would like to see happen," he concluded.

The other attorney was visibly impressed, even a bit shaken, and the conversation continued, ending with the opposing counsel agreeing that the best way for his clients to save face would be by putting the whole matter up to the stockholders. The next day, a compromise was reached. The directors agreed to let the stockholders decide the issue, and they made a gentleman's agreement that there would be no bitter, acrimonious proxy battle. Each side would merely state its position and views in a simple, straightforward letter. Both letters would be sent in the same envelope at the same time to all shareholders, and they could then decide and give their proxies to whichever side they wished.

In the event, it turned out differently. The letters were written and sent —but a week before the date on which the proxies had to be filed, the opposing side sent out a second letter to the stockholders. It was a bitter attack on the Getty forces. Apparently, the opposition believed the Getty group would not have time to counter this move. But the directors reckoned without the loyalty and energy of my aids and associates.

A letter countering the surprise one that had been sent to the stockholders by the opposition was quickly prepared. A volunteer emergency "task force" worked straight through the night reproducing the letter, addressing envelopes, and inserting the individual letters in them. The replies to the opposing side's attack were in the mail to the stockholders the next morning, and they elicited a highly satisfactory response.

The stockholders' meeting was held on May 13, 1937. The proposal to distribute the Tide Water Associated stock held by the Mission Corporation was beaten down by an overwhelming vote. Mission's management officials—Tide Water's controlling directors and their associates—were repudiated and voted out of office.

The Getty interests continued to buy Tide Water stock whenever it became available. The campaign continued until 1951, when the Getty interests finally obtained clear-cut numerical control. Two years later, the Getty group elected all the company's directors, and the long fight, which lasted almost twenty years, was over.

In 1932, the assets of Tide Water Associated totaled $192,000,000. Today, they total nearly a billion dollars and, among its many properties, the now-renamed Tidewater Oil Company has the world's most modern refinery, located near Wilmington, Delaware.

I think that this is as good a place as any to make some things clear about the Tide Water campaign and to pay some tributes where they are due.

First of all, I want to make it very clear that I feel no rancor or resentment against any of the executives of Tide Water who opposed me through the years of the battle for control of the company. They had their views on how the company should and should not be managed. Mine and those of my associates differed from theirs. In the last analysis, the fight was decided by democratic means, through the vote of the stockholders themselves.

As for William Humphrey, who for many years after 1934 was the president of Tide Water, I can truthfully say that I liked, admired, and respected him. A top-notch lawyer and businessman, his direction of Tide Water's affairs proved profitable to all the company's stockholders, the Getty interests among them. The differences that Bill and I had were all over business matters, and they were long ago adjusted and forgotten. Any corporation, no matter how large, would have been fortunate to have a top executive of Bill Humphrey's caliber on its management roster.

The "victory" of the Getty interests was brought about largely by the loyalty, confidence, and support I received from my aids and associates. They stuck by me and trusted me and my decisions even when the situation looked bleak—and mighty bleak it did look on several occasions and at several stages of the campaign.

David Hecht, my brilliant and tireless attorney until his untimely death in 1959, guided the myriad transactions and operations which were involved through labyrinthine legal mazes. E. F. Hutton & Company brokers Ruloff Cutten, Don Phillips, and my old Harvard Military Academy schoolmate, Gordon Crary, worked miracles for me by their adroit handling of stock purchases and transactions on the New York Stock Exchange. Fero Williams, Harold Rowland, H. P. Grimm, Norris Bramlett, and Emil Kluth are only a few among many others who gave me moral—and, on occasion, even material—support when I needed it most. Without these men, this major triumph of my business career might have become my biggest failure.

My associates, aids, allies, and I planned our moves as carefully as any general and his staff would plan the strategies and tactics in a military campaign. We had to. We could leave little or no margin for error. We were too small in comparison to the opposition arrayed against us to take any unnecessary chances.

At first glance, it might seem as though the campaign to gain control of Tide Water involved nothing more than going into the market and buying the company's stock. It wasn't that simple or easy.

There were millions—more than five million shares at the beginning and even more after the incumbent management issued additional shares— of Tide Water Associated common outstanding. Only a relatively small percentage of these were ever on the market at any given time. Great blocks were held by individuals and interests desiring to maintain control over the company. Many other shares were owned by people who just didn't want to sell for any of a number of reasons. Others who might have sold hoped the contest for control would run up the price of the stock, and they determined to hold on to their shares and see what happened.

Consequently, our campaign had to be conducted on several fronts simultaneously. First, we had to buy as much stock as we could when it became available on the market—subject, of course, to the availability of funds for that purpose. Then, it was necessary to obtain voting proxies from stockholders who did not wish to sell their shares.

Naturally, these stockholders had to be shown that it was to their advantage to give the Getty interests their proxies. They had to be convinced that control by the Getty group of independent stockholders would benefit the company, increase the value of their stocks and mean larger dividends for them in the future.

Also, considerable blocks of Tide Water stock were held by other companies such as the Mission Corporation. It was therefore necessary to conduct another and entirely separate effort to gain control of Mission Corporation in order to obtain control of the Tide Water stock which Mission owned.

There were countless ramifications and complications at every step of the way. New problems and obstacles seemed to present themselves constantly as the campaign progressed.

My associates and I worked tirelessly and around the clock during many critical stages of the contest. All-day meetings followed by all-night conferences again followed by all-day meetings were not unusual during vital phases of the Tide Water campaign. Once again, I want to emphasize that I shall always be grateful to my associates who, bone-weary and hollow-eyed as they frequently were, nonetheless always somehow managed to find the strength and energy to do just a little bit more, a little bit extra.

Insofar as I personally am concerned, I think the principal qualities which made it possible for me to achieve my goal were determination, persistence, and mulish stubbornness. I knew why I wanted to control the Tide Water Associated Oil Company. I had a program for the company's operation and expansion clearly in mind—a program I was certain would benefit its stockholders, employees, customers, and the general public.

The stakes were high, well worth the risks taken and the money and energy expended. Within a few years after the campaign began, I could sense that the contest was slowly moving in favor of the Getty interests, and, as has been seen, after approximately nineteen years, it ended in complete success.

Overnight successes in business are rare enough to be considered unique.

Any recipe for success in business must contain generous amounts of imagination, determination, patience, tenacity—and above all, hard work.

Sooner or later in his business career, every businessman encounters large and promising opportunities. He must be able to recognize them when they present themselves and possess the tenacity and capacity for hard work to make the most of them.

I don't believe that these are necessarily innate traits or abilities. I think that in the great majority of instances, they are formed and developed by one's experience and experiences in one's business career. Having seen his opportunity and set his goal, a businessman can hope for success if he lays his plans with care, is fortunate enough to have loyal and enthusiastic associates, and then gives all his efforts and energies to the tasks he has set for himself.

By so doing, he has the battle three-quarters won. The remaining one-quarter is the variable and unpredictable factor, the unknown quantity that puts the zest and excitement into business. Without that element of uncertainty, the bringing off of even the greatest business triumph would be a dull, routine, and eminently unsatisfying affair.

Such were the lessons I learned from the Tide Water campaign. I would apply them to advantage in the years that followed.

24

IT HAD long seemed that there were too many "Getty companies." Some of them had been formed by my father, others by me. By 1936, it appeared advisable to do some tidying up and eliminate duplications and overlaps, reduce administrative overhead and improve general efficiency. Consolidation and dissolution were the obvious answers.

Any such programs necessarily involve a massive amount of legal, accounting, and other paper work. The steps taken are largely routine, but nonetheless very complex. I suppose the best and easiest way to relate this part of my story is simply to list the steps taken in chronological order.

Early in 1936, the headquarters of George F. Getty Oil Company, Minnehoma Oil and Gas Company, George F. Getty Petroleum Corporation, Getty, Inc., and Sandoma Gasoline Company were moved from Los Angeles, California, to Jersey City, New Jersey.

In December of that same year, the directors of three of the Getty companies—George F. Getty Oil Company, George F. Getty Petroleum Corporation and George F. Getty, Inc.—took under consideration the advisability of consolidation. After careful study of the pros and cons involved in such a step, they recommended consolidation of the three firms and drew up an agreement which set forth the terms and conditions under which it was to be accomplished. The proposal was approved by the stockholders of the companies that same month, and the effective date of consolidation was set as December 30, 1936.

A new company, retaining the name George F. Getty, Inc., was formed. Into it were taken the three former companies which, on date of consolidation, had assets valued at a total of more than $27,500,000. Stockholders in each of the former companies received stock in the new company in proportion to their investments in the old.

In August, 1937, the directors of Getty, Inc.—the company I formed in 1933 to manage the securities I had purchased—and George F. Getty, Inc., considered and approved a merger of the two companies. Getty, Inc., was merged into George F. Getty, Inc., on August 31, 1937. The assets of Getty, Inc., at the time of merger exceeded $7,600,000.

On December 21, 1937, the Sandoma Gasoline Company merged into another of the companies I had previously formed, the Santa Fe Investment Company. And on July 20, 1938, George F. Getty, Inc., purchased the entire capital stock of the Santa Fe Investment Company.

On December 14, 1938, the directors of the Minnehoma Oil and Gas Company recommended that the company be liquidated. From a sentimental standpoint, the decision to dissolve this company was a very difficult one to make. Originally organized in 1903 as the Minnehoma Oil Company, it had been the pioneer Getty company, on which the Getty oil business and the Getty fortune were founded.

The name "Minnehoma" was sufficient to evoke countless associations and memories of my childhood and youth—and above all, memories of my father. Minnehoma Oil Company had drilled the first producing well on Lot 50 in Oklahoma. It had been as a Minnehoma Oil Company employee that I served my apprenticeship in the Oklahoma oil fields. Although I was over forty-five in 1938, I must admit that the thought of liquidating the Minnehoma Oil and Gas Company, successor to Minnehoma Oil, caused sharp tugs at my heartstrings.

But the company had been inactive for some time. Its field offices had been closed down the previous May, and since then its properties had been operated by the Skelly Oil Company of Tulsa on a fee basis. There was no practical and logical way to avoid liquidation of the company, and an agreement of dissolution was made on December 20, 1938. All necessary approval was quickly obtained and, on December 28, Minnehoma Oil and Gas Company assets were distributed and the company passed out of existence. The sentimental attachment to the name "Minnehoma" remains, however. I have given it to other companies I have since formed and also to one of the giant super-tankers which form the present-day Tidewater tanker fleet.

There were other developments, too, during the period when so much of my time and energy was consumed by the Tide Water and Mission Corporation battles which I have described in detail in the foregoing chapters. One important and disheartening event in my personal life had been the failure of my marriage to Ann Rork; by 1935 I was again—and for the fourth time—a divorced man.

On the business side, there was a highly surprising and most pleasant development which grew out of the 1937 "victory" of the Getty interests in the struggle to gain control of the Mission Corporation. By gaining control, the Getty group of independent stockholders received a truly fantastic bonus.

Early in 1935, Standard Oil of New Jersey had unexpectedly transferred its controlling stock interest in the Skelly Oil Company to the Mission Corporation. To our surprise, we learned that, in addition to its huge block of Tide Water Associated shares, Mission held no less than 57 per cent of the common stock of Skelly Oil!

Thus, in gaining control of Mission, and through it control of well over a million shares of Tide Water common, the Getty interests had also gained secure control of the Skelly Oil Company, a midcontinent major oil company with headquarters in Tulsa, Oklahoma. The value of this "bonus" acquisition may be seen when it is known that in 1937, Skelly Oil had a net income of $6,400,000. Nowadays, its assets exceed $300,000,000, and its net income runs around $25,000,000 per year. Mission Corporation, I might add, still holds the controlling interest in the company.

Among Skelly Oil's subsidiaries was the Spartan Aircraft Company, which was destined to play a very large and important part in my life and business career during and immediately following World War II.

In the spring of 1937, I went to London to see the coronation of King George VI. Tide Water and Mission Corporation matters being safely squared away for the time being, I felt I could afford a much-needed vacation and, after the coronation, went on to spend a few weeks on the Continent.

I went to Europe again in May, 1938, and this time remained abroad for several months. I maintained constant contact with my companies and close supervision over my business interests by letter, cable, and transatlantic telephone.

While in Europe, I received a transatlantic call from an acquaintance, a real estate agent in New York City, who informed me that the Hotel Pierre was for sale. He offered it to me and quoted a price. Although I had never owned a hotel before and knew little if anything about operating one, I sensed that the Pierre would make a fine investment. A businessman's instincts being what they are, I heard the real estate agent out and, when he was through speaking, signified my interest and made a counteroffer of a price considerably lower than that which he had quoted. This is how I took my first flyer in a going business which had no connection with the oil industry. I quite literally bought the Hotel Pierre over the telephone. Naturally, it took some months for the deal to be closed, and the Getty interests would not take actual possession of the hotel until May, 1939.

According to an apocryphal tale, a perennial favorite among gossip columnists, I bought the Hotel Pierre because I was rankled by the poor service I received while lunching there one day. According to this fanciful version, I ordered my lunch and, when it was brought to my table, found it unsatisfactory. I then supposedly complained to the waiter and, upon receiving a rude reply, stalked from the dining room in a rage. That same afternoon, the story goes, I purchased the hotel in order to fire the offending waiter and the headwaiter and manager to boot.

I suppose it's a good enough story, and I rather doubt that I've heard it or seen it in print for the last time. There's only one thing wrong with it. It simply isn't true.

I bought the Hotel Pierre because it was available at a low price. So great was the bargain that I cannot to this day understand why someone else didn't snap it up long before I even heard that the property could be purchased. The only reasonable explanation I have ever been able to give is that confidence and ready cash were still in short supply. There were many such bargains for sale at the time.

The luxurious, forty-two-story Hotel Pierre, located on a choice plot on Manhattan's swank Fifth Avenue at Sixty first Street, was then the most modern hotel in the entire city. It had been built in 1929–30, and originally cost more than $10,000,000. In 1938, it could be purchased for $2,350,000, less than one-quarter of the amount that had been spent on building, equipping, and furnishing it in the first place.

I did not need any crystal ball to tell me that this was a bargain. The country was rapidly emerging from the Depression and its aftermath; business conditions were improving rapidly. Business and personal travel were bound to increase greatly and create large demands for hotel accommodations. There had been very little significant hotel construction in New York City for years, and no new hotel construction was being contemplated by anyone in 1938. These factors alone were enough to justify buying the Pierre.

Negotiations for the purchase of the Hotel Pierre, which were being handled most ably for me by my attorney, David Hecht, moved slowly at first. This was due to difficulties and complications which developed on the seller's side. My diary entries covering the period of my 1938 trip abroad are studded with references to cables and telephone calls I received —in Paris, Lausanne, Berlin, and other cities—from Hecht in regard to the Pierre transaction.

At last, on October 11, 1938, the preliminary negotiations finally reached a more or less firm stage. A special meeting of the Board of Directors of George F. Getty, Inc., was held to consider the purchase. After due study and consideration of the Pierre situation, the directors—H. L. Rowland, Millard F. Tompkins, and Charles E. Krug, Jr.—passed a resolution which called for the purchase of the hotel "for an aggregate consideration of $2,350,000," the amount of my counteroffer.

Still more months would pass before the Getty interests, as represented by the Getty Realty Corporation, a wholly owned subsidiary of George F. Getty, Inc., took actual possession of the hotel.

I returned to the United States in early November, 1938. As late as mid-April, 1939, when I was in Los Angeles, I was receiving telegrams and telephone calls from Dave Hecht and Charles E. Krug, Jr., informing me of various additional complications which had developed.

On May 3, my diary entry shows: *David Hecht phoned. We talked about an hour re: the Pierre . . .*

It wasn't until May 5 that my diary entry would read: *Got a wire from Krug saying Pierre is in our possession today.*

At current (1963) land and construction costs, between $25,000,000 and $30,000,000 would be needed to duplicate the Hotel Pierre, which is now one of the two Getty hotels.

The years 1938–39 also marked the period during which I first began seriously to collect paintings and objects of fine art. Not that I hadn't long wished to do so. My deep interest in and desire to some day own fine works of art date back to my youth, having been awakened during my first trip to Europe in 1909, when my mother, father, and I visited the great museums and galleries in England and on the Continent.

My interest increased and my knowledge and taste improved through the years and during my subsequent visits to Europe. I'd taken a few tentative steps toward assembling an art collection of my own as far back as 1931, when I'd attended the Goldschmidt-Rothschild sale in Berlin and bought some Old English prints, a small oil painting, and an antique rug. Two years later, I purchased a group of twelve paintings by the leading

Spanish Impressionist, Joaquin Sorolla y Bastida, at the Thomas Fortune Ryan sale held at the Anderson Art Galleries in New York City.

There was little time or opportunity for me to continue my collecting in the extremely busy years which followed. I had to content myself with viewing the paintings and art objects owned by others in public and private collections. I found this to be a rather unsatisfactory substitute for the pleasure and gratification one derives from owning beautiful things of one's own.

Then, by what was to prove a fortuitous circumstance, in November, 1936, I found myself in need of a home base in New York City. After considerable casting about for a suitable apartment, I leased the large penthouse at One Sutton Place. The penthouse was owned by Mrs. Frederick Guest. A lady of exquisite taste, she had furnished the apartment with a fine collection of eighteenth-century French and English furniture. During the months I lived there, I increasingly felt the influence of the graceful furnishings and the tasteful elegance of the décor.

This, I suppose, more than anything else motivated me finally to begin what I might otherwise have continued to put off from year to year. I determined to start my own collection. But I also determined to avoid the pitfalls which confront the art collector. I made up my mind that I would buy no art objects without the advice, general and specific, of the best authorities and experts. Even before and beyond this, I wanted to expand and increase my own knowledge.

I had received a fair general art education at school, at the universities I'd attended, and through extensive reading and by making frequent visits to museums and galleries. However, I felt there was much more I should know. To this end, I retained several highly regarded art historians and experts to tutor me in the finer points of judging and buying art, particularly art and antique furniture of the Renaissance and the eighteenth century.

When I met Mitchell Samuels, the renowned art expert and dealer with French & Company in New York, I knew almost immediately that I'd met a man I could trust implicitly. I authorized Samuels to keep his highly trained and discerning eye open for any good pieces and to start assembling a collection of eighteenth-century French furniture for me.

In June, 1938, the great Mortimer Schiff Collection was placed on sale at Christie's in London. I was in England at the time and attended the auction. To my amazement, most of the people at the sale appeared to be there as spectators, not as purchasers. Perhaps their reticence to bid was caused by their concern over the rumors and alarms of impending war which were filling the air. In any event, I discovered that I would be able to purchase some priceless treasures for almost shamefully low prices.

I began bidding and, before the sale had ended, had bought most of the collection. The exceptionally fine pieces of French eighteenth-century furniture I purchased, along with a magnificent Louis XIII Savonnerie carpet, when added to those pieces which Mitchell Samuels had already acquired for my account, made me the possessor of an outstanding collection.

But the collecting of fine art is an insidiously habit-forming avocation. When one acquires beautiful paintings, art objects, or pieces of fine antique furniture, one finds that possessing them only serves to whet one's appetite even further.

This is not a manifestation of any "pack-rat" trait, for most large-scale collectors, I among them, donate their acquisitions to museums or place them on permanent exhibit so that they may be seen and enjoyed by the general public. It has long been my theory that an individual who buys a beautiful painting or *objet d'art* is very much like the one who cannot resist buying a puppy in a pet shop window because he fears that the next buyer along won't give the animal as good a home and treatment as he, himself, will give it.

I made many other important purchases during 1938. I managed to secure Thomas Gainsborough's portrait of James Christie through Colnaghi's in London. I acquired Rembrandt's "Marten Looten" for a bargain price of sixty-five thousand dollars at the Mensing sale in Amsterdam. But perhaps the most important acquisition of all was the historic, almost legendary, Ardabil Persian carpet, which had been made on the royal looms of Tabriz in 1535. Moslem Persians had considered this fabulous eleven-by-twenty-four-foot carpet so beautiful that they said it was "too good for Christian eyes to gaze upon."

Nevertheless, "Christian eyes" had often "gazed upon" the Ardabil carpet—and had marveled at what they saw.

"It is worth all the pictures ever painted," the American artist James Whistler declared after seeing the Ardabil.

The carpet, a symphony of glowing colors executed with unsurpassed artistry and fantastic in its detail, is generally acknowledged to be one of the two finest carpets ever made.

In 1910, the Ardabil sold for twenty-seven thousand dollars. Nine years later, it was purchased by the famous art expert and dealer, Lord Duveen, who paid fifty-seven thousand dollars for it. I bought the carpet from Lord Duveen for sixty-eight thousand dollars.

Had I wished to resell this great carpet, I could have realized a very high price for it in later years. I received many offers for it. Among them was one tendered presumably on behalf of the then King Farouk. I was approached personally and asked if I would sell the Ardabil to King Farouk, who wanted to give it as a present to his sister, Fawzia, when she married the Shah of Iran. It was indicated that price would be no object, but I turned the offer down, along with all the others I had received. I did not wish to sell, for I did not want the carpet to leave the United States. I donated the Ardabil carpet to the Los Angeles County Museum some years ago. Museum authorities consider it one of the museum's principal treasures.

Although I will have more to say about my art and antique furniture collection in later chapters, a few more of the pieces I acquired in Europe during my visits there in 1938 and 1939 might bear mention.

I purchased some particularly fine examples of Georgian silverware, including outstanding pieces by the great eighteenth-century London silversmith, Paul Lamerie. I acquired the Beauvais Boucher tapestry "Bacchus and Ariadne" and the famous Persian sixteenth-century "Coronation Carpet," which some authorities believe is a near rival to the Ardabil. In Rome, I obtained some fine examples of early Greek and Roman sculpture.

Altogether, by the time I returned to the United States in November, 1939, I owned a collection of considerable scope, range, and value.

25

W HILE in Rome during November, 1939, I married Louise "Teddy" Lynch, an American girl I had known for several years who was then studying singing in Rome.

The demands of business and the new economic situations and problems which had been created by the outbreak of war in Europe the previous September required my return to the United States immediately after the wedding ceremony. Teddy stayed behind. She had given up her New York Social Register status a few years before to become one of the first and best of the "society" nightclub singers who achieved considerable popularity in the mid-1930's. Now she was unalterably determined to become an opera singer and insisted on remaining in still-neutral Italy to continue her lessons.

Hence, I reluctantly sailed alone aboard of the S.S. *Conte di Savoia* from Naples. I arrived in New York on Thanksgiving Day and had Thanksgiving dinner there with my absent bride's family. I spent several days in New York City attending to matters concerned with the Hotel Pierre and taking care of other urgent business.

I left New York for Tulsa on December 5, and arrived in Tulsa two days later. There I conferred with Bill Skelly, founder and president of Skelly Oil Company, and other company officials. During the day, I drove out to the Spartan Aircraft Company plant. Its aircraft manufacturing operations were somewhat limited; only some sixty workers were employed in the factory. But the affiliated Spartan flying school was much more active. It was, in fact, the largest privately owned flying school then operating anywhere in the United States.

The school was headed by Captain Maxwell Balfour, a crack flyer and veteran combat pilot who had served in the U.S. Air Corps with great distinction during World War I. Under Captain Balfour's brilliant direction, the Spartan flying school had achieved an enviable record and reputation.

At the time I visited the plant and school in 1939, the Spartan school boasted more than 50 instructors and over 50 airplanes. Some 160 U.S. Army Air Corps cadets were receiving their primary flight training there under a contract between Spartan and the War Department, and another 140 students of various categories were also being trained.

By an odd coincidence, I made my visit to Spartan on December 7, two years to the day before the Japanese attack on Pearl Harbor would plunge the United States into World War II. I was gratified by what I saw at Spartan and felt that the aircraft manufacturing operation had many potentials that could be further exploited. Naturally, I had no reason to guess that, when war came, Spartan would become and long remain my first and foremost business responsibility.

Completing my work in Tulsa, I went on to Los Angeles. Following a happy reunion with my mother, I pitched into the work that had accumulated during my absence. Christmas was one of the high spots of the entire year. My children by my previous marriages were all in Los Angeles for the holiday. On Monday, December 25, 1939, I could write in my diary: *Christmas—We had a lovely tree and heaps of presents in Mother's sitting room. Mother enjoyed it like a youngster. My four wonderful sons came to visit us. We are very proud of them.*

Having fought his way to certain objectives, a military commander is likely to halt his forces and, instead of ordering them to continue their drive, will set them to work consolidating the positions they have gained. In similar manner, I spent most of 1940 taking care of the details and filling whatever gaps remained after the Getty companies achieved their many goals in the immediately preceding years. In other words, I, too, was "consolidating" my position and that of the Getty interests in the business world.

Came November, and I felt the need for a change of scenery and a short holiday. I decided to take a motor-trip to Mexico and invited my cousin, Howell "Hal" Seymour, to accompany me.

Four years my senior, Hal had been my very close friend and, with spasmodic frequency, my boon companion ever since childhood. It has been my good fortune to meet and know many picturesque individuals in my lifetime. However, although many may have been Hal's equals,

I doubt if any of them could be considered more colorful and ruggedly individualistic than Howell Seymour.

Hal was a born adventurer. He had worked in the oil fields, navigated ore-ships on the Great Lakes, prospected for gold and silver in Nevada, Alaska, and Mexico. A fine still and motion picture photographer, he was also an excellent violinist and trumpet-player. He had played in several name bands and, for a time, was one of Bing Crosby's accompanists.

Hal delighted in dabbling in many different fields of endeavor and in mastering many trades. On the other hand, he refused to be tied down, as he put it, and stubbornly refused to surrender an iota of his personal freedom for the success that could have been his in any of several fields. It could not be said that business bored Hal, for there was little that ever bored him unless it was insincerity or pretension. Up until the day of his death in 1959, when he was over seventy, he took an intense interest in all that went on around him and lived a vigorous, active life that left him completely independent of anything or anyone. But the mere thought of an existence centered on any desk-bound, nine-to-five routine was always enough to make my cousin recoil in horror.

Hal Seymour cared nothing about making any more money than was essential for his comparatively modest needs. I recall that at one point in his checkered career, he married a widow of considerable means who prevailed upon him to start a realty business with her. The enterprise was instantly successful, and Hal suddenly found himself earning several hundred dollars a week.

The shock and fear that he might grow rich and thus become tied down by wife and wealth were too much for Hal. He was soon without both bride and business.

Whether one was traveling or not, one could find no better companion than Hal Seymour. His wry humor was perpetually amusing; his energy and enthusiasm—and his store of stories, both factual and apocryphal—were inexhaustible. I was greatly pleased when he agreed to drive with me to Mexico City in late November, 1940; I knew that my planned vacation would be infinitely more enjoyable because of his presence.

We arrived in Mexico City on Monday, December 2, 1940, and checked into the Hotel Reforma. Somehow, I got a cinder in my eye. I couldn't dislodge it—or even find it, for that matter—and made the familiar mistake of rubbing my eye to alleviate the discomfort. The eye became badly inflamed, and when the doctor Hal finally insisted on calling for me arrived at the hotel, he told me that a minor operation would be necessary in order to remove the offending cinder. The operation was very simple and quickly performed, but I was advised not to drive or travel for about a week afterward. When, at last, I was pronounced completely fit, Hal and I left Mexico City and drove a lazy, meandering course to the southwest. I had already made up my mind to extend my vacation, and I wanted to spend it by the sea.

My cousin Hal and I reached Acapulco in late December. Finding climate, scenery, surroundings, and the swimming all to be perfect, we agreed it would be senseless to travel further. I decided to stay awhile—for a few days, according to my first estimates. Then, as Acapulco and the easy pleasant life there grew on me, I repeatedly extended the period.

"Just another week," became a familiar refrain.

I had left my business affairs in good shape north of the border. Whatever orders had to be given or decisions had to be made could be transmitted by letter, telegram, or telephone. Acapulco was a paradise, and I was content to be an affluent beachcomber who issued forth from his comfortable rented apartment each morning and spent most of the day swimming and sun-bathing.

One evening, entirely by accident, I met another tourist who exuberantly informed me that he had discovered the world's most beautiful beach several miles south of Acapulco and invited me to visit it with him and his party the next day. I said I would go and wished I hadn't when told we would have to take a truck through some miles of tangled tropical forest and then proceed by canoe to reach the place.

But I dragooned Hal Seymour into coming along, and we all went, clinging grimly to the sides of the ancient truck that bounced and banged along a dirt track which cut uncertainly through the forest. My first glimpse of the magnificent spread of sea and sand was in itself generous reward for any discomfort I had experienced during the ride.

My tourist friend had not exaggerated.

Revolcadero Beach—for that was its name—was, without question, the world's most beautiful beach.

It was completely natural and unspoiled, preserved by the remoteness of its location and the fact that it was entirely ringed by dense tropical forest on the landward side. These factors had prevented its discovery by anyone save a few local Indians and, of course, a few tourists.

The beach itself was a long, broad expanse of fine white sand. A few miles inland, a range of mountains that rose to several thousand feet formed a protective wall against winds which might otherwise have brought extremes of weather and temperature. The immediate area was laced by sweet-water lagoons.

It was all ideal, perfect, more beautiful than anything I had ever seen anywhere. Not even the Italian Riviera, where the Ligurian Alps meet the Mediterranean, could compare with it.

After several more visits to Revolcadero Beach, an idea began to grow in my mind. I thought of buying several hundred acres of the land and visualized building a fabulous resort that would attract visitors and tourists from all over the world. The more I thought of it, the more I liked the idea, even though there appeared to be countless all-but-insuperable obstacles to realizing it.

The land was completely undeveloped. It was virgin land covered by thick forest and tangled underbrush. It would cost a fortune merely to clear it. Roads and utilities were nonexistent. Certainly the cost of building the kind of roads suitable for a luxury resort would be staggering. Then, paradoxically, the very features and elements which made Revolcadero Beach so attractive in the first place contrived against it as a resort area. It was unknown and off the beaten path; a great many people would be reluctant to pay luxury-class hotel rates at a resort that wasn't already fashionable and situated in a readily accessible location.

The type of resort I envisioned would need boat landings and a yacht basin. Another fortune would have to be spent in building and dredging these. The acquiescence and even co-operation of the Mexican government would be required before work of any sort could commence. Beyond all this, Europe was already at war, and the international situation was hardly such as to warrant the investment of large sums outside one's own country.

Nonetheless, I believed the project was feasible. Development of the land would alone serve to increase its value greatly over whatever price I paid for it. The natural beauty of Revolcadero Beach and the building of the sort of hotel I envisioned would go a very long way toward making the resort "fashionable." The comparatively low labor and material costs which obtained in Mexico would offset at least in substantial part the added expense involved in building from scratch on virgin land.

Details of purchase and appropriate negotiations with the Mexican government would have to be handled by a competent attorney. Having made my decision to buy and build, I put through a long distance call to the ever-reliable David Hecht and told him to leave New York immediately for Acapulco. We wasted no time after his arrival, and the Mexican company in which I was interested purchased some land at Revolcadero Beach. Dave and I returned to the United States in mid-March. Hal Seymour remained behind and took care of a thousand and one preliminary details.

But the United States would be forced into war nine months later. My plans for Revolcadero Beach would have to be shelved for the duration. They would be further delayed for various reasons beyond my control after the war ended.

The Revolcadero Beach project was nevertheless implemented and completed. The Hotel Pierre Marques finally opened in 1956. When it did, the hotel proved to be all that any of us who had been involved in its planning and building had anticipated.

The instantaneous success of the Hotel Pierre Marques exceeded all hopes and expectations. The Pierre Marques is, of course, the other hotel in what some overzealous columnists have been wont to describe grandiosely as "the Getty hotel chain."

Returning to Los Angeles from Mexico in March, 1941, I immediately turned my attention back to my oil business. It was a hectic and uncertain period for the American petroleum industry. The world situation was worsening rapidly and steadily. France had fallen the year before; Britain and her empire stood alone against the rampaging Axis.

Increased purchasing by the British, whose war machine required vast quantities of oil, and stepped-up defense requirements at home served to raise the demand for petroleum products of all kinds. And, since it was becoming increasingly clear that the Axis was aiming for world domination, the question of whether the United States would become involved in the war was rapidly changing to one of when it would become involved.

In May, President Franklin D. Roosevelt declared a state of unlimited national emergency, a move with which I wholeheartedly agreed. The next month, Hitler invaded Russia. In August, 1941, I wrote in my diary: *I have concluded that Hitler's treacherous attack on Russia has cost him the war.*

In June, American troops were sent to Iceland at the request of the Icelandic government. On August 14, President Roosevelt and British Prime Minister Winston Churchill signed the Atlantic Charter.

The possibility that America could remain out of the conflict grew dimmer with each passing day. Totalitarian aggressions would not be limited to any single continent or hemisphere. It would only be a matter of time before one or another of the aggressors would strike at the United States, the richest and most tempting prize of all.

Leaders of the petroleum industry were fully aware that if the nation entered into the war it would be necessary to produce crude oil on a far greater scale than ever before in history. Warships, troop transports, freighters, fleets of airplanes, mechanized and motorized military units— all would consume great oceans of petroleum in the form of fuel and lubricants.

On May 28, 1941, the day following his declaration of an unlimited national emergency, President Roosevelt appointed Secretary of the Interior Harold L. Ickes as petroleum co-ordinator for national defense. Secretary Ickes was directed to unify and co-ordinate the various parts and phases of the petroleum industry so that any conceivable wartime demands for oil could and would be met. Ralph K. Davies of the Standard Oil Company of California was appointed deputy co-ordinator.

Within two months, the Office of Petroleum Co-ordinator was a functioning agency of the United States government. Its principal departments included Production, Refining, Transportation, Conservation, Marketing, Foreign, and Research. The agency, renamed the Petroleum Administration for War in late 1942, operated with great efficiency throughout the emergency and the war.

Fortunately, the oil industry was in a good position to expand its production rapidly. Unitization, proration, and other voluntary or state-regulated conservation measures had served not only to limit the number of wells drilled over the preceding years in producing fields, but had also held down the production of a sizable percentage of existing wells by limiting the quantities of oil they could produce. The nation's petroleum reserves had been conserved. Wells producing at less than their maximum possible rate could be brought to full production practically overnight; this alone would greatly increase available stocks of crude oil. Then, many additional wells could be drilled rapidly in producing fields where existing wells were widely spaced to conform with conservation regulations, thus increasing output even further. And, if still more petroleum were required, exploration and drilling crews stood ready to fan out across the country or across the continent to locate new reserves and open new fields.

Petroleum industry technology was also equal to whatever demands might be made of it in the event of war. Great scientific and technological strides had been made during the 1920's and 1930's. Instruments such as the seismograph, magnetometer, torsion balance, and gravimeter took a considerable portion of the guesswork out of oil prospecting. Rotary rigs and the machinery and equipment used in drilling oil wells had been immensely improved through the years. Towering 176-foot steel derricks, high-speed rigs, improved tools and bits, special drilling muds, revolutionary new refining methods and processes—these and a thousand and one other scientific and technological advances helped to make the American petroleum industry ready for whatever might happen.

Like a great many other Americans, I had at first hoped that the United States would be able to stay out of the war. And, like so many of my fellow countrymen, I grew to realize that no free nation could long continue to exist if the remainder of the world was controlled by totalitarian powers. The following excerpt from my diary reflects the course my thinking had taken by the latter part of 1941:

> November 29, 1941—The 10 P.M. radio newscast said that President Roosevelt returned hurriedly to Washington today. If this means war with the Axis, I am for it. The time has come for the U.S. to be united in support of the President's foreign policy. He said from the beginning that appeasement wouldn't work with the Axis, and we must ruefully admit that he was right.

I, by the way, do not happen to be one of those businessmen to whom Franklin Delano Roosevelt's name is anathema. I agreed with many of his views and supported many of his policies, foreign and domestic, and I voted for him. Many charges have been leveled against Franklin Roosevelt, among them that he harmed or weakened or sought to destroy the American free-enterprise system. I, for one, consider any such allegations to be patently ridiculous. In my opinion—and I believe economic facts, figures, and statistics will bear me out—the free-enterprise system, American business, and American businessmen derived many benefits and made many gains during the years that FDR was in office. I, personally, admired him as a man and as a President, and, by late 1941, I was fully convinced that his foreign policy was the only rational one possible under the world conditions that prevailed.

There was little that could be or needed to be done to prepare the Getty oil companies for the exigencies of war. All were functioning smoothly and efficiently. Executives and employees were seasoned, hard-working individuals who knew their jobs and did them well. The companies were producing sizable quantities of petroleum and petroleum products. They were geared to produce considerably more very quickly if the need arose.

And the need arose soon enough. War came with the Japanese sneak-attack on Pearl Harbor on December 7, 1941.

26

On DECEMBER 7, 1941, I sent the following telegram to Under Secretary of the Navy James Forrestal, whom I had known personally for many years:

I AM FORTY-NINE BUT IN GOOD HEALTH, HAVE OWNED THREE YACHTS AND AM EXPERIENCED IN THEIR CARE AND MAINTENANCE. IF NAVY CAN USE ME IN ANY CAPACITY, PLEASE ADVISE. REGARDS. PAUL GETTY.

Jim Forrestal's reply came the next day:

YOUR MESSAGE APPRECIATED. REFERRED TO BUREAU OF NAVIGATION. FORRESTAL.

Civilians are often apt to become impatient with the speed at which government bureaus and agencies move. I was no exception. When I'd heard nothing from the Bureau of Navigation by December 11, I wrote Jim Forrestal a letter reiterating my desire to serve in the Navy. Two days later, I decided to take matters into my own hands and presented myself at the Navy Recruiting Station, where I underwent physical examinations, had several interviews, and filled out reams of forms and questionnaires.

On December 17, I learned that my eyesight did not measure up to the Navy's stringent requirements and that I would have to obtain glasses to correct my vision to the 20/20 minimum standard.

Three days later, on Saturday, December 20, my beloved mother became ill. She was nearing eighty-nine, and as I rushed home from downtown Los Angeles to be by her bedside, I realized that it was the first time in my life that I had known her to be ill. Gamely, the grand old lady fought back against illness. By midafternoon, she insisted on sitting up in her favorite chair and asked me to take her for her usual drive. It was difficult to find plausible excuses for not granting her wish. I could not bring myself to tell her that the doctors forbade her leaving the house. I dared not let her know how seriously ill she really was.

I remained with her throughout the weekend, doing whatever I could to amuse her and make her more comfortable. On Monday, I should have gone to my office to sign some checks and papers. I felt a cold, premonitory chill when Mother's attending physician heard of my intentions and said, "Don't go."

That night, I wrote in my diary: *About 6:00 p.m., Mama improved and seemed quite comfortable; at 10:00 p.m. she is still the same. It seems like a miracle. I was so discouraged all the afternoon.*

Tuesday and Wednesday passed without much change in Mother's condition. On Thursday—Christmas Day—she took a turn for the worse, but nonetheless gathered enough strength to insist that I leave the house and deliver the Christmas presents I had chosen for my four sons and some of my close friends. I was gone only a short time, and found her in the same condition as when I'd left.

Christmas Day was a sad one because of Mama, I wrote in my diary. *She is very ill and has, I am afraid, little chance to recover. I was hopeful until this afternoon, but then became alarmed. Mama took three cups of hot water from me. She kissed me. Afterwards I went out of the room and cried.*

My mother's condition grew worse the next day, but in the evening, she seemed to get a bit better. I sat next to her, holding her hand. She squeezed my hand and, in a soft voice, asked me to leave her alone for awhile. I thought that perhaps she wanted to sleep a little and left her. I went outside the house and walked in the garden beneath her bedroom windows. After several minutes, I suddenly noticed that one of the servants was drawing the curtains of Mother's bedroom windows.

I understood immediately.

The shock was great, the sudden pain of grief all but intolerable. I realized that my mother was gone and that her final act had been one of great love for me. She had mustered her last strength to ask me to leave her room, so that I would be spared the sight of her going.

There are no words, no phrases—no matter how well turned—to describe what one feels at the loss of one's mother. It is useless to try and express the sensation of utter loneliness, the magnitude of the sorrow that can find no outlet. I moved through the days that followed numbly, mechanically, not yet able to comprehend my loss fully, not yet able to realize fully that both the parents I had loved and respected so deeply throughout my life were now gone.

My mother, Sarah McPherson Risher Getty, was born on January 29, 1853, in Delaware, Ohio. Her entire life had been one of service and of devotion to those she loved. She was a schoolteacher when she met my father, whom she married in 1879. From then until his passing, she was his constant companion and his partner in all things.

Their first child, Gertrude Lois Getty, an older sister I never saw, died during a typhoid epidemic in Minneapolis two years before I was born. From the time of my birth, Mother shared her life with Father and me, her only living child. Yet there was always room in her heart for the multitude of others—relatives and friends—who were dear to her.

On December 28, 1941, I wrote in my diary: *How I miss her! No one ever had a better mother.*

The years have done little to lessen my sense of loss.

My cousin, Hal Seymour, had rushed back to Los Angeles from Mexico after I had telegraphed him about Mother's illness. He and other relatives and friends did all they could to ease my sorrow. Hal stayed with me and insisted on accompanying me when I received instructions to report to the Navy Recruiting Office on December 31. I was required to take additional medical tests and was told to return the following Friday. Hal and I went back to the Wilshire Boulevard house, now so silent and empty, and spent a sad, contemplative New Year's Eve there.

The status of my wife, Teddy, was also a matter of deep concern to me at this time. She had remained in Rome, continuing her voice lessons and working as a correspondent for the *New York Herald Tribune.* Italy had declared war on the United States soon after Japan attacked Pearl Harbor. Teddy had been arrested, then interned as an enemy alien in Rome. I had done everything humanly possible through neutral diplomatic channels to secure her release, but without avail. It would not be until June, 1942, that she and other internees would be repatriated aboard the Red Cross ship *Gripsholm.*

Although I passed the Navy physical examination on January 3, 1942, there were further delays in the processing of my application. On January 5, the head of the local Petroleum Co-ordinator's office suggested that I would be of more service to my country exploring for oil than by serving in the Navy. I pointed out that my companies were well organized and efficiently run by the men who formed their executive and managerial staffs. They were entirely capable of running the companies at peak efficiency without me. I wanted to serve in the Navy, and I wanted sea duty. But there was still no decision from the Navy Department.

There was no way in which I could determine how long it would be before I received word from the Navy. I decided to utilize the waiting time by enrolling in a course of instruction in Navigation and Seamanship then being offered at the University of Southern California. Thus, at the age of forty-nine, I began attending classes at the same university at which I had, for a time, studied as an undergraduate thirty years before.

As I'd said in my December 7, 1941, telegram to Navy Under Secretary James Forrestal, I had at one time and another owned three different yachts. The first was the 102-foot *Sobre las Olas*. Its successor was the 160-foot *Jezebel*. The third and last had been the 1,500-ton, 260-foot *Warrior*.

I had bought and sold these vessels in succession. Each time I bought a yacht, I held high hopes of being able to take long, leisurely cruises and ocean voyages aboard it. Somehow, due mainly to the coincident demands and pressures of my business affairs, I had never been able to realize my hopes. Save for a few brief voyages, each of the vessels had for the most part remained in port. Since I had sold my last yacht, the *Warrior*, in 1936, I feared that my knowledge of ships and seamanship might have gotten rather rusty. I wanted to refresh my memory and bring myself up to date on any new advances and developments; I didn't want to be a duffer in the event that I was accepted for service by the United States Navy.

I attended the classes for nearly three weeks, and still there was no decision. The war situation was bad and seemed to be growing worse by the day. United States and Allied forces were being battered and defeated by the Japanese in the Pacific. Despite successful Russian counterattacks, the Nazis were still deep inside Russia and far more than merely holding their own in North Africa. On the high seas, German and Japanese U-boats ravaged Allied shipping, sending large numbers of vessels to the bottom each week.

My impatience increased and, finally, I went directly to Washington in hopes of expediting action on my application. From February 6 to 17th, I went from one Navy Department office—and Navy Department official —to another. The answers I received were unanimously discouraging. It appeared that sea duty was out of the question insofar as I was concerned. I was too old to serve as a junior officer aboard a warship and did not have sufficient experience to qualify for higher rank in the combat branches of the U.S. Navy.

I could, I was told repeatedly, obtain a commission in some supply or administrative branch, with the understanding that I could not hope to be assigned anywhere but to shore duty in the "ZI"—the Zone of the Interior. This would mean that my chances of ever leaving the continental limits of the United States on Navy service were so obscure as to be nonexistent.

I have no idea what the final outcome might have been if I hadn't met Jake Swerbul of Grumman Aircraft in Washington. Jake knew that the Getty interests held control of Skelly Oil, which, in turn, owned Spartan Aircraft. Spartan was doing some subcontracting work for Grumman and, he reluctantly informed me, doing it very badly. He said the aircraft manufacturing end of the Spartan operation was poorly organized and managed. He showed me a confidential report which stated that the NP-1 Primary Trainer being built by Spartan was nose-heavy, badly welded, and that deliveries of completed airframes were running nine months behind contract schedule.

Swerbul's information astounded and shocked me. I had kept a close eye on the management and operations of the various oil companies owned or controlled by the Getty interests, and I knew that these were in tiptop shape. Spartan, however, was a subsidiary of Skelly Oil and so, in a manner of speaking, twice removed from being properly a Getty operation.

I had made no changes in Skelly Oil management after taking control of the company, because it was headed by its founder, William G. "Bill" Skelly, and operating at peak efficiency. But evidently, no one at Skelly was riding close enough herd on the Spartan Aircraft manufacturing operation. I, personally, was not aware of what went on at Spartan. Up to that time, I had received no reports directly from this Skelly Oil subsidiary. Its operations were, by all rights, the responsibilities of Skelly Oil. However, having heard what Jake Swerbul had to say, I determined to make some major changes without delay.

I promptly requested an interview with Colonel Frank Knox, the Secretary of the Navy. An appointment was made for me for 11:45 A.M. the next morning, February 20. I went to Secretary Knox's office and found him to be a most able, intelligent, and friendly individual who was apparently fully aware of the troubles at Spartan. The flying school was doing well, but the aircraft manufacturing end was not doing so well.

"The Armed Forces must have every aircraft factory in large-scale production as soon as humanly possible," Colonel Knox told me. "The most important service you can render your country is to drop all your other business activities and take over direct personal management of Spartan."

He called in Jim Forrestal and several other civilian officials and high-ranking naval officers. All agreed that the management of the Spartan manufacturing operation should be improved.

Two days later, I was in Tulsa, where Spartan Aircraft and the Spartan Aeronautical School were located. The relative conditions of the two were the same as they had been when I was there a little more than two years earlier. The school was thriving. Well managed by Captain Max Balfour, it had expanded greatly. New barracks, hangars, and other structures had been built and were abuilding. Now the school was training Royal Air Force cadets as well as fledgling American pilots. Six auxiliary fields had been built, many more planes and instructors were available, and student enrollment was climbing steadily.

The Spartan Aircraft Company—the manufacturing company—was a far different story. Still geared for minimal peacetime civilian production, it was limping along with a single 235-by-340-foot factory building.

On February 24, I was elected President of the Spartan Aircraft Company and of the Spartan Aeronautical School. As the school was in excellent shape, I decided to leave its management in the highly capable hands of Captain Balfour and concentrate on the manufacturing company.

Now, my knowledge of airplane manufacture was virtually nil. About all I knew about airplanes was that they had wings and engines—and that if they were properly built and piloted, they flew.

Up to that time, my business activities had been largely concerned with the finding, producing, refining, and marketing of petroleum products. Yes, I'd made a few tangential essays into other fields, among them real estate and the hotel business. I had never been a manufacturer before, and certainly not a manufacturer of airplanes and airplane parts.

On February 21, while I was en route from Washington to Tulsa, I had made the following notation in my diary: *I have an important job-getting the Spartan factory into mass production for the Army and Navy.*

It was with no small degree of trepidation that I faced this job. This was no normal, peacetime venture. Spartan would not be producing everyday items for civilian consumption. Its products would be highly important, even vital, to the nation's war effort. Airplanes are not porch-swings or doorknobs. They are extremely complex mechanisms whose every part and component must be manufactured with infinite precision. There could be no margin for error. Even the smallest mistakes or miscalculations—errors of a thousandth of an inch in machining or grinding, for example—could weaken a vital part and result in the loss of human life.

Would I be able to handle the task of getting the Spartan factory into mass production?

I'd asked myself this question a thousand times in the two days that followed my interview with Secretary Knox in Washington. Soon after I got to Tulsa, I made a thorough inspection of the Spartan plant, studied the company's books and records, and conferred at length with its executives and employees.

I soon had the answer to my question.

My job, as I saw it, was principally to expand manufacturing facilities and improve the quality and quantity of production at the Spartan Aircraft plant. I believed that I could do it. First of all, I felt that I could because it had to be done. Also, it seemed to me that the principles involved were no different from those involved in expanding an oil company or in increasing oil-field or refinery production.

Granted, there were many and great differences in the technical aspects —in the details. Drilling a thirty-five-hundred-foot oil well with a rotary rig is one thing. Precision drilling an engine-mount bracket to a one-one-thousandth of an inch tolerance is quite another. It doesn't matter much if a tool shed is roofed with tar paper or galvanized iron. But there can be no substitutions of materials in building an airplane; one cannot use nickel steel when the engineering specifications call for a certain gauge and type of aluminum alloy.

I was also acutely aware that time was short and materials scarce, and that workers would have to be recruited in a highly competitive labor market and trained very quickly. But I'd had experience with similar problems before, during the great Oklahoma and California oil booms.

My primary aim would not be to build the company or to make profits, but to do anything and everything possible to help win the war. But old-fashioned business principles were still applicable. Spartan had to turn out top-quality products at maximum speed and at the lowest possible prices to meet a huge and exigent need.

Once I viewed my responsibilities and duties as head of the Spartan Aircraft Company in these lights, the problems of getting the company's operations into high gear and of expanding its plant and its productive capacity were brought down to manageable proportions. I realized that I needed to apply the same principles, rules, and yardsticks that I had always used throughout my business career. I found that they worked as well in manufacturing as they had when applied to the oil business.

By March 21, the quantity and quality of production had risen appreciably. On that day, seven NP-1 trainers were completed and accepted by the Navy. Before long, Army and Navy representatives were accepting Spartan's estimates of the time needed to get into production on various items, considering them more reliable than those of experts who had been sent to Spartan to make studies and surveys.

In one instance Spartan received a subcontract to manufacture tail-boom assemblies for Lockheed P-38 fighter planes. The experts predicted it would take the factory at least fifteen months to tool up, train labor, and get into full production on the booms. They backed their estimates with the usual Everests of charts, graphs, and tables.

The war situation was anything but bright. The Philippines had fallen. The United States and its Allies were on the defensive on every front; the Axis powers were celebrating triumphs large and small. Under such circumstances, fifteen months seemed an unconscionably long time to get into production on tail booms for urgently needed fighter aircraft.

I wasn't overly impressed by the forecasts of the experts. I've often found that the trouble with many experts is that they're technicians, not businessmen; they frequently seem to lack the built-in enterprise and competitive spirit that motivate businessmen to beat deadlines and achieve results quickly.

I talked the entire question over with Spartan executives, supervisory personnel, and line workers. All recognized the challenge and the need for speed. We slashed the time-lag estimate down to six months. Needless to say, the experts protested in disbelief that this was impossible.

Although Lockheed and AAF representatives were somewhat skeptical about Spartan's ability to begin deliveries within six months, they agreed to go along with our estimates and co-operate in every way possible.

My production chief and I promptly picked fifty of our best workers and sent them to the prime contracting Lockheed Aircraft Company's plant in California. There, they received intensive on-the-job training in the most efficient means and methods of producing tail booms for the Lockheed fighters. In the meantime, we began tooling up feverishly at Spartan. By the time the men returned to Tulsa, we had ten jigs ready for operation. Spartan was in production on the Lockheed subcontract in slightly less than the six months we had estimated.

When I had completed the first two years of my stint at Spartan, I had ample reason to feel proud of the company's achievements and its contribution to the nation's war effort. And I would have even more reason to be proud before the war ended.

27

O<small>N</small> February 14, 1944, I could note in my diary that Spartan Aircraft had produced an impressive array of items for the Army Air Force and the Navy. Among them were:

Rudders, ailerons, and elevators for some 3,000 B-24 heavy bombers.

Wings for 155 Grumman Wildcat fighters.

Cowls for 650 Curtiss dive-bombers.

All the control surfaces for 1,100 Douglas dive-bombers.

Ninety NP-1 Primary Trainer aircraft.

By about the same date, the Spartan School of Aeronautics, which had grown to be one of the largest privately-owned flying schools anywhere in the world, had graduated more than fifteen thousand U.S. and Allied pilots. The gallant young men who were trained at the Spartan school went on to advanced training and then to combat operations in every theater of war. Three Spartan "grads" flew in the B-25 bombers which, launched from the carrier *Hornet* and led by the then Colonel Jimmy Doolittle, carried out the first daring raid on Tokyo on April 18, 1942. Wherever U.S. warplanes operated, it was certain that some of the pilots who sat in their cockpits were Spartan graduates.

The entire Spartan operation had been greatly expanded in two years. More than 300,000 square feet of factory space had been added to the Spartan Aircraft plant. Employment had soared, until over 5,500 highly skilled workers were working round the clock on production lines that had few equals for speed and efficiency anywhere in the aircraft industry.

Anyone who had any manufacturing experience during the war years knows that it was a constant struggle to maintain production in the face of materials shortages, transportation problems, and countless other bottlenecks and obstacles. Strict government controls, priorities, shortages, materials allocations, and other factors made it necessary to improvise often. I remember one occasion when the expanding engineering department needed more space. By rights, a new building should have been built to accommodate the engineers, their drawing boards, and other paraphernalia. But this would have required the use of too much scarce material and would have taken too much time. We solved the problem by adding a spacious mezzanine against one wall of the plant.

In another instance, we received a subcontract to produce twenty-five hundred engine mounts for Republic P-47 Thunderbolt fighter planes. At first it seemed that, in order to handle the contract, we would have to build an entirely new plant and obtain a large quantity of special machine tools. There were more than two dozen lugs on the engine-mount casting that had to be simultaneously machined to a one-thousandth of an inch tolerance.

Such a new plant would have cost a fortune, and the cost would have been passed on to the government in the form of necessarily higher prices for the engine mounts. More than that, it would have taken months to build the plant and obtain the necessary machine tools. The delay would have meant an equal delay in the production of Thunderbolts, which were badly needed on the war fronts.

There appeared to be no way out of the dilemma. I pondered long over the problem and finally came up with what seemed a possible solution. Why wouldn't it be feasible to use a boring mill and rotary table that had been set up to mill all the lugs at the same time?

I fell back on a tried and true last resort that had always served me in excellent stead in the oil fields. Instead of conferring with high-powered experts or engineers, I went down into the plant and put the suggestion to the machinists on the production line.

"What do you fellows think?" I asked after I finished telling them about my idea.

It was like the question of how to solve the "insoluble" problem of the "impossible" lease at Seal Beach many years before. And, just as before, the skilled workmen picked up the ball and ran with it.

"Sounds all right, boss," an old master machinist finally spoke up. He wiped his hands on his coveralls and dug a chewed pencil stub from his pocket. "Got a piece of paper?" he asked. Someone handed him a sheet of what looked like wrapping paper.

"I can't see why it won't work," the machinist grunted, making some quick sketches and doing some fast computations. "I say we ought to give it a try."

The machinery needed was already in the plant. Less than forty-eight hours were needed to set up the first machine according to off-the-cuff specifications. The improvised expedient worked—so well that Republic and government inspectors expressed amazement when they found that the parts thus produced met all specifications and tests.

I remained in active and direct charge of Spartan's operations throughout the war years, living in Tulsa and making my office in the factory. By V-J Day, Spartan's production record was, I like to think, a creditable one.

In addition to the parts and components I've already mentioned as having been produced during the February, 1942–February, 1944 period, Spartan turned out the following major items:

Nearly 3,000 more rudder, aileron, and elevator sets for Consolidated-Vultee B-24 Liberator bombers.

2,500 P-47 engine mounts.

Several hundred tail booms for Lockheed P-38 Lightning fighters.

Several hundred more wing sets for Grumman fighters.

Components and subassemblies for Boeing B-29 Superfortress Very Heavy Bombers.

Between February, 1944, and the end of the war, the Spartan School of Aeronautics turned out an additional ten thousand pilots, making a grand total of more than twenty-five thousand for the period 1939–45.

The wartime performance of the two Spartans—the manufacturing company and the flying school—brought high commendations from the Armed Forces, and words of praise from the prime contractors for whom parts and subassemblies had been manufactured. These were tributes laboriously earned and greatly deserved by the thousands of loyal, efficient men and women who had worked for the companies and did their unstinting best to help win the war.

I believe that a word about the high morale of Spartan's employees is in order. In my entire experience as a businessman, I have seldom if ever seen a group of workers whose morale and enthusiasm reached and held a level equal to that shown by the men and women on the wartime Spartan payrolls. Much of this, of course, was due to the fact that they were all acutely aware that there *was* a war going on. Almost every employee had relatives or close friends serving in the Armed Forces. Each worker seemed to understand what was at stake in the conflict.

But even so, morale might have sagged and enthusiasm waned had it not been for the fact that Spartan's workers were led, rather than pushed, by executive and supervisory personnel. People in positions of authority were chosen carefully, and it was made clear to them that if they hoped to stay on at Spartan, they would have to set examples for their subordinates.

There was no late arriving or early quitting for Spartan management personnel. They were expected to be on the job at the prescribed time and to stay until the quitting whistle blew—and, preferably, to get to work early and leave late if there was any unfinished work to be done. I established a minimum ten-hour-a-day schedule for myself, and generally, my workday would stretch out to twelve and even more hours.

Then, it was soon made clear to all that no goldbricking on the job would be permitted and no petty larcenies of time or material would be tolerated. The object lessons were taught at the top, and those in the lower echelons quickly got the point. Executives who dawdled unnecessarily long over lunch or read newspapers on company time—and the U.S. taxpayers' money—were likely to find that their salaries were docked. When one executive collected some scrap material around the plant to build a dog kennel for one of his pets, I not only saw to it that he was billed for the material at its full value plus a heavy surcharge for overhead but also made certain that the rank and file got wind of the incident.

The lower echelon employees got the message—that there was only one set of basic rules and regulations and that it applied with equal vigor to everyone, regardless of his position on the company's organization chart. Morale—and production—soared as a consequence.

Withal, Spartan Aircraft did not show a profit through the war years. It wasn't supposed to. To make a profit was hardly the object of the exercise. The point and purpose of the entire operation was to produce vital war materials at the lowest possible cost. The Spartan School of Aeronautics did make profits, but these were invariably plowed back into the manufacturing end.

All the other companies owned or controlled by the Getty interests worked at top speed and efficiency during the war years. The oil companies produced milions of barrels of petroleum which helped to satisfy the awesome demands of the United States and Allied war machines everywhere in the world.

Tide Water played its part in the construction miracle of the Big Inch, the transcontinental pipeline which solved the troublesome west-to-east-coast petroleum shipping problem. Eleven major companies organized War Emergency Pipelines, Inc., to build the 1,254-mile-long line of twenty-four-inch-diameter pipe extending from Texas to Pennsylvania. Competitive rivalry between companies was shelved for the duration, and, in addition to Tide Water, the following oil companies were "in" War Emergency Pipelines, Inc.: Standard Oil of New Jersey, Cities Service, Sun, Atlantic, Socony-Vacuum, Pan American, Shell, Texas, Consolidated, and Gulf.

Prices obtained for crude oil and refined products were, of course, strictly controlled by the government. There was no opportunity for profiteering in the petroleum industry and, I might add, the petroleum industry wanted none. All responsible individuals in the industry realized that World War II was a war of oil, that neither side could fight without it, and that ample oil stocks could win the war, while shortages could lose it.

Some of the nation's oil companies made only the most slender of profits during the war years, yet all pitched in without reservation to insure that there could not possibly be an oil shortage on the Allied side. Crude oil production soared from 1,400,000,000 barrels in 1941 to 1,700,-000,000 barrels by 1945. Refinery capacities also increased tremendously, and petroleum industry scientists worked wonders in developing new processes to produce better and more powerful fuels, especially for aircraft.

Great strides were also made in the petrochemicals field. Synthetic rubber, made from petroleum-derived butadiene and styrene, was one of the most important of the wartime petrochemical products. During World War II, about 85 per cent of U.S. rubber produced was the copolymer of styrene and butadiene widely known as Buna-S.

One Getty enterprise that did enjoy great prosperity during the war years was the Pierre Hotel. There was a tremendous increase in travel, both military and civilian, during the war. In New York City, where there had been little or no important hotel construction for several years, hotel rooms were even scarcer than in other large cities. As a consequence, the Pierre was always booked to capacity, and this was inevitably reflected in its profit and loss statement.

There were several developments in my personal life during the war years. In June, 1942, my wife, Teddy, was repatriated from Italy, where she had been interned for six months. She returned to the United States aboard the neutral Swedish vessel *Gripsholm*, which brought back several hundred other Americans who had been held in Europe after the United States entered the war.

My oldest son, George, was eighteen in 1942. He enlisted in the Army Reserve and was called up for active duty early in 1943. After going through his basic training, he was sent to OCS. Commissioned an Infantry second lieutenant, he was sent to the Pacific theater, and spent a total of more than four years in the Army.

My other three boys were growing rapidly. I saw them as often as I could, but this was infrequently enough, what with the need for constant supervision over Spartan and the many other difficulties posed by wartime conditions.

Jean Ronald—Ronny—was five years younger than George. Like all boys in their midteens, he chafed because he was not yet old enough to enlist. Soon after having a long visit with George, prior to his leaving on active service, I saw Gordon and Paul and noted with no little surprise that while Gordon was ten, a year younger than his brother, he outweighed Paul by fully ten pounds.

By the spring of 1945, it was clear that the Axis was beaten and that the fate of Japan was sealed. Spartan's backlog of military and naval orders had begun to dwindle early in the year. By April, government procurement agencies were ordering cutbacks and canceling contracts.

Plainly, the end of the war was in sight. I had to give some thought to what I would do when it was over. The decision I finally made was a great surprise to many people, myself included.

28

IN 1945, every U.S. manufacturing company that had been engaged in turning out war materials had to face up to the problem of reconverting to peacetime production.

For most companies which had been engaged in the manufacture of civilian goods before Pearl Harbor, the problem was a comparatively simple one. It was largely a matter of switching back, of picking up where they had left off. The production of almost all civilian goods had been severely curtailed during the war years. While there had been full employment and workers had earned good salaries, there had been relatively little to buy. Thus the pent-up demand for virtually every conceivable type of manufactured item was enormous.

The question of reconversion was a far more complex one for such companies as Spartan Aircraft. Before the war, Spartan had been a tiny manufacturing concern employing a handful of workers. Its product had been airplanes, but the volume of its production had been small.

By any yardstick of measurement, Spartan had expanded a hundredfold during the war. Where before Pearl Harbor a few dozen workers had literally hand-produced a few airframes a year, in 1945 busy production lines were spewing out thousands of parts and components for military aircraft.

As war contracts began to dry up, Spartan's management had to decide on what course of action they would follow when the war was over. At first, it seemed natural to think in terms of producing civilian aircraft. There would doubtless be an unprecedented demand for airplanes of all kinds. The nation had become air-minded during the war. There would be a big market for light planes, executive models, cargo and passenger craft of all kinds.

Before the war, Spartan had turned out the Executive, an all-metal monoplane with a top speed of 190 miles per hour, designed as its name implied for use by busy business executives. The craft was ahead of its time in the prewar era; people were not yet sufficiently air-minded, and the managements of most companies were not yet ready to invest large amounts in airplanes.

There was no doubt that the picture had changed greatly in the intervening years. Countless thousands of executives had traveled aboard airplanes during the war; the tempo of business had been speeded up to a point where fast-flying aircraft would soon be a necessary adjunct for any company which hoped to keep up with its competitors by covering large market areas and getting the right people to the right place quickly.

Initial Spartan reconversion plans called for the production of a much-modernized Executive model with fully retractable tricycle landing gear, greater speed and radius, and equipped with the latest navigational and safety devices. To supplement this model and round out the Spartan line, we planned to build the Spartan Skyway Traveller, a six-to-eight-passenger aircraft which would be ideally suited for use by feeder airlines and larger business organizations.

Such, at any rate, were the initial plans. At first glance, they looked good, very good indeed. On closer, more careful examination, I could not help but feel that many serious drawbacks and pitfalls were concealed beneath their promise.

Thousands, even tens of thousands, of airplanes suitable for rapid conversion and modification to civilian use had been produced for the Armed Forces between 1941 and 1945. By law, the government would have to place many of these on sale as war-surplus goods. The prices charged for them would be far below any at which a company could profitably produce like or equal models for purely civilian use. It would take the market several years to absorb all the aircraft thus made available to potential airplane buyers.

Such aircraft as the twin-engined Beech AT-11 or Cessna AT-17 and several other models could be modified admirably for the same purposes and uses as those for which the Spartan Executive was designed. Furthermore, as the war drew to a close, it became apparent that feeder airlines would demand planes of greater capacity than the six-to-eight-passenger Spartan Skyway Traveller. Inquiries and information received from the feeder airlines indicated that most were standing ready to snap up such transports as the Douglas DC-3, which had been built in tremendous numbers under the Army Air Force designation of C-47 and the Navy designation of RD-4.

Lastly, and distasteful as this was to me, I had to admit that Spartan had lost a vital public-relations battle by default during the war. The names of such aircraft manufacturers as Boeing, Douglas, Cessna, Beech, Northrop, North American, and others had become household words throughout the country. These firms had been the prime contractors for aircraft models originated by them and thus bearing their names. U.S. newspaper readers and radio listeners had read and heard the names thousands of times in accounts describing the achievements of American and Allied flyers.

Like the names of most subcontractors producing components and parts, or even those which produced complete airplanes under license, the name "Spartan" had gotten lost in the shuffle. In short, people immediately recognized such a name as, say, "Douglas," but no bells would ring for the majority at the mention of "Spartan."

Much as I would have liked to enter into what I knew would be a keenly competitive and challenging postwar civilian aircraft manufacturing industry, I did not feel that I could gamble with the jobs and futures of Spartan's employees or with the investments and welfare of its stockholders. The need was to reconvert to civilian production by manufacturing some item for which there would be a fairly steady and lasting demand.

The directors of the company and I considered—and discarded—many possibilities. Among them were refrigerators, home appliances, home-heating units, and at one point, we even considered manufacturing automobiles. In the end, after much consideration and study, it was decided to convert the Spartan Aircraft manufacturing facilities to the production of mobile homes, or house trailers.

There were two principal reasons behind the choice of product that Spartan would produce.

First of all, the most pressing postwar consumer need would be for housing. Very little housing had been built during the war, and millions of families would be frantically looking for homes, among them the young families of servicemen returning to civilian life. No matter how quickly or vigorously the building industry reconverted to home construction, it would still be a long, long time before there was enough new housing to meet the immense demand.

Secondarily, the United States had become a highly mobile nation. Soldiers, sailors, airmen, and war workers, and very often their families, had gotten accustomed to the idea of moving great distances, of shifting from one city or state to another. The American people had once more gotten used to the idea of traveling to wherever there was the most and best opportunity, or simply traveling for the sake of seeing new places.

There was no question but that assembly lines could turn out high-quality, comfortably appointed mobile homes at a far faster rate than contractors could build even the smallest and flimsiest bungalows. The buyer of a mobile home would not be faced with the sometimes very difficult problem of selling one house and then trying to find another when he moved from one city to another, as countless young couples would indubitably be forced to do in the postwar period.

I realized that in the past, many house trailers had been rather sleazy affairs. Whether intended for permanent living or not, their designers and builders had seemingly thought of them as being little more than shacks on wheels which could be used for vacationing in the mountains or by the seashore. In my opinion, Spartan could manufacture a product that lived up to all that was implied by the words, "mobile homes."

The house trailers would be real homes for those who bought them—designed and built for comfortable, pleasant living. And they would be mobile in the sense that the spacious, tastefully appointed and decorated housing units could be hitched to an automobile and towed from one location to another.

Spartan's designers and I envisioned these house trailers as radical departures from most of those built previously. They would have large windows, ample ventilation, and heating facilities and furnishings that would emphasize the "home" more than the "mobile."

But a factory does not switch from the mass production of aircraft parts to the mass production of house trailers overnight, particularly not under the circumstances that prevailed in 1945. War contracts had to be terminated and renegotiated. Machinery, equipment, and raw materials were all still in short supply, and manufacturing companies engaged in a wild scramble to obtain whatever was available. New equipment and machinery had to be moved in and set up. Workers had to be retrained.

Although I was highly enthusiastic about this new project, I did not want Spartan to get out of the aircraft business entirely. I did not share the smugly confident view of those who felt that the surrender signed by the Japanese had heralded the end of all wars for all time. Having seen the dismal aftermaths of one "war to end all wars," I could not rid myself of the gnawing suspicion that there would be other international crises, other situations which might require the United States to guarantee its safety and security by building up its military strength.

With this consideration in mind, the directors of Spartan and I decided to set up an aircraft repair and modification operation and to maintain the Spartan School of Aeronautics on at least a standby basis. This would serve to keep a nucleus of skilled personnel on the payrolls, just in case. The decision was to pay unexpected dividends. Civilian demand for aircraft repair burgeoned in the postwar years, as did civilian and military demand for flight-training facilities. Parenthetically, this Spartan aviation division was to earn a total of nearly eight million dollars in profits between 1946 and 1959.

The final winding up of the Spartan aircraft parts-manufacturing operation and the preparations for the production of Spartan Mobile Homes all took time. It was not until early 1946 that the first house trailers began to roll off the assembly lines.

By rights, I suppose I should have left Tulsa and gone back to work expanding my oil business. That I did not and remained at Spartan directing what, after all, was only a small subsidiary of one of the companies I controlled, is due to the fact that I had come to regard Spartan as my personal responsibility. I had taken over the company in 1942 and had nursed it through its many and varied wartime growing pains. I'd helped it expand and reach its maturity as a major war-plant. I could not bring myself to abandon it in what, in a manner of speaking, was its time of need during the reconversion period. My personal interest in Spartan was far too keen, and my pride in its achievements too great to allow me to do that.

Damned if I'll just blow the whistle and have the Spartan factory turned into an ice-skating rink, I had written in my diary in mid-1945.

By March, 1946, Spartan Mobile Homes production reached seventy-two units for the week. By November, the factory had turned out more than two thousand two hundred trailers and output was nearing seven hundred units monthly. Pridefully, I read the letters from buyers who expressed their complete satisfaction and the reports received from impartial observers who referred to Spartan Mobile Homes as the "Cadillacs of the trailer industry" and stated that Spartan led the field in design and quality.

I suppose another of the reasons why the all-metal Spartan Mobile Homes gained such swift and widespread public acceptance was the generous service policy initiated by the company. Whether justified or not, a charge often leveled against some trailer manufacturers was that they did not provide adequate service. Spartan assembled and trained crack service crews. Buyers' complaints, few as they were, received immediate attention. Spartan warranted its products and lived up to its warranty. If there was anything wrong, a service team was dispatched to rectify the trouble without charge to the owner of the mobile home.

Spartan production was in full swing when serious problems arose in totally unexpected directions. Mobile home buyers were finding it increasingly difficult to obtain financing or insurance on their house trailers. Some of the nation's banks and insurance companies apparently thought of trailer-owners as irresponsible nomads.

The banks and insurance companies did not seem to be impressed by facts and figures which proved conclusively that the vast majority of trailer-buyers were solid, hard-working individuals. For some reason, many bankers and insurance men had developed blind spots and could not believe their own statistics, which showed that the buyers of house trailers were excellent risks. Perhaps their prejudice stemmed from the mobility of the trailer; it wasn't an object that was fixed to the ground with concrete foundations.

When lending institutions did deign to finance house-trailer purchases, they called for terms which made it difficult for the average worker, serviceman, or retired person—the people who accounted for the bulk of trailer sales—to buy them. The minimum down payment was set at 40 per cent of the purchase price. Interest rates ran as high as 10 per cent per annum. Installment payments could not be spread over any period greater than thirty-six months. Insofar as insurance on house trailers was concerned, premiums were high, and limiting provisions written into the policies were many.

Spartan had sold thousands of its mobile homes, and I'd had experience with buyers, having made it a point to become personally acquainted with as many of them as possible. I knew that trailer-purchasers were, for the most part, entirely honest and reliable people. I thought the attitude assumed by many banks and insurance companies was not only ridiculous but also a calculated and undeserved insult to a sizable segment of the country's population.

The Bank of America agreed with me. With that institution's co-operation and assistance, I organized the Minnehoma Financial Company and the Minnehoma Insurance Company. Spartan then began selling its mobile homes on reasonable terms within the reach of most people. The down payment was reduced to 25 per cent of the purchase price. Financing costs were slashed. Buyers could spread their payments over five-year periods, and later, when the feasibility of long-term contracts had been proved to the satisfaction of all, this was further extended to seven years. Insurance was sold at low rates, and with far fewer ifs, ands, and buts written into the policies.

The confidence my associates and I had in the people who bought mobile homes was not misplaced. Both the Minnehoma Financial and Insurance companies soon showed profits. These were not great, but it was not intended that they should be. The purpose of organizing the companies was to permit deserving people to buy and insure their housing units at reasonable rates. But the fact they did show profits was all the proof needed to bear out the contention that the buyers were completely stable and trustworthy individuals. Naturally, when the fact had been so clearly established, other trailer manufacturers and lending institutions paid the customary sincerest form of flattery by following suit.

In its first sixteen months of volume production, Spartan made and sold some seventeen million dollars' worth of trailers. In the decade following V-J Day, production of five basic types, ranging from the small Spartanette to the luxurious Spartan Royal Mansion, totaled some forty thousand units.

Postwar retooling and the first year's operations were costly, and Spartan's mobile home building operations lost nearly two million dollars in 1946. By 1947, however, the company was showing a profit, and three years later all losses had been wiped out and the company was safely in the black.

Early in 1945, I'd made one of my frequent wartime visits to some of the southern California aircraft companies for which Spartan was producing parts on subcontract. For various reasons, I had to remain in Los Angeles for two or three weeks and, during this time, heard of a highly tempting real estate bargain.

Some sixty-five acres of land—part of an old Spanish land-grant ranch—

located on the Pacific Coast Highway near Malibu Beach, were being offered for sale at a rather low price. The property, which fronted on the ocean, had a generous and lovely stretch of private beach and included a mansion-sized Spanish-style ranch house.

Now, my fifth wife, Teddy, to whom I had been married since 1939, was busy with her coast-to-coast concert engagements. I, myself, was to a great extent tied down to my work in Tulsa. Nonetheless, I decided to buy the property. I planned to build a new, larger ranch house on it, preserving some of the sound, graceful portions of the beautiful old house and incorporating them into the new structure. I intended to begin construction as soon as the war was over and materials and labor once more became available for home-building.

Work on the house began in the spring of 1946. My original plans had, in the interim, been considerably expanded. Teddy was expecting a child, and I wanted to make the Ranch House a home of which we could all be proud.

My fifth son, Timothy, was born on June 14, 1946. A seven months' baby, he weighed less than five pounds at birth. I rejoiced at his arrival but was very much upset and deeply concerned about the baby's health. Timmy suffered from anemia at birth. He was brought home on July 10, but three days later Teddy and I had to rush him to the hospital for a blood transfusion. We spent long, anxious hours until the doctors announced that the post-transfusion danger period had been passed.

It was with great joy that I altered the plans for the Ranch House to provide a nursery for Timmy. While waiting for the house to be completed, Teddy and Timmy—and I, whenever I was in Los Angeles—lived in the beach house on the Santa Monica oceanfront.

The Ranch House, which is still my home, was completed in 1948. Into it I moved the bulk of the art and antique furniture I'd collected over the years. With the Spartan operation in the black, and trailer sales—more than four thousand units in 1948—booming, I was able to take a short respite and spend some time with my wife and son.

The pleasant, peaceful interval did not last long, for in 1948 I was on the threshold of seizing the greatest opportunity and taking the biggest gamble of my entire career.

29

AS I have said, I had lost out on a tremendous opportunity in the 1930's by failing to obtain an Iraqi oil concession which was offered me for the proverbial song.

In the years immediately preceding World War II, and during the war itself, it became increasingly evident that the Middle East was the key to the world's oil future. Exploration and drilling in Iran, Iraq, Bahrein, Saudi Arabia, and Kuwait proved that the region was fantastically rich in petroleum—that, in fact, the major portion of the world's oil reserves were in the Middle Eastern countries.

As far back as 1920, the famous San Remo Agreement had sought to apportion all Middle Eastern oil rights among British and French companies. The American government, conscious of the importance of the Middle East, made countless official protests against this British-French monopoly and urged American oil companies to obtain Middle Eastern concessions.

It wasn't until 1927 that Gulf Oil obtained options on old British concessions in Kuwait and Bahrein. The following year, the Iraq Petroleum Company was formed with American participation. In 1933, Standard Oil of California obtained a Saudi Arabian concession.

By the end of World War II, I, like all oil producers, knew that it was highly important, even essential, for my companies to gain a foothold in the oil-rich Middle East. Unless they did so, my companies would be hard pressed to meet the heavy competition that would soon develop for overseas markets.

There was a wild scramble by the oil companies of all nationalities for Middle Eastern concessions after the war ended. I followed these developments from my detached vantage points in Tulsa and Los Angeles and waited for the smoke to clear.

I knew this was a risky policy. My companies might miss out completely. On the other hand, I suspected that patience would be more rewarding in the long run than any precipitate action taken without proper preliminary survey. That I was correct in being cautious was shown by the experience of some oil companies which grabbed at concessions in North African desert areas that had been fought over by the British and Rommel's Afrika Korps during the war. By some incredible oversight, these firms failed to realize that the areas covered by their concessions were thickly sown with land-mines. These had to be cleared at staggering cost before prospecting operations could commence. To make matters worse, when the mines had been cleared and oil exploration got under way, the territories covered by the concessions failed to show any signs of bearing oil.

By 1948, much of the dust that had been kicked up by the Middle Eastern concession-scramble had settled. Most of the available concessions had been parceled out to various companies. Most, but not all. Among those still available was one covering an undivided half-interest in the oil concession for the Neutral Zone, an arid, trackless fifteen-hundred-square-mile wasteland lying between Saudi Arabia and the Sheikdom of Kuwait on the Persian Gulf.

The oil rights in the Neutral Zone were and are owned jointly by Saudi Arabia and Kuwait. His Majesty, King Saud of Saudi Arabia, and His Highness, Sheik Abdullah as-Salim as-Subah of Kuwait, each held control of an indivisible half of these oil rights. In 1948, the Sheik of Kuwait granted a concession on his half-interest to the American Independent Oil Company, commonly known as Aminoil.

Aminoil, a consortium of ten United States oil companies in which Phillips Petroleum held the largest share, paid $7,250,000—cash down—for the concession and agreed to pay royalties and make other payments.

But Aminoil's concession was for an *undivided* half-interest in Neutral Zone oil. The company could not begin operations until His Majesty, King Saud, granted a concession on the other undivided half-interest.

I was aware of this. I also knew the United States State Department was especially desirous that another American company obtain the concession on the Saudi Arabian half-interest. I sent Dr. Paul Walton, one of the finest geologists I have ever known, to look over the Neutral Zone for the Getty interests. Obtaining the necessary permission to make the flight from authorities in both Saudi Arabia and Kuwait, Dr. Walton made an aerial survey of the Neutral Zone. The next I heard from him was a terse, cabled message:

STRUCTURES INDICATE OIL SIGNED WALTON

Such was my faith in Dr. Walton's knowledge and judgment that I immediately instructed my representatives to begin negotiations for obtaining the concession. Other companies, including Aminoil and the Royal Dutch-Shell combine, also wanted the concession. Bidding ran high, but I confidently increased my offers until the other bidders gave up and dropped out of the competition.

I secured the concession for the Getty interests—represented in this instance by the Pacific Western Oil Corporation—by topping all bids. The terms under which I obtained it made me realize with a start that I had come a very long way since the days when I had employed a stratagem to buy the Nancy Taylor Allotment Lease for five hundred dollars. On February 20, 1949, attorney Barnabas Hadfield, acting for Pacific Western, signed a voluminous agreement with the Saudi Arabian government in Riyadh. Under its provisions, Pacific Western agreed to:

1. Pay the Saudi Arabian government an immediate cash consideration of $12,500,000.
2. Pay an annual $1,000,000 advance on agreed 55-cent-per-barrel royalties on all oil produced.
3. Pay 25 per cent of net profits to the Saudi Arabian government.
4. Build a 12,000-barrel refinery and 150,000-barrel-capacity storage facilities in Saudi Arabia.
5. Deliver 100,000 gallons of gasoline and 50,000 gallons of kerosene annually to the Saudi Arabian government after the refinery was in operation.
6. Allow Saudi Arabian government representatives to attend Company board meetings; pay the salaries of government inspectors and certain other personnel including police, Customs, and Quarantine personnel who would be concerned with Company affairs.
7. Provide pension, retirement, insurance and other "fringe" benefits for all Saudi Arabian personnel employed by the company, and give them free medical care and hospital facilities.
8. Provide educational, vocational training, and other facilities for the children of Saudi Arabian employees.
9. Build and maintain housing and office accommodations for some gov-

ernment personnel as well as build a mosque, telephone and telegraph facilities, roads, a post office, and provide an adequate water supply system.

These were the main considerations. In return for them, Pacific Western was granted a concession on the Saudi Arabian undivided half-interest in Neutral Zone oil for a period of sixty years.

"Preposterous!"

"Outrageous!"

"Far too steep to ever allow any profit!"

Such were some of the opinions other oil men voiced when they heard of the terms under which the concession had been granted. There were many individuals in the petroleum industry who, for the umpteenth time during my career, freely predicted that I would bankrupt my companies and myself.

"Getty has ruined himself for sure this time," was a view expressed quite often in the next few years.

And, for a time, it would look as though I made a gargantuan mistake. That, however, is getting ahead of the story.

Although the United States is a net importer of crude oil, the principal and most natural markets for Middle Eastern crude lie in the Eastern Hemisphere. Understanding this, I thought it was time for me to begin making plans and preliminary preparations for disposing of the large quantities of petroleum I hopefully anticipated the Neutral Zone would produce. It was for these purposes that I went to Europe in 1949. The trip was my first in nearly a decade.

The sight of war-ravaged cities and of people still dazed and dislocated by the effects and aftereffects of the conflict shocked and depressed me—and made me determined to do whatever I could to help in rebuilding the shattered economies of the affected European countries. Oil would play an important part in making possible the rehabilitation of industrial Europe and thus of countries, cities, and people. My 1949 visit to Europe was comparatively short, but I accomplished much.

The same could not be said for operations in the Neutral Zone.

Aminoil and Pacific Western each owned an undivided half-interest in the over-all Neutral Zone concession. Technically, this meant that the two companies would share equally in every drop of oil brought to the surface by either. In practice, it meant that when and if oil was discovered and produced, meticulous records would have to be maintained and the oil or the net money value received for it apportioned between the two companies.

Since Aminoil was owned by a number of major oil companies, among which there was one larger than those controlled by the Getty interests, it could draw on greater technical, personnel, and organizational resources than Pacific Western. Aminoil was also the senior company in the sense that it had obtained the Kuwait concession before Pacific Western got the Saudi Arabian concession and had been the first to "go into" the Neutral Zone.

In addition to these arguments, it was pointed out that it would be wastefully expensive for the two companies to duplicate prospecting and drilling operations. It was proposed that Pacific Western send only a skeleton staff to the Neutral Zone in the beginning. Aminoil would take the lead, conduct the exploration and initial drilling. Pacific Western's role in the early stages would be limited mainly to picking up its share of the bill. This arrangement, it was contended, would greatly benefit both companies by eliminating the staggering expense of running parallel and overlapping operations. And, since all production had to be shared equally in any event, Pacific Western would gain much through such an agreement.

I'm not much of a believer in allowing others to take my responsibilities or do my work for me or my companies. However, I allowed myself to be talked into the arrangement, and operations proceeded on the basis I have outlined. When 1949 passed without any oil being discovered by Aminoil exploration teams, while Pacific Western's share of the expense ran into several millions, I began to wonder if I hadn't made a serious mistake.

In March, 1949, I sent my oldest son, George, to the Neutral Zone. After finishing his Army service, George had taken a much accelerated course at Princeton. He showed a remarkable aptitude for business in general and for the oil business in particular.

In the Middle East, he spent several months inspecting the operations of other oil companies there. George recommended that Pacific Western take a more active part in the exploration and drilling operations. The soundness of this advice was heavily emphasized by the fact that at the end of 1949 the Neutral Zone still had not produced a drop of oil.

Exploration and drilling operations in the Neutral Zone are not nearly as easy as some might think.

The Neutral Zone is probably one of the most barren, arid, and uninhabitable areas on the face of the earth. Summer temperatures there soar to 125, 130, and even 135 degrees. There are only five natural water wells in the entire 1,500-square-mile territory, and these give pitifully small quantities of water.

Between November and March, there are sudden and violent rainstorms which cause flash floods and inundate large areas, but by April, the land is again parched and waterless. Men working in the Neutral Zone must constantly wear heavy boots or risk sickness or even death from the poisonous stings of giant scorpions or the deadly bites of the triangular-headed vipers.

In order to commence operations in the Neutral Zone, Pacific Western would not only have to construct an entire new city but, literally, build a modern civilization where there was nothing.

Shelter would have to be provided for prospectors and drillers. But before that could be done, facilities would have to be built to land the materials from cargo ships on the coast and roads constructed so that imported trucks could carry them to construction sites. Even before any of this could be accomplished, the problem of providing fresh water and of disposing of sewage and waste would have to be solved.

Nor would tents or flimsy hutments suffice to house the workers. Men who get no sleep cannot work, and sleep is impossible in temperatures such as those encountered in the Neutral Zone. Thus, heavy insulation and heavy-duty air-conditioning equipment were absolute musts—and to run the air conditioners and provide electricity for light and power, there would have to be generators.

And so it went. The lists of items and materials needed to establish Pacific Western in the Neutral Zone would—and did—fill entire volumes. The lists of machinery and equipment required for exploration and drilling filled others.

It all took time and cost staggering sums.

A total of more than $18,000,000 would be spent in the Neutral Zone by the Getty interests before the first drop of oil was brought up from the ground.

The progress of our operations was eyed closely by many companies and individuals in the oil industry. It wasn't long before the rumors began to make the rounds.

"Getty is going bust in the Middle East."

"Pacific Western is on the verge of bankruptcy."

"Paul Getty is finished."

The rumors, as Mark Twain is supposed to have said about erroneous reports of his death, were greatly exaggerated. Eventually, the prophets of my financial doom would have to eat their words.

But we still had a long way to go before that would happen. There were still innumerable headaches, worries, and crises to be faced before the Neutral Zone proved itself to be one of the world's most valuable oil properties.

30

ALTHOUGH no oil came out of the Neutral Zone in 1950, I nonetheless remained certain that important discoveries would eventually be made there. Geologists' reports, the considered opinions of veteran oil men in whose judgment I had confidence, and my own strong feelings—my hunch, if you wish to call it that—all supported the belief that the area would prove immensely rich in petroleum.

It was necessary to remain patient and to continue pouring huge amounts of capital into the over-all Neutral Zone operation. Luckily, my associates and I had sufficient reserves of these. I will admit, however, that the strain on patience and capital and on ourselves increased tremendously as the months went by without any tangible results being reported from "The Zone."

No positive results were obtained in 1951 or in 1952, either. Exploration and drilling crews reported finding encouraging signs and indications during the course of their prospecting operations. The men on the crews and my field supervisory representatives on the scene continued to have high hopes. But that was about all. There was still no oil being produced.

In the meantime, I made a number of trips from the United States to Europe. My main purpose was gradually to firm up plans and programs against the day when the Neutral Zone would finally begin producing petroleum. This was scarcely what one could call a simple or easy or even clear-cut task, for as things stood, the entire project remained at best an extremely speculative one.

I had no way of knowing when Aminoil or Pacific Western exploration crews would locate any oil deposits worthy of exploitation. Truth to tell, I had absolutely no assurance that they would ever find any oil at all.

Under such circumstances, whatever plans I made had to be very flexible; any programs envisioned necessarily had to be highly tentative.

On the other hand, the Getty companies could not afford to be unprepared when and if oil was discovered on the land covered by the Neutral Zone concession. Facilities would be needed to handle the crude; there would have to be markets for it. Pipelines, storage tanks, and all the myriad, costly appurtenances of oil production, transportation, and refining cannot be built overnight. Vast amounts of preliminary planning and preparation are necessary before the first foot of pipe can be laid, particularly in an area as remote and undeveloped as the Neutral Zone.

The size of the gamble I had taken became more and more apparent as time passed. The costs of the Neutral Zone operation mounted in multiples of tens of millions of dollars.

The story of the search for oil in the Neutral Zone is much like the sagas of oil exploration conducted by countless other companies in the more rugged and remote regions of the world. It is the story of loyal, persevering men laboring endless months under the most trying and difficult conditions and undergoing considerable hardship and even danger. Four long years and very many millions of dollars were spent before the operations of the Getty companies in the Neutral Zone culminated successfully in the first of a series of great discoveries in 1953. The final pay-off was made possible by the men in the field. Whether Americans or Arabs, truck drivers or geologists, timekeepers or riggers, success was due to the on-the-spot employees who did their jobs in the barren desert despite the hellish heat, ghastly climate, and the lack of comforts and conveniences. But then, these men have always been the largely unsung heroes of the Petroleum Age; without them there would be precious little oil anywhere above the ground.

The initial 1953 strike in the Neutral Zone was made in a spot located in, roughly, the middle of the area covered by the concession. A test well drilled to thirty-five hundred feet reached the Burghan Sand and proved a fine producer. It and the wells drilled subsequently in this particular field produced nearly seven million barrels of crude oil in their first full year of operation.

A little more than eighteen months after the first well came in, another important discovery was made in the same general area. This time, test-drilling went considerably deeper, to about seven thousand feet, and tapped another oil horizon, the Ratawi Limestone. The first and second wells drilled to the Ratawi produced at the rate of more than three million barrels annually.

These discoveries were only the beginning, but the very first producing well occasioned great changes in the operations of the Getty companies and changed the entire complexion of their future.

At last, with the first well completed to the Burghan Sand and producing oil in 1953, my associates and I knew definitely that there *was* petroleum in the Neutral Zone.

Our judgment—and what, I suppose, might be termed our stubbornness—in continuing exploration operations over four fruitless years had been vindicated. The staggering investments we had made in the Neutral Zone project were shown to be at least partially justified. Now we had to make new decisions and take new action.

We had to determine how the potentials of the Neutral Zone could be best and most economically, effectively, and advantageously exploited. We had to decide where, when, and how to pour out the gigantic additional investments that would be required to make the concession most productive and to insure that all concerned would be benefited and profit to the maximum possible extent.

We were not thinking or working blind, however. Basic plans and the broad outlines of programs flexible enough to be adapted to almost any eventuality had been made during the preceding years. It was now necessary to narrow them down, to tailor them to the specific conditions and situations that were developing in the Neutral Zone as new finds were made and additional producing wells came in.

Continued exploration and drilling were soon to prove that part of the Neutral Zone was like an enormous layer cake, with numerous separate and great reservoirs of petroleum sandwiched between strata of rock and soil at various depths beneath the surface of the ground.

There was the Burghan Sand horizon at about thirty-five hundred feet.

The Ratawi Limestone reservoir lay deeper—at around sixty-eight hundred feet.

Then, there were three additional Eocene limestone reservoirs at different levels ranging from as little as six hundred feet below the surface of the ground to depths of about twenty-five hundred feet.

This fantastic geological layer cake has proved to be rich in oil. Impartial petroleum geologists and engineers who have surveyed the Neutral Zone fields recently estimate—and by their own admission, the estimate is a conservative one—proved crude oil reserves in place in the area covered by the concession at about eleven billion barrels.

But at first, the expansion of our Neutral Zone operation was necessarily a slow process. One of the biggest obstacles was the difficult logistical problem involved. Almost without exception, every item and pound of machinery, equipment, building materials, and supplies—every nail and frozen steak and can of peas—had to be transported thousands of miles by sea or air from the United States or Europe to the Middle East.

Before any of these things could be properly unloaded from ships or before any crude oil could be pumped into tankers, facilities for anchoring the vessels had to be constructed on the Persian Gulf coast, and an operational base had to be built at Mina Saud. Looming large was the most basic problem of all—a fresh-water supply. Fresh water would have to be obtained in ever increasing quantities; the nearest practicable sources lay in Kuwait. Water for the needs of the men working in the desert would have to be piped or trucked to the drilling sites.

Luckily, there was a cheap and readily available power source in the form of natural gas which came from the wells. However, before this gas could be utilized, it was necessary to build a pipeline to transport it from the fields to the Mina Saud base.

I do not doubt that I could fill a volume considerably larger than this one with a detailed list of the major and minor problems that had to be solved and the jobs and tasks that had to be done before Neutral Zone production reached anything approaching a profitable rate. Suffice it to say that slowly, gradually, the obstacles were overcome, the necessary work was accomplished, and the goals that were set from time to time were accomplished. It was all done at the best possible speed under the circumstances which prevailed.

The proof is there. For instance, the base at Mina Saud consisted of a bleak cluster of four bungalows when it was first established. It has grown to the proportions of a not-so-small small town. Among the structures and installations at Mina Saud are two spacious office buildings and a fifty-thousand-barrel-a-day capacity refinery. There are housing units and barracks for supervisory, administrative, and field employees. A post office and a mosque for devout Moslem Arab employees and their families have been built. A large commissary is stocked with a wide range of consumer and other goods. Appropriate housing and other facilities have been provided for the Saudi Arabian officials and representatives who work so closely, and, I might emphasize, so co-operatively, with the Getty Oil Company (to which Pacific Western had changed its name).

A submarine pipeline makes it possible for giant tankers to anchor off-shore and take on their cargoes of crude or refined petroleum. Other pipe-lines lace the wastelands and carry crude from the fields to Mina Saud. There are also ample accommodations for workers at the drilling sites. Housing units are air-conditioned, and everything possible is done to provide employees with the maximum of comfort and convenience.

Incidentally, we made excellent use of house trailers in the Neutral Zone. We found the mobile homes to be ideal housing units, not only in the field and on the exploration and drilling sites but also at the Mina Saud base. We used considerable numbers of them from the very start. Each trailer had its individual air-conditioning units, and the men who lived in them without exception expressed their satisfaction. Veteran oil-field workers who recalled the days when tents or tar-paper shacks served as housing in the fields marveled at the comfort and convenience of the mobile homes. Perhaps it is needless for me to say that the house trailers we used in the Neutral Zone were all products of the Spartan factory in Tulsa, Oklahoma.

As new discoveries were made, additional wells were drilled, and Neutral Zone production increased by leaps and bounds after the initial discoveries in 1953, I realized that the time had come for the Getty com-panies to take several giant steps forward on several business fronts.

31

I HAD set out to obtain control of the Tide Water Associated Oil Company in 1932. It was not until 1951 that I succeeded finally and could say that I held clear-cut control over the company.

With control established and a board of directors sympathetic to my ideas and aims, I could at last proceed to implement the programs of improvement and expansion that I had long envisioned.

Tide Water owned two refineries, one at Bayonne, New Jersey, the other at Avon, near San Francisco in California. The Bayonne refinery had been originally built before the turn of the century. Although units had been added to it since, it was still hopelessly outdated and inefficient. It was utterly useless to attempt any modernization there. It would have to be abandoned. The Avon refinery was in much better shape, but it needed considerable modernization.

Tide Water, owning seaboard refineries, obtained a substantial portion of its crude oil from foreign sources. To transport the oil, it had to charter tankers. A thorough study of this aspect of the company's operations showed that large savings could be effected if Tide Water had its own tankers to transport its crude oil and refined products.

Tide Water Associated Oil Company's needs ran into the hundreds of millions of dollars. Among the items required in order to keep Tide Water abreast and somewhat ahead of its competition were a fleet of super-tankers and an efficient new refinery.

The refinery project was a gargantuan undertaking. It would cost $200,000,000 before the 130,000-barrel-a-day capacity refinery, the most modern in the world, "went on stream," that is, went into operation.

The shipbuilding project called for more modest outlays in each of its programmed stages, but over-all it, too, would involve a staggering investment.

By early 1954, the preliminary requirements and specifications for the new refinery had been set, the site for it had been chosen, and engineering, architectural, and construction firms were assiduously plying slide rules and straining computing machines, readying their bids on the work to be done.

At about the same time, orders were let for the construction of the first of a series of up-to-date, 46,500-ton tankers. The very first vessel, christened the *Veedol*, was delivered before the end of 1955. Within the next three years, eight more supertankers, including four fifty-three-thousand-tonners, would slide down the ways, and the shipbuilding program would go on from there.

By 1953, my business interests had spread over two hemispheres. I thought it advisable to transfer my own base of operations to Europe, where I would be midway between my enterprises in the United States and those in the Middle East. Besides, I sensed that Europe would prove one of the large markets for Neutral Zone crude. I wanted to be on the spot, develop the markets, and take full advantage of the many tempting business opportunities the European market offered. The idea of either buying or building a refinery on the Continent was already taking shape in the back of my mind.

Thus, by the end of 1953, I had established what would become a routine of several years' duration. Confident that my associates and the executives of the various Getty companies could adequately handle matters in the United States, I maintained direct personal control and supervision over operations and activities in the Eastern Hemisphere. I traveled from one key city in Europe and the Middle East to another, remaining in each for the weeks or months needed to transact the business at hand or to start new projects and enterprises.

I lived in hotel suites, maintaining contact with my companies in America by transatlantic telephone, cable, or letter. Naturally, when there were exceptionally important or urgent matters to be settled, the appropriate executives of the companies concerned would fly over from the United States for meetings and conferences.

My hotel suites were, to all intents and purposes, the field headquarters of my companies and enterprises. The rooms were invariably cluttered. Reports, documents, correspondence, books, papers, and publications of all kinds were always stacked high on every flat surface and generally piled knee-high on the floors to boot. The telephones rang incessantly, and there were few hours in any working day that there wasn't someone waiting in the lobby to see me.

These activities necessitated physical separation from my young son, Timmy, and my wife, Teddy. My wife did not want to live in Europe. She preferred to stay in California at the house I had built at Malibu Beach. Beyond this, she was still pursuing her career and did not believe there would be much opportunity for her to further it in Europe. She wanted me to return to America.

I contended that it would be a great mistake for me to go back to the United States then or in the immediate future. I argued that I was on the threshold of accomplishing all my hopes and ambitions for my companies and of accomplishing them on a scale far greater than any I could have dreamed possible even a few years before.

I considered my continuing presence in Europe and the Middle East essential to the success of my efforts to create and build an integrated, smoothly functioning oil business which would span both hemispheres. While it has never been my particular conceit to think that I was indispensable to my companies, I did believe that I could contribute most and do the best job by remaining in Europe.

Why? Well, first of all, I am fairly fluent in several languages—French, Italian, Spanish, and German among them. By that time, I had also learned some Arabic. I could thus communicate readily with the people with whom my companies were doing or would do business in Europe and the Middle East. Perhaps even more important was the fact that I knew Europe and the people themselves. I'd had more than ample opportunity to make their acquaintance during my frequent trips abroad, trips that dated all the way back to 1909. Then, there was what I considered the psychological advantage of being strategically situated midway 'between my two principal spheres of business interest—namely, the United States and the Middle East.

It soon became clear that no compromise was possible between my wife and myself. She did not want to live away from the United States; I did not feel that I was justified in dropping everything to return. The result was an impasse and the beginnings of a rift that would widen in the ensuing years.

I remained in Europe, traveling extensively from one country to another. I kept very busy, indeed, guiding the multifaceted expansion programs of the companies I owned or controlled and further developing my plans and ideas for extending and increasing Getty company activities in Europe and the Middle East.

In the early spring of 1955, construction of the new Tide Water Associated Oil Company refinery began. (In 1956, Tide Water was contracted into a single word and the word Associated was dropped from the company name.) The five-thousand-acre refinery site had been selected with great care from among the scores of locations which were considered and inspected by qualified company representatives. The final choice, a site on the Delaware River, not far from Wilmington, was inspired by several important factors. The location was ideal, in the heart of one of the nation's greatest industrial complexes and near such shipping and business centers as New York City, Philadelphia, and Baltimore. Transportation facilities were excellent. Then, an oil refinery requires enormous quantities of water for its operation; the available water supply was entirely adequate to any conceivable need. The Delaware River provided easy, deep-water access to the refinery for the large tankers which would bring crude oil from abroad and transport bulk shipments of refined products elsewhere.

The land on which the refinery was to be built was largely unimproved. About one-sixth of it was low-lying swamp. Hence, its per-acre cost was extremely low—so low, in fact, that the "useless" swampland could be reclaimed and, even with the cost of reclamation added, the total price paid for the land would still be far below that being asked for outwardly more attractive but actually less valuable properties in the area.

Design and engineering of the refinery were handled by Tidewater personnel and the crack engineering firm of C. F. Braun and Co., which company also won—hands down, I might add—the contract for the construction work. I have said that the project was a "gargantuan undertaking." Some idea of its magnitude may be obtained from a few random facts and figures about the preparation of the site and the building of the refinery itself.

For instance:

More than three million cubic yards of earth had to be moved to level one section of the construction site.

A ship-channel three miles in length, four hundred feet in width, and forty feet in depth was dredged.

Nearly fifteen million cubic yards of sand and earth dredged up in order to make the channel were utilized as fill to reclaim the eight hundred acres of "useless" swampland and raise its level an average of twelve feet above the water. In other words, by using the waste dredged up in the building of the channel, Tidewater and Braun and Co. literally created eight hundred valuable acres of land at practically no cost.

Over ten thousand freight-carloads and nearly seventy-five thousand truckloads of supplies, materials, and equipment were delivered to the site and used in construction or erected or installed.

When work on the project reached its peak point, there were some nine thousand men employed on the site.

Specifications called for the construction of a petroleum refinery that was very much advanced, even revolutionary, in concept and design. When the project was still in its preliminary talking stages, I had said that I hoped we could build a refinery that would not only be years ahead of any other when it was completed, but one that would remain ahead for a long time afterwards. There can be no denying that Tidewater and Braun and Co., and all the other firms and the individuals who had any part in its construction, produced all that and more.

When it was finished in May, 1957, the Tidewater refinery in Delaware was hailed as the wonder and the envy of the entire petroleum industry. The industry's authoritative trade publication, *The Oil and Gas Journal*, called it "the refinery of the future" and went on to describe it as "the most modern refinery ever built—and the largest ever built in a single integrated step."

The huge plant's principal refining units extend in a straight line for nearly a mile. The refinery is about as completely automated as any refinery can be at the present time or for many years to come. Even such details as the temperatures of boilers or the rate at which crude oil or water flow through pipes are monitored, governed, and controlled by sensitive electronic devices. The refining units utilize the latest processes to produce the highest quality fuels, lubricants, and other petroleum products. Among them is the huge fluid coker which has solved the problems of refining heavy crude oil, of which there is much in the Neutral Zone, into high-octane (100-octane) gasoline.

The refinery cost Tidewater about two hundred million dollars, but it was a bargain. The refinery was designed around units, processes, equipment, and machines which were new and revolutionary, and had been but recently invented, developed, or perfected. Their practicability and efficiency had been proved in the laboratories or by the operation of manufacturers' sample or pilot models. However, until Tidewater came along, no oil company had been willing to take the risk of making huge capital outlays by purchasing and installing the highly advanced equipment.

Of course, the Tidewater Oil Company did not buy blind or leap into any purchases just because prices quoted were advantageous. The best technical brains in the company and the finest outside technical consultants gave every item and process a meticulous, exhaustive study, checking and double-checking before any contracts were let or purchase orders were issued.

Once again, the old adage that it pays to pioneer proved true. The astounding efficiency of the Tidewater refinery, certified by independent survey to be over 100 per cent of preconstruction estimates, created an instant and huge industry-wide demand for all the revolutionary things which made that success possible. It might be of interest to note that less than 1 per cent of the entire plant or production operation required any alteration, modification, or correction from original plans or specifications after the refinery went on stream. This in itself is remarkable for any project of its size and complexity, but even the cost of all changes was fully covered by insurance which Tidewater prudently obtained before construction began.

The Delaware refinery put Tidewater a good distance ahead of the competitive field. Its true worth cannot be gauged by its cost. In the first place, the increases in costs and prices which have been registered since 1955–57 would now increase the construction bill by 20 per cent. But when considering petroleum refineries it must be remembered that a refinery which may be comparatively cheap to build is very likely to prove costly in operation.

There are varying grades and gravities of crude oil. High-grade, high-gravity crude oil can be refined more easily than low gravity grades. The equipment needed is less complex and less costly than that needed to refine low-gravity crudes efficiently.

The Tidewater refinery at Delaware City has the most modern and finest equipment. It can refine high-gravity crude with peak efficiency, and it can do an equally good job with low-gravity grades, which usually sell for a substantially lower price than the high-gravity grades.

A refinery such as the one at Delaware City can and does save as much as 20 cents per barrel in refining the lower grades. Since the Delaware City refinery uses some fifty million barrels of crude oil per year, it is obvious that it does not take long for the extra equipment to pay out.

The efficiency of the Tidewater refinery in Delaware can be shown by the simple fact that the value of the top-quality products obtained from each barrel of relatively low-priced, low-gravity crude oil is almost identical with the value of the products obtained from a barrel of comparatively high-cost, high-gravity crude.

The Delaware City project was not Tidewater's only refinery investment during the period. The company's West Coast refinery at Avon was given a thoroughgoing overhaul and modernization. This cost another sixty million dollars. It did not make Avon into another Delaware City, but it certainly brought the Tidewater Company's California refinery up into the ranks of the best and most efficient pre-Delaware City refineries in the United States. Among the new installations at Avon is a forty-two-thousand-barrel-a-day fluid coker, the largest in the world.

In short, within the space of a very few years, the Tidewater Oil Company invested a total of $260,000,000—over a quarter of a billion dollars—to increase the efficiency of its refining operations and to improve the quality of its products.

Nevertheless, even the most modern and costliest petroleum refinery is only a worthless mass of concrete and metal unless there is, so to speak, crude oil pouring in at one end and fuels, lubricants, and other refined products pouring out at the other end. And, there must be markets for those products.

All the necessary steps were taken to insure that Tidewater would have ample supplies of both domestic and foreign crude oil. About half of the latter comes from the Neutral Zone. All foreign crude is transported with notable economy by Tidewater's own tankers, some of which, incidentally, occasionally turn a neat profit for the company from charters to other oil companies!

The expansion of markets went hand in hand with refinery and tanker programs. Not only were the efforts of Tidewater's crack sales department intensified, but there was a corresponding expansion of the company's retail operations. Existing "Flying A" and Veedol service stations were refurbished and modernized and many new ones were built in carefully selected locations in the eastern and western sections of the United States.

All things considered, Tidewater has responded very favorably to the new broom.

32

32

MY POSTWAR travels around Europe, the Balkans and the Middle East taught me several valuable lessons which, I believe, would be equally valuable to any American businessman. When I drove, as I frequently did, my car, a long, shiny Cadillac, the classic symbol of "capitalist wealth," marked me as an American and a rich one. When I traveled by train, the ordinary people in the cities and towns in which I stopped also recognized me as an American and generally, for one reason or another, saw or sensed that I was wealthy.

Mind you, much of this was at times when the Cold War between East and West was at one of the taut, threatening name-calling stages, and many United States officials and publications were protesting or bewailing the rise of anti-American feeling abroad. Whatever governments and their leaders were doing or thinking, I certainly encountered no anti-American feeling among the everyday people I met, no matter where I went, and I have covered quite a bit of territory.

Whenever people stopped and spoke to me, as they very often did, they showed polite, intense interest in me, the clothes I wore, or the objects I carried, my car and the things in it. Their conversations invariably reflected their admiration for the United States and its many achievements and their often almost desperate eagerness to achieve a standard of living approaching that enjoyed by Americans. Time and time again, I heard wistful expressions of desire to emigrate to the United States or at least to visit the country some day.

My travels to various parts of the world have always impressed upon me that most people are not particularly pro or anti any political philosophy or belief. Save for small, stridently vocal activist groups in every country, the people really don't care very much about world politics per se. All they want and care about is achieving a better life for themselves and for their children. They want food and clothing and shelter, and they long for the comforts and luxuries of life which the vast majority of Americans take for granted. It is for the promise of bettering their lot and living conditions, not because of any obscure political dogma, that the masses of people lend their sympathy or support to any political party or movement. The groups or parties which deliver on such promises are the ones which reap the lasting loyalty of the majority.

The lessons are clearly there for the astute businessman to learn. A great demand for goods and services of all kinds exists throughout the entire world. These are precisely the things which the industry and commerce of free societies and free-enterprise economies can best provide. Therein should lie tremendous incentive and stimulus for enterprising American businessmen. They should accept this as a challenge, rather than seek shelter from what so many are often wont to label "anti-Americanism," "burgeoning socialism," or "the Red Menace" abroad.

I found much to vindicate my policy of expanding my business during my talks with everyday people in Europe and the Middle East. My travels have provided me with far more proof and justification than I could have found in any library filled with glowing trade association or State Department pamphlets and releases.

My visits to the Neutral Zone have been particularly instructive in these regards. I made the first in 1954, going to Basra by train and driving from there to Mina Saud and reversing the process on the return trip. I made my second visit two years later.

April, 1956, found me in Paris, staying in my usual and favorite suite at the Hotel George V. Early that month, developments in the Neutral Zone made it advisable for me to go there and personally supervise operations. Again, I went by rail to Turkey and drove on to the Neutral Zone.

Arriving in Mina Saud in late April, I established myself in one of the company bungalows that had been built near the seashore and set to work.

I began by paying my respects to the two key Saudi Arabian officials at Mina Saud, and conferring with them on problems and projects in the Zone. I first called on His Excellency, Sheik Mohamet Nasser al Ghosn, who had been appointed Saudi Arabian Governor of the Neutral Zone by His Majesty, King Saud. Next, I talked with Sheik Abdullah al Shagawi, the Saudi Arabian labor representative. What few minor problems existed were swiftly and amicably ironed out over cups of strong, sweet coffee.

The next step was to make a thoroughgoing firsthand inspection of company installations, facilities, and operation.

There was an administrative and liaison headquarters in Jiddah, Saudi Arabia, capably headed by Edward Brown, a brilliant young attorney fluent in Arabic. Following my lifelong policy of keeping administrative overhead and thus administrative cost to a minimum, the staff there was small. But, in reiterative proof that Parkinson's Law is valid in reverse, too, the level of efficiency there was high, and I was primarily interested in production and field operations.

It has always been my contention that the executives and heads of companies should at least occasionally move out of the insulated, ivory-tower environment of paneled offices and board-rooms. Periodic visits to and even participation in the various phases of company activity will teach them more about their business, its strengths, weaknesses, and needs, and the problems faced by their employees than will the reading of Everests of reports and memoranda and years of committee meetings.

Once again practicing the preachments I had long dinned into the ears of my subordinates, I spent most of my first two weeks out in the field and many days and nights with the exploration and drilling crews. I thus obtained invaluable firsthand knowledge and experience of the conditions under which the company's employees worked.

I was greatly impressed by the difficulties and hardships the crews encountered and the typical, oil-field workers' ways in which they over-came or disregarded them.

"I just tell the boys the nearest supply store is six thousand miles away," one sun-baked driller told me good-naturedly. "That makes 'em take doubly good care of their equipment—and they learn to make do with what we've got."

"Is there anything in particular you need or want out here?" I asked him. The reply proved that oil-field workers were the same, whether employed in the Middle East or in Oklahoma, and as much infected by oil fever in 1956 as they had been in 1906.

"Hell, yes!" the driller replied. "You could start off by sending over Sears, Roebuck and the Rockettes and work your way down from there." He laughed, then said in level tones, "Seriously, boss, what we want mainly is the same thing you want—more oil."

I have been aware since childhood of the lure and fascination that oil holds for all men, and of the universally epidemic nature of oil fever. Hence, I was not overly surprised to find that the Arab workers, of whom 138 worked alongside the 40-odd American employees in the fields, had not been immune to the infection, either. Conscientious, efficient workers all, they too labored with unflagging zeal to speed the process of finding and producing more oil.

Talking with them—my largely self-taught Arabic by then being equal to most routine conversational demands—I was struck by their enthusiasm and enterprise. When I told one young Arab roustabout that I myself had once done the same work, he shrugged his shoulders as though it was no more than he expected.

"I don't intend doing this work for the rest of my life either, *Inshallah*," he replied, grinning.

Withal, my visit to the field and inspection of activities at Mina Saud turned up many things I felt needed to be done or improved. This did not imply slackness or any lack of attention or efficiency on the part of personnel on the scene. Rather, it was that, as always, the "boss" notices things that subordinates with understandably less knowledge of the overall situation, the "big picture," are liable to miss or misinterpret. Then, the "boss" can make recommendations, give orders, and authorize expenditures which individuals junior to him are unable or reluctant or hesitant to do.

Three of my most trusted associates—Melville "Jack" Forrester, Norris Bramlett, and Mrs. Penelope Kitson—were also in the Neutral Zone, each having a large variety of specific tasks to perform there. Nevertheless, I dragooned the futilely protesting Norris Bramlett, who, for many years, has been my chief accountant, into acting as a sort of combination stenotypist and Man Friday. Thrusting pad and pen into his hands, I took Norris with me everywhere, dictating memos, orders, suggestions, and ideas to him.

Norris, long-suffering and resigned to his fate, consequently had to burn large quantities of midnight oil, and, I presume, burned out more than one adding machine catching up with his own accounting work at night after having spent the day uncomplainingly driving or trudging across the sands from one drilling site to another.

As I say, I found many matters with which to concern myself. Construction of the refinery at Mina Saud had not yet begun in the spring of 1956. I took immediate steps to insure that work would commence without further unnecessary delay and that, once started, it would proceed rapidly and expeditiously. I also noted and took action to alleviate the need for additional pipelines, more equipment, more buildings, and other installations and facilities. Altogether, Norris Bramlett jotted down instructions for improvements and expansion involving capital outlays in excess of twelve million dollars.

April and May passed. One Friday, shortly after noon—on June 1, 1956, to be exact—Bramlett, Jack Forrester, Mrs. Kitson, and I were relaxing on the beach in front of the company bungalow that Jack and I were sharing for the duration of our stay in the Neutral Zone. It was a hot, clear day, and the light breeze blowing off the Persian Gulf was a welcome novelty. We weren't doing much of anything—mainly staring across the placid waters and chatting, as I recall.

Suddenly, one of us spotted a large steamer apparently sailing toward Mina Saud. There were no tankers or other cargo vessels due; passenger ships almost never made an appearance. We spent several minutes idly speculating about the identity of the ship and its purpose in heading for Mina Saud. If memory serves me, it was Jack Forrester who first recognized the vessel.

"Holy smoke!" he exclaimed, leaping up from the folding canvas chair in which he had been sprawling lazily. "That's King Saud's yacht!"

There was no one on the beach or even moving about in the vicinity, save for the four of us. Everyone else was taking their traditional Middle Eastern post-luncheon rest indoors. As for us, we were all in casual sports clothes, hardly the sort of garb suited for wear when meeting and greeting a reigning monarch.

Yet, there was no time for us to change. The ship had by then drawn in to shore as far as its draught would allow, which was not very close, because the shore at Mina Saud shelves very gradually. Already, davits were being swung out and a large launch was being lowered. There was nothing for it but to wait for His Majesty King Saud to come ashore and hope for the best.

His Majesty's surprise visit to Mina Saud and the Neutral Zone had indeed taken us and everyone else by surprise. A tall, imposingly regal figure of a man, clad in rich, traditional robes, His Majesty did not even flicker an eyelash at our comparatively unkempt appearance. He returned our greetings with as much dignity and aplomb as if we had been formally dressed for a court reception. Then, after visiting in my bungalow for a few minutes, he invited us to dine with him aboard the Royal yacht that evening.

The yacht and the dinner served aboard it were like something out of an Arabian Nights' tale. Even the gangway slung against the yacht's side was carpeted with thick, priceless Oriental rugs. There were considerably more than a hundred guests in a huge dining salon. Dinner—course after course of it—was served on the finest porcelain, each plate and dish decorated with the Saudi emblem, a sword and palm tree. A good-sized army of retainers was posted around the dining salon, ready to wait on the King and guests.

The sumptuous feast, marked by all the color and grandeur befitting the court of an Oriental potentate, lasted nearly three hours. When it ended, His Majesty signified his evident satisfaction with matters in general by graciously accepting a return invitation to a party which would be given in his honor in the near future by oil companies to which he had granted the Neutral Zone concession.

I extended my stay in the Neutral Zone, remaining there for somewhat over two additional months. Then, in August, feeling that I had taken care of everything which required my personal attention, I returned to Europe, where other urgent business matters awaited me. I left the Neutral Zone totally unsuspecting that, within a few months, the Middle East—and, indeed, the entire world—would be brought to the brink of catastrophe.

33

COUNTLESS millions of words have been written about the 1956 Suez affair, its background, causes, aftermaths, and repercussions.

Now, I hardly consider myself either qualified or justified to volunteer any observations or opinions about the history or broad implications of this dismal incident. I do not, however, think it would be remiss at this point to say a few words about the immediate and direct effects that Suez had on the oil business. At the same time, it might be worthwhile to digress momentarily and take a quick glance at the general situation of the world petroleum industry before and after the Suez affair.

Almost as soon as World War II ended, the oil-shortage alarm was once again sounded in many countries around the globe. In the United States, the shortage was most strongly felt during 1947 and 1948 by firms and individuals who used oil as industrial or home heating-fuel.

The reasons behind the shortage, as is usual in such instances, were simple and fairly obvious. Postwar demand for petroleum products of all kinds had skyrocketed. But wartime conditions, restrictions, and control had prevented the oil industry from making the necessary preparations for the greatly increased consumption that developed after V-E Day.

There was no real shortage, not in the sense that the United States or the world was running out of crude oil. The actual shortages were in new wells and in refining, transportation, and storage capacity.

Somehow, it is not possible to explain these things to most people. Almost invariably, an appreciable shortage—even though only temporary—of almost any refined petroleum product sets off rumors that the nation (or the world) is "running out of oil."

American and foreign oil producers proved that this was not happening during the postwar years, and that it probably could not happen for many, many decades. Once peace made free movement throughout much of the world possible, and wartime restrictions were lifted, large-scale exploration and drilling operations started again on a gigantic scale on every continent.

By 1950, supply was equal to demand and gradually edging past it in some places. The Korean War slammed the pendulum back to the other extreme. Military consumption of petroleum soared, and demand once more outstripped production, giving rise to yet another round of oil-shortage rumors.

About a year later, Iran, which had long been an important source of crude for the Eastern Hemisphere, went through some violent political convolutions culminating in nationalization of the Iranian petroleum industry, which had been developed there largely by British interests. This had the effect of taking tremendous quantities of petroleum off the world's markets. The Iranians were unable to operate their newly nationalized oil industry at anywhere near capacity. The refinery at Abadan, the largest in the world, was closed down. Furthermore, Britain boycotted what Iranian oil was being produced.

The Korean War and the Iranian situation spurred oil companies to expand their production. There was a noticeable increase in wildcatting operations all over the world. More wells were drilled, more new fields were opened, and the output of existing wells was increased. This was the period during which big discoveries were made by American companies engaged in offshore United States drilling. Exploration and drilling operations were expanded in Canada, South America, and, of course, in the Middle East.

All this activity served not only to restore the balance between production and demand, but also to prove to the world that there were still great oceans of crude oil below ground, that the day of any conceivable oil shortage was far off.

By 1954, the tangled Iranian situation had been cleared up. A consortium of British, American, French, and Dutch oil companies—in which consortium, incidentally, Tidewater and Getty Oil Company each hold a 0.417 per cent interest—reached a working agreement with the Iranian government. On August 5 of that year, the Iranian government and the consortium signed a twenty-five-year contract, renewable for an additional fifteen years. Under its terms the consortium would operate the Iranian oil industry, paying Iran 50 per cent of all its earnings. With this, the great Iranian fields began producing again, and the giant Abadan refinery was reopened.

Two years later, on July 26, 1956, the Egyptian government seized the Suez Canal, the vital artery connecting East and West, through which moved the tankers carrying crude oil from the Middle Eastern fields to Europe, Britain, and the United States. The situation deteriorated rapidly, culminating in open conflict in late October and early November. Egyptian authorities ordered that a large number of ships be scuttled and sunk in the Suez Canal itself, thereby effectively blocking it and preventing the passage of traffic through the canal.

The Suez remained blocked even after the United Nations imposed a cease-fire order which brought hostilities to an end. Many months would pass before the canal would be completely cleared of sunken ships and other obstructions. In the meantime, the entire world's petroleum industry was dislocated and thrown into confusion.

Tankers loaded with crude oil or refined products from the Middle Eastern fields and refineries could not use the Suez short cut. The only route open between the Middle East and Europe was via the long way around the Cape of Good Hope, the southernmost tip of the African continent. This meant a voyage of more than eleven thousand miles each way.

Thus, the distance a ship had to travel in order to deliver a cargo was tripled. And so, of course, was the distance it had to travel to pick up a fresh load of oil. And, where the distance tripled, the time involved in getting from source to market and back was also multiplied three times. In effect, this cut the carrying capacity of the tanker fleets operating from the Middle East, and thus Britain's and Europe's Middle Eastern oil supplies, down to one-third their normal level. It also more than tripled the transportation costs on every barrel of oil shipped from the Middle East.

There was not enough tankerage available to take up the slack. With winter and the consequent rise in demand for oil for heating purposes rapidly coming on, Britain and most European countries found themselves facing very real and very serious shortages. As the stocks of crude and refined products dwindled, western hemisphere producers strove to meet the deficits, shipping huge quantities of crude and petroleum products from the United States and South America.

Eventually, of course, the Suez Canal was cleared and reopened for normal use. But in the meantime, no small degree of havoc had been caused in the Middle Eastern oil fields. With lack of transportation sharply reducing the outlets for their crude, most companies in the Middle East had to curtail production once their limited storage facilities had been filled to capacity. The production of some wells had to be cut drastically, while others were shut down completely. In many instances, the drilling of new wells had to be suspended.

One does not turn an oil field or a refinery on and off like a popcorn machine. It costs money to shut down, more money is lost during the period when there is greatly curtailed or no production, and the costs of restarting operations and bringing them up to previous levels are very high. For these and other allied reasons, the operating costs and expenses of companies operating in the Middle East soared during the Suez crisis and for months afterwards.

There was, of course, one immense consolation. Suez did not develop into the global war that seemed to threaten during October and November of 1956. The fact that such a holocaust, or even a limited war, was averted made all the costs and dislocations pale into meaningless insignificance.

By mid-1957, most Middle Eastern operations were back to normal, as were the levels of British and European petroleum stocks which had been largely depleted during the Suez crisis and the ensuing period during which the canal was being cleared.

The Getty Oil Company's activities in the Neutral Zone were once more moving ahead under a full head of figurative steam. On the coast, at Mina Saud, construction of the refinery and other buildings, installations, and facilities were proceeding apace.

Inland, at Wafra, the settlement in the center of the Neutral Zone fields, more wells were being drilled. In point of fact, two wells were brought in during March; drilled to the first Eocene limestone at a little more than one thousand feet, they came in for combined initial daily production in excess of four thousand barrels.

Also at Wafra, additional storage tanks, soon to provide total capacity of nearly half a million barrels, were gradually being assembled to rise above the barren desert and dominate the flat landscape. Then, a swimming pool, an everyday commonplace to most Americans at home, but a previously undreamed-of luxury in the Neutral Zone, was also abuilding.

The other Getty companies were also having a busy year. In 1956, Tidewater and two other oil companies had joined together to form a consortium to prospect for oil in Turkey. Tidewater, with one-third interest, was also designated as the company to conduct the exploration operations on the more than three million acres covered by the permits the Turkish government issued.

Tidewater was also interested in exploration and drilling operations in Central and South America, Canada, and Pakistan, all of which kept the company's field personnel hopping.

There were other developments, too.

The first of Tidewater's 46,500-ton tankers—the *Veedol*—had been delivered by its Japanese builders as far back as December, 1955. By 1957, it and several sister ships were veterans of the world's sea-lanes, which they plied with their cargoes of crude oil and refined petroleum products.

These were among the most modern vessels of their class and tonnage, capable of cruising great distances economically at relatively high speeds. They were also outfitted to provide the maximum of comfort and convenience for their officers and crews. There are no dreary, poorly ventilated fo'c'sles aboard these tankers. Crew members as well as officers have comfortable staterooms and sleep on beds that compare favorably with those found aboard passenger liners. Each ship carries a reading library and a wide range of recreational equipment for the use of the men who sail aboard her during such long voyages as that from the Middle East to the United States.

Yet, despite their modernity and comfort, these ships were bargains. Contracts for their construction were let before the cost of building ships took a sudden and sharp upswing, in some cases more than doubling the price of a tanker. In other words, the price of these Tidewater tankers was about half of what their replacement value became within a year or two after they were completed!

Much the same is true of the next-in-size supertankers constructed under the Tidewater shipbuilding program. These vessels—fifty-three-thousand-tonners—incorporated even more features which experienced seamen considered exceptional. Delivery on these ships began in 1957. With more space, it was possible to provide a private stateroom for each and every crew member aboard them. Fast, capacious, the fifty-three-thousand-ton ships were built in French shipyards. I named the first of these vessels that came off the ways the *George F. Getty*, in memory of my father, and the second the *Minnehoma*, after the company he formed in 1903 and which provided the basis of his and my fortunes in oil.

The fifty-three-thousand-tonners were also ordered before shipbuilding prices went up. Thus, they too were worth more than their cost from the moment their keels were laid.

I was not entirely satisfied with the decoration of the earlier 46,500-ton ships. This may seem like a small and unimportant item, but I've long maintained that even the most utilitarian of objects can be attractive. There is no earthly reason that I can see why a tanker should be any less attractively decorated than one's home or office. After all, the tanker is both home and office for weeks on end to the men who sail aboard her. They—officers and crew alike—deserve to spend at least their off-duty hours in surroundings that are as pleasant as it is possible to make them.

Besides, as psychologists and time-and-motion engineers have pointed out so often, human beings do their best and most efficient work, with less resulting tension and fatigue, when their immediate surroundings are attractive and comfortable. Hence, I called upon Mrs. Penelope Kitson, my close friend and a decorator of note in England, to consult with the builders and advise them on the decoration of the living quarters, messing and recreational rooms aboard the tankers.

Mrs. Kitson adroitly managed to add a subtle woman's touch without in any way impairing the essentially masculine quality that any ocean-going vessel with an all-male complement must possess. Officers and crews have been unanimous in their praise and even gratitude for the warmer, pleasanter atmosphere that consequently prevails aboard the ships.

As the fifty-three-thousand-ton vessels proved themselves under all conditions, it became quite clear that, within certain limits, the larger the supertanker, the more efficient and economical it was. Carefully tailoring specifications to the particular uses intended for each vessel and still letting contracts on highly advantageous terms, Tidewater ordered sixty-seven-thousand-ton, sixty-eight-thousand-ton, and finally seventy-three-thousand-ton ships.

One of the giant seventy-three-thousand-tonners, built in a French ship-yard, was launched in late 1960. I would like to say at this point that I was not a little moved by the tribute inherent in the Tidewater directors' resolution, passed by them in the United States and then mailed to me, which directed that the ship be named the *J. Paul Getty*. Like most men, I cannot help but feel that such gestures by one's associates are tantamount to votes of confidence, and they are at once handsome rewards for the services I have rendered and incentives which inspire me to redouble my efforts.

The Tidewater fleet now totals more than a million tons of modern tankerage. The building program has not ended. There are more and, if possible, even better ships to come.

I have taken an intense personal interest in the program since its inception. Part of the reason, I suppose, is that I have always had an interest in ships, but mainly because I wanted to be certain that Tidewater and its stockholders got their money's worth when they invested tens of millions of dollars in new tankers. What knowledge I already had, I applied. What I did not know, I sought to learn from expert naval architects and shipbuilders.

By keeping a close check on every phase of construction, and even, in some instances, on such relatively minute details as the number of coats of paint applied to bulkheads, I believe that I was able to insure that the strength, seaworthiness, and safety of the vessels were at least the equal of any ship afloat.

During the Suez crisis, every tanker that could chug from one port to another was, of course, almost literally worth its weight in gold. Within a little more than a year, the picture would change completely. The petroleum industry, its markets by then glutted with oil, would suddenly find itself with more tankers than it needed. With the United States government initiating a system designed to limit the import of Middle Eastern crude to protect domestic producers in 1957, the tanker situation would worsen, and scores of vessels would be laid up indefinitely because there were no cargoes for them.

Luckily, the Getty companies and the Tidewater fleet were not for long seriously affected by what became known as the "tanker-glut." My associates and I were not taken unawares; we were not unprepared for the possibility that such a situation might develop. The story of how the problem was met and solved belongs in a later chapter. I have already leapfrogged ahead of the story, an integral part of which is the account of an entirely different kind of building program, this time on dry land—and in the United States.

34

THERE is an old story about the harried chain-store executive who rushes into a railroad depot and loudly demands that the counter clerk sell him a ticket immediately.

"Where to?" the clerk asks.

"It doesn't make any difference." The man shrugs. "We've got stores everywhere."

I'll grant that the story isn't particularly funny, but in a way, it does reflect the position in which I found myself in 1957. I didn't have "stores everywhere," but as head of the rapidly burgeoning Getty companies and enterprises, my business interests were spread over dozens of countries on five continents.

I have already touched upon such activities as the stateside refinery construction and modernization projects at Delaware City and Avon, the supertanker construction program and oil exploration and drilling operations in Pakistan, Turkey, North and South America.

Things were humming elsewhere as well. The Hotel Pierre Marques had opened at Revolcadero Beach near Acapulco, Mexico, the previous year, and its success had been immediate. Products bearing the Veedol trademark were being sold in more and more countries around the globe as marketing activities increased. Tidewater had a 50-per-cent interest in a Japanese refining venture which would soon have a refinery with a capacity in excess of fifty thousand barrels a day in operation at Kawasaki. Plans were being considered to build or buy a refinery on the European continent. The Getty companies were even taking interest in uranium-prospecting ventures and conducting research in processes for the extraction of petroleum from shale, owning as they did an estimated fifteen billion barrels of shale oil reserves in Colorado.

These were but a few of the varied intercontinental activities of the Getty companies in the mid-1950's. With such widespread operations and continuing growth and expansion, it was only natural that the managements of those companies should have given attention to providing adequate home-office headquarters for them. Thus, among the many matters with which I had to concern myself in 1957 were the multimillion-dollar building construction programs which were in various stages of progress in the United States.

These activities were centered in three cities: Los Angeles, California; Tulsa, Oklahoma; and New York City. In describing them, perhaps it would be easiest to consider them in order, from West to East.

Back in the 1930's, when Los Angeles real estate values had plummeted to rock-bottom lows, I had made several property purchases. Among the properties I bought was a fine, large site on Wilshire Boulevard. I paid a bargain price for it and held on through the years, resisting the temptation to sell at a considerable profit during the post-World War II Los Angeles real estate boom that sent property values spiraling up toward the stratosphere. The site was too good to sell to anyone else; I held on to it against the day when one of the companies I owned or controlled could put it to use and derive the maximum benefit from it.

By the mid-1950's, Wilshire Boulevard was solidly established as one of the richest, most glamorous thoroughfares in the world, comparing favorably to New York's Fifth Avenue or the Champs Elysées in Paris. The property in question was situated in the heart of the glittering Wilshire District's most elegant and exclusive section. It was worth several times what I had originally paid for it, as was evidenced by the many offers I received for the property from southern California real estate firms.

Then the management of the Tidewater Oil Company indicated it would like to build a new headquarters building on the property. The site was ideal for the purpose intended, and I gladly agreed to the request.

Tidewater certainly deserved its own spanking-new office building. The company could boast of having some 10,000 employees, nearly 30,000 stockholders, and more than $800,000,000 in assets. Its products—100-octane Flying-A gasoline and Veedol lubricants among them—were used by millions of satisfied customers. In 1956, the company's profits came close to reaching the $39,000,000 mark.

Preliminary plans for the new Tidewater Building called for a 14-story, 155-foot-high structure that would be the largest office building in Los Angeles. An unexpected hitch developed immediately. City zoning restrictions, due to expire in a few years, but still in effect at that time, limited construction to 6 stories, to a total height of only 85 feet. This left the Tidewater management and me in a quandary, faced with three obvious alternatives, each of which we considered and discarded.

First, we could have abandoned all plans to build on the Wilshire Boulevard property and looked for another site. We rejected this possibility because it was highly doubtful that we could find any other site that was as desirable and well-suited as the one we already owned. Even if we did find a satisfactory property, its price would unquestionably be much higher than the original cost of the Wilshire Boulevard property.

Second, we could order the plans changed drastically and thus, in effect, recast the entire program for construction of the Tidewater Building. This alternative was vetoed because the original plans provided for maximum and most efficient utilization of the property. We did not feel that we wanted to settle for less.

Third, the start of construction could be delayed until such time as the zoning restrictions had expired. This meant that Tidewater would have to wait for years before having its own building. That in itself would be uneconomical, for the company would simply continue to pay for leased space. Beyond this, it was clear to all that the trend of all construction costs was up and would remain so for the foreseeable future. To delay construction only meant that the company would have to pay just that much more when work finally did commence.

Having rejected all three of these alternatives, we hit upon and adopted a fourth course of action. It was decided that construction would begin on the Wilshire Boulevard site as soon as possible and as previously planned. There would, however, be a difference, and a big one. Only the first six floors of the structure would be built. The remaining floors, which had been conceived as a central tower section surmounting the six-story base, would be added on when the Los Angeles city zoning restrictions expired.

Since a considerable portion of the projected building was intended for rental to other tenants, Tidewater, which required only four floors for its own use, would have ample space in its own building, which would be located on one of the choicest sites in all Los Angeles. And, the deeply excavated foundations and the main base structure would be built at prevailing labor and materials cost levels. If costs rose as expected in the future, the increases would affect only the construction of the tower section.

This is how the block-long Tidewater Building was built. Completed and opened for occupancy before the end of 1958, it cost nearly ten million dollars. It is expected that the limiting zoning laws will soon expire, and that the eight-story tower section may be added to the existing structure. In the meantime, Tidewater's management can feel satisfied that it made the right decision by going ahead with the project. The company has already made a paper profit on its building, for anticipated increases in construction costs and property prices have raised its replacement value to a level appreciably higher than the amount spent.

As for the building itself, it is a handsome structure consisting of two massive wings joined by a slender central tower which houses the elevator shafts and the exterior of which is emblazoned with the Tidewater Flying-A trademark. The exterior of the building is a gleaming white accentuated by a baseband of black granite that sheathes the building to the top of its first-floor level. The ground floor is set back several feet from the sidewalk on the Wilshire Boulevard side. Thus, there is a second-floor overhang, which creates the effect of a cool, shaded arcade.

Two large banks—the Security First National and the Bank of America —have branch offices located on the ground floor. And so does the brokerage house of E. F. Hutton & Company, a firm with which I have had close and pleasant relationships for three decades.

Southern California sunshine being what it is, there is an exceptionally large number of windows in the Tidewater Building, made of special-process, heat-resistant glass. The spacious lobby is decorated with large murals which depict, as is only fitting, various phases of oil industry activity.

Farther east, in Tulsa, Oklahoma, the Skelly Oil Company was also planning a new building in 1957. There being no zoning or other restrictions to hamper the imagination of the architects and designers, the plans called for a strikingly beautiful, fifteen-story skyscraper of advanced, even revolutionary, concept.

When I inspected the architects' sketches and blueprints which were sent to me in Europe in 1957, I immediately recognized that the projected building would be worth every penny of the more than ten million dollars which had been allotted for its construction.

Actual work on the Skelly Building did not start until the beginning of 1958. It was completed and fully ready for occupancy shortly after New Year's Day, 1960, and was widely hailed as one of wealthy, bustling Tulsa's most attractive and impressive office buildings.

Fronting on Boulder Avenue, the building is set well back from streets and sidewalks. The space thus provided is landscaped with trees, bushes, and flowers. The first floors form a huge platform which serves as a base for the soaring tower. The building is extremely modern in its design, with simple, clean lines, yet with none of the harsh, angular hardness that characterizes so many modern buildings. Despite its size, it has an airy, elegant quality. It has none of the heaviness that one sees in so many sky-scrapers. On the contrary, its main bulk—the tower—seems to float easily on its spacious base.

Oklahomans, no less than Texans, are accustomed to thinking big and keeping ahead of the times. Thus, it is hardly surprising that the roof of the Skelly Building is designed to permit the take-off and landing of heli-copters, and that four floors of indoor garage parking space have been provided for the use of those who work in the building. There is an audi-torium comparable in size to a fair-sized theater; it comes in equally handy for sales meetings or for employee Little Theater productions.

The final seal of approval was placed on the Skelly Building by the Tulsa Chamber of Commerce, which presented the company with a formal commendation, citing it "for the beautification of its property, thus further enhancing Tulsa's reputation as 'America's Most Beautiful City.' "

Most involved—and costliest—of the Getty companies' stateside ven-tures into office-building construction was the one involving the erection of the twenty-two-story Getty Building in New York City. This project had a rather long history.

Almost as soon as I had bought the Hotel Pierre in 1938–39, I began to think in terms of acquiring all the land on the block partially occupied by the hotel. It seemed to me that this block, bounded east and west by Madison and Fifth avenues, and north and south by Sixty-first and Sixtieth streets, would lend itself admirably to the construction of a sort of vest-pocket-sized Radio-City-type skyscraper complex. Naturally, I shelved any such ideas when World War II began and did not again give them any consideration until 1951 or so.

I consulted with my attorney, David Hecht, and with various real estate men and builders of my acquaintance, asking their opinions about the feasibility of any such project. All seemed to agree, at least in principle, that the idea was essentially sound, but warned that buying up the land-parcels and demolishing the existing buildings would be a long, complicated, and extremely expensive process.

It is difficult to guess what I might have done had it not been for situations and developments entirely beyond my control. Inquiries among the owners of the various lots comprising the block indicated that some would sell, others might do so, and some would not consider anything of the kind.

It became evident that only with the greatest difficulty could I even hope to assemble the land-parcel I wanted and that the hold-out owners would very probably make it utterly impossible for me to do so. There matters stood until Dave Hecht one day learned that the Rothschild interests had succeeded in assembling a parcel in the block and were willing to sell it for $1,500,000.

This was only part of what I had hoped to purchase, but the property adjoined the Pierre, and I decided to buy it. Once I owned this parcel as well as the property on which the Hotel Pierre stood, I thought I might be able to persuade the recalcitrants among the other owners in the block to sell. It was a futile hope. One lot was owned by a real estate operator who flatly refused to sell. Another lot was owned by an exclusive club; at first, it seemed that I would be able to buy, then my offer was turned down with a polite finality which clearly spelled the end of my hopes in that direction.

In the end, I was left with a property consisting chiefly of the corner of Madison Avenue and Sixty-first Street. It was at about this point that the Eastern Marketing and Refining Division of the Tidewater Oil Company became pressed for office space. Requirements added up to approximately 120,000 square feet.

It seemed to me that the soundest and most economical way of solving both problems—what to do with the property at Madison and Sixty-first and how to provide Tidewater with the space it needed—was to put up a new building which would not only supply the latter, but also provide a return on investment through office rentals. Valid as such an idea may be and simple as it may seem when stated here in a few words, it cannot be realized overnight, particularly not in a great and complex city such as New York.

Vast amounts of preliminary planning had to be done. Arrangements had to be made for the transfer of tenants in the buildings already on the property. Permits and licenses had to be obtained to demolish the existing structures and, of course, to build a new one. A thousand and one things had to be done before the first spadeful of earth could be turned for the new structure's foundations.

My associates and I decided that, while we were at it, we might as well build the best that money could buy. Selecting one of America's finest architectural firms, Emery Roth and Sons, to design and plan the building, we instructed the architects to that effect. The firm turned the project over to its top man, Richard Roth, under whose direction the Getty Building was designed and built.

A minor miracle was wrought in the construction of the skyscraper, which was completed in a record-breaking ten months, two months less than the time that had been estimated. The building, with its clear, un-cluttered lines, expresses the best in contemporary architecture. Designer Roth and his colleagues fully understood the importance of the element of fenestration in any building in which hundreds of men and women are to work. A glance at a photograph of the Getty Building gives one the impression that the tiered, twenty-two-story structure is sheathed in glass, supported by a delicate latticework of thin vertical dividers and slightly broader horizontal supports.

Inside as well as out, the building embodies the latest advances which insure optimum worker efficiency and comfort. Naturally, the building is completely air-conditioned. Offices and even corridors are sound-con-trolled. Color-correcting fluorescent lighting is provided throughout the interior of the building.

The bill for construction of the twenty-two-story structure totaled some $12,000,000. I could not help but wince slightly when I recalled that, less than twenty years before, I had paid only $2,350,000 for the fully furnished and equipped forty-two-story Hotel Pierre, which stands next door to the Getty Building.

These, then, were the three major office-building projects which the Getty companies had under way or in the final planning stages during 1957. Eventually, they involved a total investment of more than $30,000,000.

I have indicated that 1957 was a very busy year for me. Checking plans, sketches, and blueprints and keeping tabs on the progress of the construction work in Los Angeles, Tulsa, and New York added just that much more to my work load.

Then, in October, 1957, a magazine article disrupted all the working and living patterns I had established over the years.

35

Up TO October, 1957, I had somehow managed to avoid the limelight of publicity. Or, to be more accurate, the limelight of publicity happily seemed to avoid me. Although I hardly lived the life of a recluse and made no conscious efforts to elude the press, I had succeeded in achieving a very large and quietly gratifying degree of personal anonymity throughout my life and business career.

Oh, there were a few exceptions to this rule of unpublicized bliss. My name sometimes cropped up in trade journals, or in the Business and Finance sections of newspapers or magazines, but such mentions, concerned as they were with corporate mergers or similar matters, held little interest for the general public and attracted little attention outside business circles. And, I must admit, accounts of at least one of the divorce actions brought against me caused brief front-page ripples, which, however, subsided quickly and were soon forgotten by reporters and readers alike.

Illustrative of the extent to which I had been able to maintain my anonymity through the years was a chance encounter with a former classmate I had not seen since my undergraduate days at the University of California at Berkeley. Meeting accidentally on a Los Angeles street in 1950, we recognized each other and stopped to reminisce for a few moments.

"By the way, Paul," my former schoolmate asked me at one point in our conversation, "who are you working for these days?"

All my life, I had been able to attend premieres, parties, or night clubs without eliciting much attention from the press. Reporters and photographers covering functions at which I was present generally detoured around me to seek more interesting game elsewhere. For all I know, they took me for one of the waiters. My name did not appear in gossip columns, and my photograph seldom if ever adorned the pages of any publications less prosaic than the *Oil and Gas Journal*.

This pleasant and peaceful state of affairs came to a halt, suddenly and forever after, in October, 1957. I was in London, staying at the Ritz Hotel at the time. I was completely unaware of the publicity storm that was about to break and totally unprepared for the sound and fury that it would occasion.

Unbeknown to me and, I was later to learn, most others whose names were involved, *Fortune* magazine's editors had decided to publish an article listing the wealthiest people in the United States. My name headed the list, and the authors of the article identified me as a "billionaire" and averred that I was "the richest American."

No doubt *Fortune* mailed advance copies of the issue in which the article appeared to various newspapers and wire-services, for even before the first copies reached the newsstands in October, the switchboard of the Ritz was swamped with calls and the lobby jammed with journalists. To my acute discomfort, the press had "discovered" me, and I had become a curiosity, a sort of financial freak, overnight. In the opinion of many reporters and editors, I had also become hot copy.

Fortune having labeled me "the richest American," it was not long before other periodicals and newspapers around the world began playing a journalistic game of one-upmanship by upping the ante and "revealing" that I was not only the "richest American," but, indeed, the "world's richest man" to boot.

Now, I for one have no conceivable way of gauging the validity of either of these grandiloquent titles. I cannot judge the extent of any other men's wealth, and, in fact, I cannot even judge the extent of my own fortune with any degree of accuracy.

Why?

Well, in the first place, such labels as "billionaire" are misleading. Despite all the well-intentioned efforts of headline writers to prove otherwise, there is no such thing as a billionaire among active businessmen, not in the sense that most people would understand the term. An individual may own or control business enterprises worth a billion dollars or even more, but little of his rated wealth is available to him in ready cash. A millionaire or billionaire does not have his millions on deposit in his personal checking account. The money is invested in his businesses.

It is impossible for him to know what his investments are really worth at any given time. The values of a businessman's holdings fluctuate greatly. The price of stocks may rise or fall, corporations may show major increases or decreases in their net worth, innumerable variables may multiply the value of an investment or wipe it out completely.

The *Fortune* magazine article made all this very clear, emphasizing that it had rated the wealth of those mentioned on the *estimated* value of their investments and such invisible and unmeasurable assets as ore, oil, or mineral reserves. Unfortunately, many journalists who came to interview me at the Ritz and the fantastic numbers of people who read the stories they wrote afterwards were either unable or unwilling to understand this.

More than one reporter came to my hotel suite and, it seemed, appeared surprised that there were no bundles of currency stacked on the table tops and floors. Many of the newshawks wanted to know exactly how much money I had.

"My editors want a dollars-and-cents figure."

"How much of your fortune do you keep in checking, and how much in savings accounts?"

"How long would it take you to count up your money?"

Such were the demands and questions. My replies, which explained that the vast majority of my fortune was working as investments in the companies I owned or controlled, were brushed off impatiently.

Within a few days after the general-circulation press had discovered a new sensation for its readers in J. Paul Getty, "the world's richest man," the flood of begging and crank letters began to pour into the Ritz. The letters, thousands of them, came from people who were total strangers to me. They came from practically every corner of the globe, written by men and women in almost all walks of life. Some pleaded, others were insistent, and others were downright demanding.

The vast majority of these letter writers wanted me to send them money because they'd read that I was a billionaire and America's—or the world's—wealthiest person. Some asked for a few dollars, others wanted hundreds, thousands, or even millions. In the case of one enterprising chap, the request was for a mere $200,000,000.

He proposed building a canal across Nicaragua to compete against Uncle Sam's Panama Canal. In a burst of generosity, the man offered me 10 per cent of the ship-toll profits in return for my "investment."

A woman in Kansas asked for $10,000 because she "wanted a vacation." Another in Brussels, Belgium, asked for twice that amount to buy her son an airplane. A Honolulu resident—a physician, no less—suggested that I send him $75,000 so that he could mount a round-the-world hunting expedition; if I would finance his sport, he promised, he would furnish me with a trophy head of every game animal known to science.

You can display them in your home and tell your friends you bagged them yourself, this mendicant medico wrote. *Part of the consideration I offer in return for the $75,000 is the promise that I will never reveal your secret.*

Letters such as these arrived by the sackful each day at my hotel. The patience and usually unflagging good nature of my then-secretary, June Cassell, were strained to the breaking point as she sifted through each morning's mountain of mail, gleaning the important business letters and correspondence from my friends out of vast quantities of chaff.

The writers of these begging letters spent their time and efforts and their postage money in vain. I do not give money to individuals who write to me for it. It would take a huge organization to investigate all the letters I receive in a steady stream since the *Fortune* article was published. If I gave to one, I would have to give to all. And this would be manifestly impossible. The total amount requested by the writers of these begging letters during an average month is between two million and five million dollars. It would not take long for me to bankrupt myself and my companies at that rate. All my contributions are made to legitimate charities which have been checked out by such organizations as the Better Business Bureau—and to these, my companies and I donate large sums each year.

But the *Fortune* article brought more than just begging letters. It set off a publicity chain reaction that has continued unabated to the present day. The press—and I use the term broadly to include not only newspapers and magazines but also radio and television—and, because of its interest, presumably the public, appear to have developed a lasting curiosity in me and my affairs.

I suppose this is understandable if for no other reason than that almost everyone is interested in money and that the average person is fascinated by absolute superlatives. Anything tabbed biggest or smallest, best or worst, most this or that, will automatically attract and hold attention. The billionaire and richest man labels that were figuratively tied on me by the *Fortune* article combined the elements of money and the absolute superlative, and I was thenceforth a curiosity only a step or two removed from the world's tallest man or the world's shortest midget.

Don't misunderstand me. I am not complaining. I have been most fortunate in life, and I am humbly grateful for all the liberal blessings I have received. But that's not the point. I am only saying that such labels can be more hindrance than help, more liability than asset.

Once a man is tagged as a millionaire or billionaire, he is thenceforward and forever marked and on a griddle that can become quite hot. Among other things, he ruefully finds himself the man who is always handed the bill.

Waiters automatically hand him the check. It's not the money I object to, it's the principle of the thing that bothers me, to say nothing of the monotony of it.

For instance, shortly after the *Fortune* article was published, I found a large group of my friends finishing their dinners in a well-known London restaurant.

"Have dessert and coffee with us, Paul," several of them asked me after hearing that I had already eaten my dinner. I joined them and we talked for about an hour.

When everyone was ready to leave, the headwaiter, who had obviously recognized me, came straight to my chair. It was almost like a reflex—he came as straight as a guided missile riding a directional beam.

"The dinner goes on your bill, of course, Mr. Getty," he murmured. It wasn't a question. It was a statement, as though putting any and all dinner checks on my bill was the most natural thing to do.

My friends had no knowledge of what was taking place. They would have been horrified had they known. But, to save everyone, myself included, embarrassment, I nodded dolefully to the headwaiter and suppressed a weary groan.

Sometimes, the people who invite me to break bread with them aren't quite so blameless or innocent of ulterior motive. On one occasion, I was invited to a dinner party at Maxim's in Paris. The affair was given for sixteen guests.

It was a neatly put-up job. Our "host" urged all present to eat and drink—nothing but the best, of course—and to damn the expense and be merry. Then, when the party broke up, he blithely told the management to send the bill to me.

To my astonishment, to say nothing of my anger, a bill for four hundred dollars arrived at my hotel from Maxim's. I immediately telephoned the restaurant.

"I think you've made an error," I told the maître d'hôtel.

"*Mais non*, Monsieur Getty!" that worthy protested. "We were in-structed to send *l'addition* to you."

Not unreasonably, I refused to pay. I may be wealthy, but that hardly means that I am a sucker or that I enjoy being bilked. Learning that I had not agreed to pay for the dinner and had attended it as an invited guest, Maxim's management apologized profusely, and the matter was forgotten.

But I guess that a man who is reputed to be very rich has to grow a tough, impervious skin and expect such things. Certainly, the October, 1957, *Fortune* article marked a turning point in my life in the sense that it had the effect of ending my existence as an ordinary private citizen and made me, for better or for worse, a public figure, or at least a person about whom the public curiosity was whetted.

Which brings up the inevitable question of just how wealthy I am— and whether or not I am in fact a billionaire and the "richest man."

To these questions, I can give no clear-cut, hard-and-fast answers.

As I have already said, it is impossible to compute a working business-man's wealth with accuracy. My business enterprises are built around a core of operating companies. The stocks in the various corporations are necessarily owned by holding companies—their management would other-wise be far too complex, unwieldy, and inefficient.

The assets of just two of the operating companies—Tidewater and Skelly—total considerably more than a billion dollars. Directly and in-directly, I own a sizable percentage of the stock in these companies. Now, how can one compute the actual value of my interests in Tidewater and Skelly?

Should the figure be the market value of the stock I own? Or should it be based on a computation of the per-share liquidation values of the companies?

In either case, the total would only be a "rated," a paper value. To realize the value of the stocks I own in cash, I would have to sell the shares, and the selling of such large blocks would almost certainly depress the prices of the shares before more than a fraction of them were sold.

To realize the per-share liquidation value of the stocks, the assets of the companies would have to be sold. No active businessman puts thriv-ing companies out of business. Thus the liquidation-value yardstick is a moot, purely theoretical, and totally unreliable one in this instance.

As for the question about my being the world's richest man, it is equally impossible for me to confirm or deny this. I repeat that I have no way of knowing how much wealth, rated or in cash and liquid assets, other individuals possess.

Certainly, if the issue revolves around the question of how much immediate, personal cash they or I possess, then there are more than a few men who have greater fortunes of their own. Such names as that of the Nizam of Hyderabad come immediately to mind as men with cash-in-hand wealth greater than my own.

To me, the important consideration is not how much cash I have or what my rated wealth is, but what the money, the wealth, is doing. If it's working to produce more and better goods and services for more people at lower prices, then all is well.

To me, this is the point and purpose of having wealth and being in business. If I have succeeded in achieving these aims and can continue to achieve them in the future, then I suppose I can consider myself very rich indeed. If, by any stretch of the imagination, I could accomplish these things better than any other businessman on the face of the earth, then I would have no hesitancy in calling myself "the world's richest man."

Until then, I'll let *Fortune* magazine do the worrying about the size of my fortune—and pay attention to my own business and my own businesses.

36

ASSUMING and hoping fervently that no madman or blundering idiot trips the triggers of nuclear war in the interim, historians of the next century will doubtless write in awe about the miracle of post-World War II Western Europe.

In 1945, most European countries were exhausted by years of war and enemy occupation. Their industrial plants were shattered, their economies dislocated. Countless cities and towns were bomb-blasted heaps of rubble; transportation and communications systems were wrecked. Unemployment and hardship, to say nothing of poverty and hunger, were widespread. The people were restive, and many governments were shaky.

I recall a scholarly survey of the European situation that was published by a leading American news magazine in 1946. In it, technical experts and political leaders gave their estimates of the time it would take for the war-ravaged Continental countries to rebuild their cities and economies.

"At least fifty years."

"It will take a minimum of twenty years merely to clear the rubble."

"There is grave doubt whether Europe will be able to achieve full recovery in the twentieth century."

Such were the discouraging assessments and predictions made by the majority of the authorities who were quoted in the survey. And, for a time, it seemed as though their pessimistic appraisals would prove correct.

Once-great commercial and industrial centers such as Naples, Vienna, the French Channel ports, Hamburg and Rotterdam—to name only a very few—were largely wastelands of bomb-blasted debris. Vast numbers of demobilized soldiers, repatriated prisoners of war, and displaced persons returning to what had once been their homes swelled the legions of jobless who could find no work in factories that no longer existed or stores that had nothing to sell.

Fully exploited by the cynical prophets of Communist Utopia, the economic chaos bred social and political unrest which threatened—promised, in fact—to engulf all Europe in the sort of bloody civil war which already raged in Greece. The over-all situation seemed to support and substantiate the views of those who grimly predicted that Europe was "dead" for the remainder of the twentieth century.

Western Europe wasn't dead yet, but it was dying rapidly from the wounds the war had inflicted on it. Even the most optimistic observers were forced to admit that complete disintegration and very probably a blood-bath would be the results if something was not done, and done quickly. The American Marshall Plan provided the last-minute help that averted catastrophe.

Massive infusions of U.S. aid shored up what remained of wrecked economies, provided the props that held up crumbling democratic governments, and raised the sagging morale of entire populations. The Marshall Plan saved the situation and Western Europe. Subsequent aid programs, loans, and other economic assistance carried the patient to the convalescent stage.

Nonetheless, the marks and reminders of war were still very evident in Europe as late as 1956, eleven years after the conflict had ended. American tourists still gaped at acres of rubble as they "did" the Continent. The pockmark-like scars left by strafing machine guns and bomb-splinters still defaced the walls of buildings in France, Italy, Austria, the Benelux countries, and Germany. Motorists driving along European highways still passed concrete bunkers and pillboxes, some even yet bearing the marks left by shells or flame-throwers, and drove carefully over temporary bridges that were poor substitutes for the permanent ones that had been destroyed during the war.

Despite these lingering scars, by 1956–57 Europe was a long way along the road to recovery. The miracle that would increase the total gross national product of the six Euromart countries alone by 20 per cent between 1957 and 1961 and raise their combined industrial output by over a third during the same period had already begun to take shape.

No one, least of all the businessmen of Europe, will deny that the foundations of European recovery were built with American dollar-aid. But, once the foundations had been provided, the people of Europe created their own economic and industrial renaissance. The vitality, energy, and enterprise shown by Europeans surprised, even astounded, many Americans who had come to believe that Europe was decadent and debilitated.

The truth of the matter is that Europe, once it had recovered from the worst effects of the war, had ample reason and incentive to strive for the same high living standards as those prevailing in the United States. Shrewd European statesmen and businessmen were acutely aware that the old Continental systems, which allowed for a tiny top segment of the very rich, a small middle class, and a huge poorly paid lower class, were obsolete. The systems had to change, for if they did not, then they would be changed through social upheaval and violence. Continental merchants, traditionally accustomed to operating on small turnovers but large markups, were conscious of the need to alter their trading habits.

Europe caught on to the American systems of mass production and mass marketing. Businessmen, big and little, realized that in the future everyone from the lowliest laborer on up would have to prosper or few would survive. Higher wages, volume output, and volume turnover—these were the elements that had created American prosperity, and they were the ones which, effectively used in Europe, made possible the great European boom that is the economic marvel of the age.

Some American businessmen foresaw these developments and moved into the European markets with their products or capital or both. That I was among them should surprise no one when it is remembered that I had spent much time in Great Britain and Europe and thus had obtained a comprehensive knowledge of the countries and the people.

In 1958, the Getty Oil Company was approached by an Italian firm which wanted large quantities of Middle Eastern crude oil for its refinery in Gaeta, a short distance north of Naples. Investigation showed that the financial situation of the Italian company was such as to make the granting of long-term credit, a customary adjunct of any producer-refinery relationship, inadvisable. As a result, negotiations to sell crude oil underwent a swift metamorphosis and turned into negotiations for buying the refinery.

The Italian company, Golfo Industria Petrolifera, S.p.A., had recently built the refinery, an up-to-date plant with a 30,000-barrel-a-day refining capacity and storage facilities for 1,300,000 barrels of crude oil and refined products.

I learned that a controlling interest could be purchased at a price that seemed fair, and the opportunity was worth investigating. A glance at a map of the Mediterranean area will show the obvious advantages that a refinery located on the Bay of Gaeta offers to any company producing oil in the Middle East. The tanker run down the Persian Gulf from Mina Saud and around through the Red Sea and the Suez Canal, then across the eastern Mediterranean to Gaeta via the Straits of Messina, is a relatively short one. And the location north of Naples was ideal for access to markets in the southern part of Europe.

Getty Oil Company decided to buy the refinery if possible. I thought that Tidewater might want to buy a half-interest, and offered it to them, but the directors of that company turned the idea down.

Getty Oil went ahead with the negotiations, a goodly portion of which I handled personally. By mid-1958, the negotiations for purchasing a controlling interest in Golfo Industria Petrolifera, S.p.A., and thus the refinery, were proceeding in a satisfactory manner.

There was other activity, too. My associates and I had previously considered the construction of a new Tidewater refinery in West Germany, where Veedol products had long enjoyed considerable popularity. After protracted negotiations, it became apparent that, for various reasons, this project was impractical and was abandoned.

We were not unprepared for this eventuality; the program for expanding Tidewater's European operations had been designed flexibly, and by early 1959, a substitute project was under serious consideration. This involved the construction of a refinery, one with a capacity upwards of 20,000 barrels daily, at Kalundborg, Denmark. Negotiations for this project were begun in 1959. They were handled by Melville "Jack" Forrester, one of my most valued business associates and closest personal friends, working with Tidewater executive personnel. Jack made remarkable progress and, within a comparatively short time, had the project completely organized and ready to roll. The Kalundborg refinery was completed and came on stream in the latter part of 1961, largely because of the efforts of Jack Forrester, about whom a few words are, I believe, in order.

Jack is one of the most colorful characters I have known—and I have encountered many who fit the description. Born on New York's East Side, Forrester started his career as a dancer. He was starred in Maurice Chevalier's *Casino de Paris Revue* in the 1920's in Paris, toured Europe and South America in the early thirties. Not long before World War II began, Jack, who had made his home in Paris for several years, organized a motion-picture production company in France. Signing such stars as

Raimu and Marlene Dietrich, he produced several fine and successful films, including *J'Accuse.*

The war—and the fall of France—wrecked Jack's motion picture business. He returned to the United States and, the day after the Japanese attacked Pearl Harbor, he was in Washington. Speaking fluent French and Spanish, he felt he would be able to perform valuable service as an undercover agent in Europe.

Forrester was finally taken into the OSS and sent to Spain. For two years, he operated as an OSS agent in the rugged Pyrenees Mountains. Recruiting a private army from among French refugees, he led his men on sabotage operations and raids across the French border. He and his guerrillas harassed the German occupation forces and rescued scores of Allied flyers who had been shot down over France. Later, when Paris was liberated, Jack was sent to the French capital, where he served as a top-level counterintelligence officer.

Jack received several decorations for heroism and meritorious service. Then, released from the OSS after V-J Day, he found himself in Paris, out of work and low on funds. He finally obtained a job as a contact man for a large investment firm, the World Commerce Corporation. Forrester toured Europe, the Middle East, and Asia, seeking out promising projects and enterprises in which World Commerce could invest its capital funds. A shrewd, astute, and personable businessman, he did so well that in a few years he was made president of the firm's French subsidiary, World Commerce Corporation of France.

I had known Jack before the war. I respected his ability and liked him, his jovial good nature, and his wry, dry sense of humor. I met him again in Paris during 1949. He told me what he had been doing since the war ended and casually mentioned that he had his business so well organized that he now had time to spare.

"How would you like to do some work for me?" I asked him.

"I don't know much about the oil business," he replied. "But I suppose I can learn fast enough."

He did learn fast and well. Since 1949, the affable, highly intelligent, and exceptionally hard-working sometime motion picture producer has successfully conducted many delicate and important negotiations for the Getty companies. He has been instrumental in securing valuable oil concessions and has prepared and smoothed the way for many other operations and transactions including the building of tankers and pipelines and, of course, construction of the Kalundborg refinery.

Jack Forrester is a good example of the best type of American business-man operating abroad. He has taken the time and trouble to learn the languages of the people among whom his work takes him. He tries to understand their problems and viewpoints and shows respect for their ideas and customs, even when these are different or strange by American standards. He is equally at home and well-received in a Paris *salon* or at a banquet given by a Saudi Arabian sheik in the Middle East. He is a highly successful businessman who had his first million within ten years after V-J Day.

None of this has changed his character or personality in any way. He has certainly retained his sense of humor, and he occasionally tries mine by telephoning me from Paris, Rome, or New York to remind me that he is a minority stockholder in some of my companies and demanding to know how many hours I've worked that particular day. So far, he has not carried out his jocular threat to buy a time-clock and have it installed in my study. Knowing Jack, I would not be surprised to see one delivered to my door one of these days.

Forrester did yeoman work in Denmark, overcoming the problems and obstacles that invariably arise when a company desires to buy large tracts of land and begin building an industrial plant on the site. He and others among my associates were simultaneously conferring with engineers, architects, builders, and manufacturers of refinery equipment, machinery, and supplies.

When completed, the Kalundborg project would go far toward round-ing out Tidewater's global operations. The company's refineries at Wil-mington, Delaware, and Avon, California, would take care of American requirements. Its 50-per-cent interest in a refinery at Kawasaki, just out-side Tokyo, gave it a good position in Japan and the Far East.

The Kalundborg refinery would provide a firm footing in the burgeon-ing European market, an outlet for Tidewater's Persian crude oil produc-tion and possibly Pakistan and Spanish Sahara production, as well as more work for its tankers. As for Getty Oil, its control of Golfo Industria Petrolifera would mean that it, too, would have access to European markets.

37

IT would be futile for me to pretend that my personal life has followed an orthodox or conventional course. My five marriages and five divorces would, in themselves, make any such claim ridiculous.

Whatever other pros and cons were involved in the breakups of my marriages, to me the most bitterly disappointing and regrettable results of these matrimonial failures were the effects they had on my relationships with my five sons. They remained in their mothers' care after estrangements and divorces and, since my business required me to travel a great deal, I sometimes did not see them for long periods.

This did not mean that I lacked feeling for them, or failed to miss them. On the contrary, as any parent who has experienced enforced separation from his children knows, the love and affection I bore for my sons were poignantly intensified by the gulfs of time and distance.

Ample provision for all conceivable needs of my children were an integral part of each separation agreement or divorce settlement. Their care, education, and futures were assured by me and further guaranteed by the trust that my mother and I had established for them in the 1930's.

Through the years, I did whatever I could under the circumstances that obtained to exert a personal influence on my sons' development. I wrote and telephoned them and saw them whenever the opportunity to do so presented itself. I'll be the first to grant that these were poor substitutes for normal father-son relationships. The fact that all of them developed into individuals in whom I could take honest and objective pride is largely a credit to their mothers and to their own innate abilities and traits of character.

By mid-1958, George was thirty-four; Ronald—Ronny—was twenty-nine; Paul and Gordon were, respectively, twenty-five and twenty-four. Timothy—Timmy—was twelve.

As each of the four older boys finished school, he had been allowed to make his own free choice about entering the family business. All had decided to do so. Each had started at the bottom of the ladder, receiving his first practical introduction to the petroleum industry through a stint as a filling-station attendant.

From the beginning, each of my four older boys had been allowed to move along, learning each phase of the oil business, his pace of advancement being governed solely by his own abilities, merits, and qualifications. Each was given no-nonsense on-the-job training in the various operations of the Getty companies—production, transportation, refining, and marketing. Each spent time in the oil fields and particularly in the tough school of the Middle Eastern Neutral Zone.

By 1958, they were beginning to make their own marks in the petroleum industry.

George, the oldest, had served with distinction as an Infantry officer during World War II. He had remained in the United States Army for an additional period in order to complete a special assignment with the U.S. War Crimes Commission in Japan. After leaving the Army and completing a one-year course at Princeton, he served a grueling apprenticeship at Spartan Aircraft and in the Skelly, Pacific Western, and Tidewater organizations that included a long stint in the Neutral Zone.

His ability and performance clearly qualified him for the position of President of Tidewater, to which post he was elected. Married not long after leaving the Army, by 1958 George and his lovely wife, Gloria, had three beautiful little daughters who, I fear, show a rare talent for bending their paternal grandfather to their whims.

My second son, Ronny, had also worked his way up through the ranks in the family business. A considerable portion of his education had been obtained on the Continent, and he speaks other languages besides English. These considerations, plus his natural aptitudes, suited him admirably for the executive position he held on the marketing side of the Getty companies' European operations.

In 1958, twenty-five-year-old Paul Jr. was completing a rigorous on-the-job executive training course. Like all the boys, he received the same nominal pay and the same treatment as any other executive trainee. He and his extremely pretty and charming wife, Gail, already had one child, Paul

Getty III, a bright, red-headed little rascal who also possesses a remarkable ability for making his grandpa obey his commands.

My fourth son, Gordon, had decided to interrupt a promising career as a concert pianist and a composer of serious music to learn the oil business. He was hard at work in the Neutral Zone, learning the production end of the petroleum industry at the Mina Saud base and in the fields at Wafra.

My youngest boy, Timmy, was only twelve, and living in New York City with his mother—my fifth wife, Teddy—to whom I was still married despite a growing estrangement that would eventually carry the marriage to the final breaking point and divorce.

Timmy was not my favorite son in the sense that I loved him more deeply than I did my four other boys. But there were reasons, readily comprehensible to any parent, why my interest in him and my concern for his welfare were more immediate and actively stronger than they were for my older sons.

In the first place, Timmy was the youngest, still a child, while George, Ronny, Paul, and Gordon were grown men. Then, unfortunately, Timmy had been a frail and delicate youngster since he was born prematurely in 1946. Several emergency blood transfusions had been needed to save his life then, and in the ensuing years he had gamely and uncomplainingly fought back against frequent illness.

A warmly affectionate, freckle-faced child who took great delight in everything around him, Timmy had visited me in England with his mother as late as 1955, but they had returned to America after I failed to persuade Teddy to remain in Europe with me. From then on, I had to rely largely on the transatlantic telephone system to keep in touch with Timmy. I called him often, sometimes daily, and talked to him for an hour or more at a time. He was reconciled—albeit reluctantly—to this arrangement, and we seldom failed to discuss our plans for what we would do the next time we saw each other.

On August 14, 1958, my son Timmy entered a New York hospital to undergo what was thought to be a simple minor operation. The operation was performed successfully, but Timmy died three days later. His death was a loss not only to his mother and me, but to everyone who knew the child.

I was in Lugano, Switzerland, conducting negotiations with representatives of the Swiss interests which held control of the Gaeta refinery when word reached me. The impact of the news stunned me. I have little recollection of the events of the next several days, which I spent in the seclusion of my hotel suite. More than a week later, when I was again able to gather my thoughts and talk to people, I ascertained that everything that it was humanly possible to do had been done for Timmy. The outcome of the operation could only be laid to the will of whatever force or destiny controls all our lives.

I shall be eternally grateful to the countless friends and acquaintances who sent or telephoned their messages of condolence and comfort and offered to help me in any way they could. I am also especially thankful to my then-secretary, June Cassell, who was also in Lugano and who unhesitatingly took a heavy load of work and responsibility on her own shoulders. The loyalty and sympathy shown by her and by my other employees and associates were a source of great solace and gratification.

Once again, work proved to be the best and, perhaps, the sole palliative for grief. Before the year ended, I had brought the negotiations for the Gaeta refinery to a successful conclusion. Early in 1959, I was temporarily established in Milan, where the administrative offices of the Golfo Industria Petrolifera were located.

I stayed at the Hotel Francia-Europa, which was only a hundred yards or so from the buildings in which the offices were housed. This enabled me to spend more time taking care of the preliminary work that had to be done before the newly formed Getty Oil Italiana, S.p.A. company could assume full and active operational control of the refinery. I wanted the details taken care of as soon as possible, for I planned to close the Milan offices and move them to Rome, which was a great deal nearer to Gaeta and thus a more logical and practical location for the company's administrative offices.

The work was done in record time, for I had a solid nucleus of experienced people to help me. Among them were my son, Paul, Jr., and June Cassell, both of whom went to Rome when the office was transferred there. They are still in Rome, directing the operations of Getty Oil Italiana, which is headed by Paul, Jr.

I, too, went to the Italian capital, but remained there for only a brief period, moving on to Paris and London where I had other urgent business to transact.

Actually, my business affairs were gradually becoming well stabilized. The Getty companies were thriving under the capable direction of their seasoned, efficient management personnel. The framework of the worldwide complex of companies had been built; it was no longer necessary for me to move constantly from one place to another laying the groundwork for new enterprises or personally helping them through their teething pains. I could actually think of staying put for months at a time, a thought as pleasant and refreshing as it was novel.

Nevertheless, eastern hemisphere operations still needed a careful eye and a guiding hand. There had to be co-ordination between the United States end and the Neutral Zone and enterprises on the Continent. In order to provide these when and where necessary, I thought of establishing a strategically located base of operations, one that was at least psychologically equidistant from the United States and the Middle East.

Furthermore, the fast-moving, globe-girdling executives and technicians of the various companies needed an Eastern Hemisphere rendezvous point where they could meet and confer. Arrangements for this were at best makeshift. There were generally several executives or experts in the Eastern Hemisphere; when they met to hold meetings or conferences, it was usually in one of the capital cities. Housing was always a problem. Europe has an acute shortage of hotel accommodations, especially in the spring and summer. It was not an unknown occurrence for six or eight executives of Getty companies to arrive in a major European city and then find it necessary to take rooms in four or five widely separated hotels. It was not easy to hold meetings under such conditions. Nor was it economical. Carrying the name J. Paul Getty and the fatal label of "billionaire," I had long ago given up hope of being allowed to stay in a hotel for anything approaching a reasonable price. My executives' individual bills were less than mine, but still mounted up to an impressive total.

About a year before, my accountants had made a study of the expenses our executives and I incurred during our sometimes necessarily prolonged stays in European capitals. To their amazement, and, needless to say, to mine, they discovered that it would be cheaper in the long run if we bought a large suburban house somewhere, converted it to our needs, and stayed there instead of in hotels.

Taking all these elements into consideration, I was thinking seriously of establishing a sort of liaison base in Paris, where I'd had headquarters at various times in the past. Paris, one of the world's great petroleum industry capitals, seemed an ideal location. It had excellent banking, transportation, communications, and other facilities linking it to the rest of Europe and the entire world.

I suppose the Getty companies' eastern hemisphere liaison center would have been established in Paris, had I not attended a dinner party in London one evening in June, 1959. I had arrived in London during the previous month, intending to stay there only a few weeks.

My diary entry for June 27, 1959, reads as follows:

> In the morning went to my shoemaker, Lobb, and then to my tailor, Kilgour, French and Stanbury. In the evening went with Paul-Louis Weiller in his Rolls to Sutton Place for dinner with the Duke and Duchess of Sutherland. There were 18 for dinner. The Duke told me he had bought the estate for 120,000 pounds sterling in 1917, and declared that he would now like to sell it. After dinner, we saw a good war film in the Duke's "Cinema Room." Paul-Louis and I drove back to London afterwards.

The Duke's remarks had a delayed action. It was only a day or two later that it began to dawn on me that London would be as good a place as Paris in which to buy a large suburban house and convert it.

London was as central as Paris. It certainly had equal facilities. If the great manor house at Sutton Place could be purchased at a reasonable price by the Getty interests, then why not establish the liaison center there?

The necessary inquiries were made of the Duke of Sutherland. The information obtained indicated that the seventy-two-room manor house was being offered at a price I estimated to be one-twentieth of its replacement value. The 750 acres of land on which it stood were being offered for their value as agricultural property. Altogether, Sutton Place seemed a bargain, and this is what tipped the scales in favor of London against Paris.

It was decided to buy Sutton Place. E. Dudley Delevingne acted as agent. Miss Robina Lund, a friend of mine employed by one of England's largest and most famous law firms, handled the legal details. Delevingne and Miss Lund quickly wrapped up the transaction. The purchase was completed before the end of 1959, and the Getty interests were ready to reap the manifold advantages of having a stately English home for a liaison center and a place where their executives could meet and talk in a relaxed, comfortable atmosphere.

38

THE manor house at Sutton Place was built during the years 1521 to 1530 by Sir Richard Weston, one of King Henry VIII's favorite courtiers. It is regarded as one of the earliest—if not *the* earliest—of mansion-type dwellings erected purely as a residence, without any consideration for its defensibility.

Sir Richard, realizing that gunpowder had rendered fortified castles obsolete, determined to build a manor house of unsurpassed grace and elegance. Having served as King Henry VIII's emissary to the French Court, he was familiar with the architectural styles then coming into vogue on the Continent. Preferring these to the more ponderous, unimaginative English styles, he brought a small army of Italian artisans to England to build his house.

Sir Richard lavished several years and a great fortune on the majestic brick-and-terra-cotta mansion which today is generally conceded to be one of the finest examples of Tudor architecture extant. The term "historic" is hardly adequate to describe Sutton Place, which is so thoroughly steeped and mellowed in historical lore and romantic legend.

King Henry himself was a frequent visitor there. It was, in fact, at Sutton Place that he first met Anne Boleyn. Anne often stayed at Sutton Place, before and after she married King Henry. Oddly enough, one of the men with whom she was accused of having committed adultery was Sir Richard Weston's son. Henry had his friend's son beheaded, but took no punitive action against Sir Richard, with whom he remained on excellent terms. Anne Boleyn's unhappy wraith is said to haunt the so-called Red Room at Sutton Place, the room she occupied whenever she was a guest there.

Sutton Place was a popular gathering place for England's great and influential personages through the centuries, even until modern times, when Edward, Prince of Wales (later the Duke of Windsor) and the late King George VI often played tennis on the estate's fine covered court.

When the Getty interests purchased the estate in 1959, the manor house was essentially the same in form and size as it had been hundreds of years before. The exterior is of brick, trimmed and embellished with molded terra-cotta details. One of the features for which the mansion is justly famous is its magnificent display of priceless painted-glass windows, some of which are believed to antedate the house by several decades and perhaps even a century or more. Miraculously, the majority of the scores of such windows Sir Richard Weston installed in the 1500's are still in perfect condition.

The manor house, set like a jewel in the middle of a sweeping expanse of velvety lawn and exquisite formal gardens, has an impressive center section and two long, graceful wings. The mansion's seventy-two rooms include more than a dozen reception rooms, fourteen principal bedrooms, ten principal bathrooms, sixteen servants' rooms and an assortment of antechambers, lesser rooms, pantries, kitchens, and even special rooms for ironing, sewing, and for the arranging of the fresh flowers grown in the extensive flower gardens on the property.

Naturally, before it was bought the entire estate was meticulously inspected. Architects and engineers reported that the main building was structurally as sound as it had been when first built more than four hundred years before. Nonetheless, it was obvious that a great deal of repair and renovation would be required before the manor house would be ready for the type of use and occupancy for which it was intended.

Reports and plans were submitted and, after the transaction of buying the property was completed, orders to have the necessary work done were issued. Mrs. Penelope Kitson, who had done such an excellent job on some of the Tidewater tankers, was asked to take charge of the decoration and refurnishing of the house.

While the building itself had remained in excellent condition, the years had taken their toll of such things as floors and ceilings. Several of these needed reinforcement or even replacement. Many of the thousands of handmade tiles on the roof also needed to be replaced.

Acres of original oak paneling which sheathed many inside walls had been covered with countless layers of paint through the centuries. These layers of paint had to be laboriously stripped off by trained artisans in order that panels would be restored to their original color and beauty.

Central heating, installed decades before, was provided by a weary old coal furnace, something which I, being in the oil business, could hardly be expected to tolerate. A modern oil-burning system was ordered for the house, another was ordered for use in heating water for the 57-by-47-foot outdoor swimming pool.

The kitchens at Sutton Place were sadly outdated. Cooking ranges still burned solid fuel. The kitchens needed a thorough overhauling and got it. American electric ranges, dishwashers, refrigerators, walk-in freezer, plate-warmers, and automatic washers for the laundry were ordered. Bright, cheerful linoleum was laid over the stone floors. Lower ceilings and fluorescent lights were installed.

Some bathrooms were dismally old-fashioned; these were completely redone and fitted with new fixtures. Unpaneled sections of interior walls were in dire need of fresh paint. And, although many extremely valuable pieces of antique furniture, tapestries, and carpets came with the house, many more items had to be purchased before the manor could be considered completely furnished and livable.

Mrs. Kitson had to buy not only major pieces of furniture, but also a dry-goods-storeful of lesser items. Among these were: 128 pairs of bedsheets and more than double that number pillowcases; hundreds of towels and dish towels and cloths by the gross.

We had been assured that all the contractors' work on the house would be completed by the end of April, 1960, but could do nothing about the delays and postponements which cropped up with infuriating regularity as the weeks went by. These snags and snarls came within a hairbreadth of causing us the embarrassment of a major social catastrophe.

A large housewarming party had been planned as soon as Sutton Place was ready. I had allowed what I thought was ample time to provide a safety factor over and above the promised completion date and set the date for the party as June 30, 1960. The guest list was made up. On it were some twelve hundred names of people from all over the world. They included Getty company executives, top management personnel of other companies in and out of the oil industry, and business friends from all over the world. The invitations were addressed and mailed in May.

April had gone into May, May went into June, and still the work at Sutton Place was nowhere near completion. We began to have unnerving visions of guests arriving for the party and banging their heads on painters' ladders and scaffolding and tripping over buckets of paint. For her part, Mrs. Kitson was verging on panic. Furniture wasn't delivered on time; suppliers called to apologize for having made a mistake—the items she had ordered weren't in stock.

And so it went.

As the day of the party approached, large sections of wall were still unpainted, and much of the great house was a jumble of heaped lumber, stacked pipe, and workmen's tools.

Somehow, possibly because Mrs. Kitson made some sort of compact with a legion or two of pixies and leprechauns, everything was presentable—if not precisely complete—with only hours to spare before the 8:00 P.M. deadline on the night of June 30. True, there were still some rooms which were unfinished; luckily, they were mainly back bedrooms and could be closed off. Some tools had to be hidden hurriedly behind drapes or huge, flower-filled vases. Doors needing new hinges had to be temporarily hung back on their old ones. Here and there, the last remaining gaps caused by the nondelivery of promised furniture were filled with pieces supplied by the catering firm which had been retained for the affair.

Despite everything, catastrophe was not only averted, but the housewarming apparently proved to be an unqualified success.

Twelve hundred guests had been invited. Nearly twenty-five hundred arrived—and it seemed more like twenty-five thousand to me after I had shaken hands with all of them as they came through the receiving line.

The twenty-five hundred seemed to enjoy themselves thoroughly. They drank almost as many bottles of champagne; ate nearly an equal number of portions of caviar, fresh lobster, and giant English strawberries and cream; and danced to the music of three orchestras until long after dawn the next day. Admittedly, the cost was high, but the great amount of world-wide publicity which resulted from the party proved highly beneficial to all the Getty companies.

Once the monumental task of cleaning up after the party was done, the remainder of the restoration and renovation work that had been interrupted was allowed to proceed to completion.

The great manor house has taken amiably to the idea of being nudged gently but firmly into the twentieth century. Although it retains its overall atmosphere and feel of Tudor-era England, the stately old home is modern, comfortable, and a very cheerful house in which to work.

My associates and executives used to grit their teeth unhappily at the thought of flying into London from various parts of the world. They braced themselves against the confusion and the endless petty annoyances they knew they would encounter in the crowded hotels and traffic-jammed city.

Now they come to London, or rather, to Sutton Place in Surrey, eagerly. They and I find it much easier to work, and we are able to accomplish a great deal more in any given period of time. There is ample space to spread out maps and charts. Sutton Place is easily accessible, yet it is isolated from the noise and bustle of the city—even from traffic, for it is at least a mile to the nearest main highway from the house.

There is no noise; there are no unwarranted interruptions. Many of the businessmen who visit Sutton bring their wives along. The ladies as well as their husbands can enjoy the ample recreational facilities available when they decide they want to relax and have fun. They can swim, depending on the weather, in either the indoor or outdoor swimming pools, play tennis or badminton, golf or croquet. If they just want to take a stroll, there are several miles of lovely English country lanes crisscrossing the 750-acre estate.

Breakfasts are served in the bedrooms. Lunch and dinner are served in the great oak-paneled dining hall, which is almost seventy feet long and can readily accommodate as many as sixty persons. At night, guests and visitors can use the well-stocked library, watch television, or even view the latest sound motion pictures. A hi-fi set pipes music to various rooms for those who desire it. Anyone yearning for the bright lights of London can travel to the heart of the city in less than an hour.

Permission to use the manor house and grounds for such fund-raising projects as balls, concerts, and fashion shows has been granted freely to charitable organizations. The organizers and sponsors of these affairs have told me that the events invariably brought in record sums for the charities involved. Through such means as these, the Getty companies have proved to the people of Surrey—and of England—that they want very much to be good neighbors.

All things considered, Sutton Place has proved to be a fine investment. I, myself, have gotten to like the house and estate so much and find it so convenient that I spend a considerable portion of my time there.

Some of the fine pieces of art and antique furniture from the Getty collection are at Sutton Place. Among these are Gainsborough's "Portrait of Lady Chesterfield," which cost $104,000; a priceless collection of gold and silver plate, many pieces in which were fashioned by the great smith,

Paul Lamerie; and Rembrandt's "Man with a Knife," a relatively recent acquisition purchased for $548,000.

Very few of the paintings, art items, or examples of antique furniture bought in past years are at Sutton Place. Truth to tell, I no longer actually own most of these. I donated some of them to the Los Angeles County Museum. Among these gifts were Rembrandt's "Marten Looten," three of my finest Boucher tapestries, and the "million-dollar" Ardabil and "Coronation" carpets.

I transferred the bulk of my remaining collection in the United States to a foundation I established in 1954. The Ranch House at Malibu, California, which is my home and residence, and where I intend to live when I retire from business, has had one wing converted into a museum. The collection is displayed to the public without charge.

Among the many objects on permanent exhibit at the Ranch House museum are the Lansdowne "Hercules," some especially fine pieces from the Elgin collection of marbles, paintings by Titian, Lotto, Tintoretto, Rubens, and other masters. Also on display are examples of French eighteenth-century furniture comprising a collection which experts have characterized as being among the finest anywhere in the world.

The knowledge that countless thousands of people can see and enjoy the beauty of the things I collected over the years is ample justification for not having them with me for my own personal pleasure. And the fact that I can now spend long periods at Sutton Place is at least partial compensation for being unable to live in my Malibu Ranch House, which, of course, I cannot very well do because of the demands of my business.

Sutton Place has become a unique showplace since 1960. Utilizing the priceless period pieces already in the manor house and adding to them with flawless taste, Penelope Kitson has achieved an extremely rare ideal result. She has produced a decorative scheme in which each of the mansion's rooms has a distinctive personality all its own, while at the same time all blend into a harmonious and lovely whole.

Take, for instance, the Long Gallery. Intended by Sir Richard Weston, the builder of Sutton Place, as a ballroom, it is 165 feet long and 22 feet wide and is said to be the longest single room in any house in Great Britain. The essential flavor of the Long Gallery has been preserved. Its oak-paneled walls are hung with early-sixteenth-century tapestries. The furniture is original Tudor. By virtue of its size alone, the Long Gallery has a formal quality when not being used by large numbers of people.

Remarkably, the effect created by its decoration minimizes this and produces a warm and inviting quality.

But any house as large and elaborate as the Sutton Place manor has its drawbacks, too. There are many problems, large and small.

Among the large ones is the problem of security. The art treasures in the house are worth fortunes; insurance rates would skyrocket if these were not properly safeguarded. But these are not the only treasures at Sutton. Since it is the "liaison center" of quite a number of companies, there are countless papers and documents in the files which would be of no small value to unscrupulous persons. For these and other reasons, the house is protected by elaborate burglar and fire alarm systems. There are also watchmen to patrol the grounds with trained guard-dogs, handsome Alsatians.

The dogs themselves have, quite literally, created additional problems. Being both male and female, they have gotten together to produce more dogs. I have been reluctant to allow any of them to be sold. As a consequence, the kennel colony and the kennels at Sutton are carrying out their share of the steady expansion which characterizes most of the units which make up the Getty interests.

Compared to such major over-all problems as security, headaches of the type which developed into the much-publicized incident of the installation of a pay telephone at Sutton Place are minor, indeed. They can, however, be troublesome and expensive.

Sutton Place is large enough to require several telephone extensions, but not so large as to justify installation of a regular switchboard and the employment of full-time telephone operators. In the beginning, all the extension telephones in the house were connected directly to outside lines and thus to the central telephone office in Guildford. The phones had access to long distance telephone service. Operators at the central office could not possibly differentiate between one person or another who called from Sutton Place to make a long distance call.

After a few months, accountants checking the telephone bills discovered that many long distance calls had been placed to numbers unknown to me or anyone connected with the Getty companies. The consequent overcharges on the bill ran high.

The conclusion was inescapable. People attending parties, charity functions, or open house receptions at Sutton Place were casually picking up the telephones they found scattered around the house and placing calls here, there, and everywhere.

The telephone central was without fault; the operators there had only done what they were supposed to do—put through all calls as efficiently and expeditiously as possible. Tracing down each individual unauthorized call and then trying to discover who had placed it would have been a bit too much. There was only one sensible way to handle the matter and prevent any recurrences: by shutting the barn doors before any more pound-a-minute calls slipped through them.

The majority of the telephone instruments in the house were adjusted so that they could only be used for local calls. The only phones over which long distance or transoceanic calls could be placed were those in rooms accessible only to authorized persons. For the convenience of casual visitors, a regular pay telephone was installed in one of the cloak-rooms on the main floor of the house.

The wisdom of these steps became apparent within the first month. Although several hundred people attended charity affairs or receptions at Sutton Place during that period, there were no more mysterious telephone calls listed on the next telephone bill.

I suppose it is understandable enough that the press had a field day with the story. After all, on the face of it, there is considerable humor in the thought that a pay telephone is installed in a house used by companies controlled by a man reputed to be the richest in the world. Within a day or two after a visiting journalist saw the newly installed pay box, the item made the newspapers from London to Los Angeles and from Paris to Port Moresby.

Notwithstanding problems large and small, I reiterate that Sutton Place has proved a fine investment and it is a fine place to stay and work.

I know that I work better and accomplish more there. Perhaps the best way to illustrate its advantages is by relating the events of one of my typical workdays.

39

I HAVE often maintained that I possess a rare talent and strong inclination to be a beachcomber. I rather imagine that if it were not for the demands made upon me by my business, I would provide living proof that a man can live quite happily for decades without ever doing any work at all.

Perhaps it is because I am subconsciously aware of this inclination and its perils that I have long since disciplined myself to follow a daily regimen and acclimated myself to working as much as fourteen or even sixteen hours a day.

I am not an early riser. I usually surface around 10:00 A.M., but I like working late, using the quiet and tranquil after-midnight hours to read and digest complex reports and documents and to do my most intense concentrating on the weightier matters at hand.

I awaken between nine and ten in the morning. When at Sutton Place I follow much the same routine as I have for many years. Having long ago established a two-main-meals-a-day regimen for myself, I start my day with at least ten minutes of vigorous exercise rather than with breakfast. After completing the usual routine of bathing, shaving and dressing, in the clothes solicitously laid out by Bullimore, the butler-valet and benevolently despotic major-domo of the manor, I am downstairs in the spacious study that serves as my office, ready to start another working day.

By then, never later than eleven, my various aids and employees have arrived at Sutton from their homes in London or nearby Guildford. Cables, important correspondence carefully culled from among a hundred or more letters which arrive for me daily, and a thick sheaf of the American, British, French, and Italian newspapers I read regularly are on the desk. They have been laid out neatly by Barbara Collings, my pert and sometimes somewhat tyrannically efficient personal secretary.

The cables and top-priority letters—many of the latter have reports or other documents enclosed—require anywhere from half an hour to an hour and a half of reading and replying time. If my luck is good, I can turn to the newspapers after this is finished, but such is seldom the case.

More often than not, some of my business associates or executives are waiting to see me. Even if they are not, then one of my administrative assistants will want instructions, information, or decisions on matters ranging from personnel changes to purchase orders involving thousands or contracts involving millions.

I have two administrative assistants, confidants who do the work of a fair-sized platoon and function as my extra right arms.

One is attractive, twenty-six-year-old Robina Lund. I hastened to put her on the payroll early in 1960 after she had so convincingly demonstrated her abilities by handling the labyrinthine legal complexities of the Sutton Place transaction in record time and with astonishing efficiency.

The other is Claus Bulow, a thirty-four-year-old English-educated barrister of Danish extraction whose rapier-quick mind, penchant for hard work, and highly personable manner have proved to be as valuable in the business world as at the bar.

Robina and Claus take a tremendous load of administrative, preparatory, and detail work from my shoulders. They perform such varied jobs and duties as those of legal and public relations advisers, buffers, highly diplomatic representatives, and a host of others. At times, they also serve as whipping boys, roles they accept with remarkable forbearance and good nature.

One or the other, and often both, will usually have something for me to see, sign, or decide before lunchtime. If it's an especially fortunate day, I can manage to get away from my desk for a fifteen-minute swim in one of the two pools at Sutton, but such days are even more rare than the proverbial one in June.

Lunch is served at one-thirty in the dining room. My personal tastes in food tend to the simple side; my lunch generally consists of fresh citrus fruit, grilled or roasted meat, vegetables, fresh salad, and dessert.

Telephone calls from and to London, Paris, Rome, and many corners of the globe punctuate my average day, but almost all conversations with the United States take place in the afternoon, following lunch, because of the differences in time. There are also more conferences, dictation, and other work after lunch and until around 5:00 P.M.

Whenever possible, I try to take a short, brisk walk before tea is served in the drawing room. The working day ends for my aids and office employees at around 5:30 P.M., unless, of course, there is some especially pressing unfinished work to be done, in which case it is not unknown for one or more of them to work around the clock with me.

I generally manage an hour or even two of work between teatime and dinner. If there are no special guests, dinner, which is served at eight-thirty, lasts about an hour, after which I head back to the study. More letters and documents have piled up there during the course of the day. I go through these, making notes of the replies to be sent, the questions to be asked and answered, and the action to be taken.

The pile is usually cleared before midnight. It is then, when everything is quiet and even the members of the domestic staff have gone to bed, that I find it the best time to concentrate on the technical and financial reports from my various companies and to do my heavy thinking. It is also the best time for me to digest the oil industry trade and technical publications to which I subscribe and which help to keep me abreast of the latest trends, developments, inventions, and processes throughout the industry.

It is usually two o'clock in the morning or later when I go up to my bedroom. There is a small pantry adjoining it and if, as is sometimes the case, I am hungry, I will make myself a late snack—waffles, pancakes, or hamburgers.

Now, I would not pretend that I put in a sixteen-hour day every day of the year. I attend concerts, the opera and theater, parties and social functions fairly often. But the sixteen-hour day is not unusual, and the days when I do no work at all are rare enough to be memorable.

Much as I would sometimes like to do so, I cannot slough off or sleep on the job. My business interests form a complex, multifaceted structure, and they add up to a heavy responsibility. My associates and the executives who direct and manage the various segments of the business and the individual companies are all seasoned, reliable, excellent men. But there has to be someone at the top to direct, co-ordinate, and, if I may be permitted use of the term, to inspire, the whole that comprises what newspapers like to call an industrial or financial empire.

Altogether, I head or control nearly one hundred corporations, large and small. I have listed only a very few of them below, but even this much-truncated list should provide some idea of the complexities and responsibilities of an international business. These, then, are some of the companies:

Getty Oil Company
Tidewater Oil Company
Skelly Oil Company
Mission Corporation
Mission Development Company
Pacific Western Oil Co., Ltd.
Getty Oil Italiana, S.p.A.
Pacwest Realty Corporation
Pacific Western-Iran, Ltd.
Getty Realty Corporation
Club Pierre Marques, S.A.
Impulsora de Revolcadero, S.A.
Veedol Marketing Companies (one in every Western European country)

Company names mean nothing unless one can realize and understand that they represent people and products and services. Each one of these companies has employees, and, in most cases, stockholders other than myself. The Boss must concern himself constantly to insure the jobs and welfare of the former and the investments and interests of the latter.

Each of my companies must directly or indirectly perform a commercial service for its customers. In order to thrive and prosper, all the companies must strive unceasingly to broaden and improve the services they perform, whether these be in producing crude oil or providing accommodations for hotel guests, and to lower the prices charged the consumer or customer wherever and whenever it is economically feasible to do so.

"Your money is only as good as what you do with it," my father told me many years ago.

This is as true now as it was then. And so is the dictum that the best thing a wealthy man can do with his money is to invest it, keep it at work providing more jobs at higher wages for more workers and producing more and better goods or services for more people at lower cost.

To accomplish these aims, the businessman himself must keep on working along with his investments. If he is willing to accept the rewards, he must also be willing to accept the responsibilities.

I believe in the validity of these basic truths and principles. Hence, although I have been actively in business for nearly five decades, I still put in more than occasional sixteen-hour days and am yet to learn at first-hand what it is to work a forty-hour week and then forget about business until the following Monday.

Even so, since I have established the comparatively well-ordered and smoothly functioning liaison center at Sutton Place, I have managed to find enough extra time and opportunity to gratify some whims of long standing and to satisfy some long-harbored ambitions.

Since all my four sons are executives in various companies in the Getty group, they, too, often come to Sutton Place. George, his wife Gloria, and their three young daughters; Paul, Jr., his wife Gail, and their now four children; and Ronny and Gordon, who are at this writing still bachelors, have all been frequent visitors at Sutton. This has been a source of tremendous pleasure and gratification for me. My boys and I have gotten to know each other much better than was possible in previous years. I have always loved my sons; now I can honestly say that I know them well enough to like and respect them as men.

Indirectly, Sutton Place has helped me realize one of my long-standing ambitions—to write. As a young man, I had even thought seriously of making writing my career. Through the years, I have managed to produce three books, but these were on specialized subjects and intended for extremely limited audiences. Needless to say, these books were written in bits and snatches as odd moments became available in otherwise full days.

Since I have been able to find a little more spare time whenever I am at Sutton Place, I have begun to write again. The reawakening, or, perhaps, the resurgence, of the urge and desire dates from 1958 and can be blamed partially on one of my friends, B. W. von Block, an American free-lance writer who has lived abroad for many years.

Von Block, who has apparently achieved a not inconsiderable degree of financial success as a writer, and I became acquainted if for no other reason than because our paths crossed often in England and on the Continent. In the course of several conversations about business and writing, he made some points which struck me as being quite sensible.

He contended that relatively few Americans really understood much about the free enterprise system, the business world, or the principles and philosophies which govern the actions and activities of businessmen and enable them to achieve success. Often fostered by groups or individuals with motives not entirely above suspicion, a great many misconceptions about all these things prevailed in the public mind.

Capitalism, business, and businessmen were often lambasted by press and public. But reasoned, factual defenses are seldom provided by the individuals best qualified to do so—namely, the nation's successful businessmen.

The average businessman confines his remarks to board meetings or Chamber of Commerce luncheons and his writings to annual reports, company house organs, or at most, to trade journals. Although he has vital and valid messages for the general public, he is usually reticent or reluctant to voice them outside business circles.

Then, Von Block pointed out, a great many young men and young women enter upon business careers without sufficient grounding and preparation. Although technically proficient in some specialized field, they frequently fail to acquire a broad, inclusive outlook of the over-all economic picture. Far too many young executives lack the fundamental understanding of the various phases and facets of business. These lacks are serious; the sooner they are remedied, the better American business, and thus the nation's economy, will be able to expand and meet the manifold challenges and threats of the present era.

"Someone has to start the ball rolling," my writer friend argued. "You've had the experience and experiences on which you could base innumerable articles that will help the public see business and businessmen in the proper perspective and which will also serve as valuable guides to beginners."

When I protested that the last thing I wanted was any more publicity, he countered with a fairly well-reasoned argument that defined the difference between publicity and writing in this instance.

"Publicity is getting your name in print for your own benefit or edification," he said. "The kind of articles you could write best would serve primarily to inform people and to make them start thinking."

I voiced my doubts that editors of general circulation magazines in the United States would be interested in publishing articles dealing with business matters.

"Nuts!" my self-appointed journalistic *eminence grise* snorted. "The public is ready and eager to hear the businessman's side. Give me twenty-four hours, and I'll prove it to you."

Von Block turned up at my hotel again the following day and blithely informed me that he'd made some transatlantic telephone calls to New York—to his able and enterprising literary agents, Joan and Joseph Foley, and to various magazine editors. He cheerfully announced that he'd obtained several tentative assignments for me. If I would do some articles within the broad scope of subjects suggested by the magazine editors, they would allow me free rein to express my thoughts and ideas.

I had previously made it quite clear that, if by any chance I ever did write any articles, I would neither expect nor accept any compensation for them. My friend must have passed on this information. Of their own volition, the various editors offered to donate sizable sums to the Salvation Army and other charities as token gestures.

This occurred in 1958, during a period when I was still traveling a great deal. I did not have the time needed to refine and polish my drafts of the articles, and Von Block good-naturedly volunteered to do these things for me. We collaborated on articles which subsequently appeared in *True*, *American Weekly, Look, This Week*, and other periodicals.

I must admit that the reaction and response to these pieces astonished me. It was quite evident from the letters and comment I received that the public *did* want to know the businessman's side of the story and that, having heard part of it, was favorably impressed and wanted to hear more.

All this led, in 1960, to a proposal from the editors of *Playboy* magazine, who asked me to prepare a series of articles on the theme, "Men, Money and Values in Today's Society." Publisher Hugh Hefner and his editor, A. C. Spectorsky, promised me carte blanche to say the sometimes unconventional, nonconformist, and controversial things that I, like a great many other veteran businessmen, had long wanted to say and felt needed saying.

There are, I am sure, many staider and more conservative magazines than *Playboy* in the United States. But these do not reach the young executives and the university students for whom the articles in the series were primarily designed and intended. Whether one likes it or not, Mr. Hefner's frisky and epidermal periodical attracts the nation's highest readership rate among young men in these two categories. And it was precisely these individuals whose thinking-processes the articles were designed to prod and even jolt.

Reader response and comment indicate that the messages contained in the pieces have been well and clearly received by those to whom they were directed. The articles have brought many complimentary, even laudatory, letters and have been widely quoted and reprinted.

I, of course, received no monetary compensation for the articles. My reward lay in the knowledge that they had been read, possibly enjoyed, and perhaps taken to heart by young businessmen and the university and college students who will one day enter careers in the business world. However, Messrs. Hefner and Spectorsky followed the lead set by the editors and publishers of my previous articles and voluntarily made substantial contributions to charity as gracious gestures of appreciation.

40

On MONDAY, May 28, 1962, the prices of most stocks listed on the New York Stock Exchange fell sharply. The Dow-Jones industrials average plummeted nearly thirty-five points, the biggest one-day drop in decades. Crashing through the 600-level for the first time since 1960, it reached a daily low of 533.

Shares traded on the American Exchange and in over-the-counter markets followed suit and also went into steep nose dives. Late afternoon headlines reflected the developments being reported by the lagging ticker.

MARKET LOSSES TOTAL BILLIONS
INVESTORS DUMP SHARES IN PANIC
WALL STREET FEARS NEW 1929 DISASTER

Two days later, several journalists representing various wire-services and publications descended on Sutton Place and requested an interview with me. They wanted to know my opinions and reactions and asked what I was doing because of the break in stock prices. I told them quite frankly that, while I sympathized wholeheartedly with anyone who had lost money because of market developments, I saw little if any reason for alarm and none for panic.

The over-all business picture was favorable and, what was even more important, gave promise of getting better in the future. There was nothing basically wrong with the American economy or with the vast majority of companies whose stocks were listed on the New York Stock Exchange. In my view, some stocks had been grossly overpriced. Irrational, emotionally inspired buying had driven their prices to unrealistic levels. The May 28 break was a natural and inevitable consequence.

As for what I was doing, the answer was quite simple. I was buying stocks, taking advantage of some of the fine stock bargains available as a result of the emotionally inspired selling wave. As I am primarily an oil man, I bought oil stocks. By the end of the New York Stock Exchange trading day on May 29, our New York brokers had purchased thousands of shares for the account of certain of the Getty companies.

My replies and the confidence I expressed in the fundamental soundness of the stock market were widely publicized. Unfortunately, few newspapers or magazines seemed to have the space or inclination to print the only good advice that I or any other seasoned investor can give to the general public—namely, that stocks should be purchased for investment and not for speculation.

In the weeks that followed, many dire prognostications of more or less imminent business recession were made by various prophets and pundits. It was being freely—far too freely—forecast that economic slump would follow on the heels of the stock market break, and far too many individuals who should have known better likened May, 1962, to October, 1929.

As these predictions of gloom and doom piled up, journalists once more approached me for my views. Speaking purely as an experienced and objective businessman-observer, I did not hesitate to express the opinion that 1962 and 1929 had very little, in fact, practically nothing, in common.

True, far too many stocks were priced far too high in 1960–62. But the nation's business outlook was generally good in 1962, and the economy was expanding at a merry clip. There were no hidden, deep-down structural flaws in the economy such as there had been in 1929.

There were other great differences. In 1929, stock speculation was done mainly on borrowed money; shares were purchased on the most slender of margins. Thus, when prices collapsed, credit collapsed, too.

Then, of course, there is the most important difference of all, the one the calamity howlers conveniently forget. The May 28, 1962 slump was not a "crash." It was a healthy, if somewhat violent and painful, adjustment that was long overdue.

I think it absolutely essential for the American public to bear in mind that:

The nation's economy was relatively sound on Friday afternoon, May 25, 1962, when the New York Stock Exchange closed for the weekend.

The U.S. economy was just as sound on the following Monday morning, when the Stock Exchange reopened.

The economy was basically no less sound when trading ended on that hectic Monday. If anything, it was on firmer ground than before because stock prices had been brought down.

Few if any industrial orders were canceled.

Few if any jobs were lost.

Few if any business establishments were forced to close their doors.

Few if any investors, large or small, were completely wiped out as so many had been in 1929.

I realize that all this is scant comfort to those who lost money when stock prices fell on May 28. It can only be hoped that they profited from the painful lesson. Perhaps they will know enough to invest rather than speculate in the future. Perhaps they will buy selected stocks at reasonable prices as investments, hold them, and allow them to increase in value at a reasonable rate.

In my view, and at this writing, the American economy is basically sound, the business picture is good, and the over-all long-term trend seems to be up. Despite any short-term upward or downward jogs of the stock market, the climate for business and businessmen seems fair, certainly no worse than at most times in our history, and just as certainly a great deal better than it has been during a great many periods.

Much concern has been expressed about such matters as the gold and dollar drains, government spending, and federal budget deficits. Rising costs, the menace of automation, the threat posed by the Communist bloc, increasing competition from abroad—these and many other related factors have also given rise to considerable worry in many quarters.

Now, I would hardly suggest that these are things which should be shrugged off or laughed at. They are problems, and very grave ones at that. But to grow hysterical over them or to adopt negative or defeatist attitudes because they exist is to deny history, ignore fact, and completely disavow the principles and strengths which have made America and the American system what it is and have enabled it to accomplish its industrial and social miracles.

The United States, like any other nation, has always faced problems and dangers. That it has been able to meet and overcome them is proved by the very fact that it has survived and thrived through some of the most difficult periods in the history of the world.

The American system is not perfect—no system ever has been or ever will be perfect. But the American system is clearly the equal of any and superior to most. True, there are economic and social weaknesses. The economy could expand at an even faster rate. There are still far too many people who do not enjoy enough of the blessings of life. There are still large segments of our population that are not yet adequately housed, or, for that matter, adequately clothed or fed. Much remains to be done in the sphere of racial relations; the fact that all our citizens, regardless of color or creed, still do not enjoy equal rights and opportunities is one of the most dismal facets of our national life and does us immeasurable harm all over the globe.

There are other problems, large and small, and there is much room for improvement.

I am not a statesman, politician, philosopher, or sociologist. I am, after all, only a businessman. I cannot offer panaceas, nor even much in the way of direct suggestion, for curing our social ills. In this regard, I can only say that common sense and an awareness of the need to keep abreast of the times and trends would probably go a very long way toward providing solutions for our social problems. History shows that those who refuse to alter their course before the winds of change are almost always destroyed by the storms that follow.

I am, however, on much firmer ground when I venture opinions about the nation's and the world's economy and economic future. My views are based on and tempered by decades of experience and seasoning as a businessman both home and abroad.

I have confidence in the economy and the economic future of not only the United States, but of the entire free world. I also have confidence in the innate vitality and resourcefulness of American business and the American businessman, both of which have always considered problems and dangers as challenges to be met and mastered.

Be the problem posed by automation, the adverse balance of foreign trade or whatever, it can, and, I believe, will, be met by the aggressive and imaginative action of the nation's businessmen. The late Franklin D. Roosevelt is credited with having said, "There is nothing to fear but fear itself." His remark was made many years ago, at a critical period in American history. The philosophy it expresses is as valid and applicable today as it was then.

In my opinion, fear and lack of confidence are the greatest threats to our economic welfare, security, growth, and future. This, I believe, applies to all fields and spheres of business. Competition, whether it comes from the shop across the street or an economic system halfway around the globe, exists only to be met and bested.

In order that this may be done, it might not be the worst of ideas for the various segments of our society to stop their pettifogging quibblings and quarrelings. Government, big as it may be, and business, big or small, had best indulge in an elaborate and sincere hatchet-burying ceremonial. Labor and management might be well advised to make their peace, too, if either hopes to survive. The members of our two major political parties could do far worse than to think first of their citizenship and only afterward of their partisanship.

There are rights and wrongs on both or all sides of any and all questions. But the niggling, picayune differences over which opposing segments are so often wont to fret and battle the most and longest can usually be compromised or adjusted easily, and so they should be, if internecine skirmishes are not to cause the destruction of the common cause.

And, speaking of things which are common, there is no better remedy for any problem than common sense, plus that priceless element which is variously called tolerance, understanding, or even a sense of humor. Liberal dashes of these tossed into the areas of fuss and friction would work and have always worked miracles.

Moving closer to home, to my own particular sphere of business activity, the oil business, I am optimistic about the future. More than a century has passed since Colonel Drake brought in his oil well at Titusville. In that time, the petroleum industry has burgeoned and grown, and the oil which a little more than a hundred years ago was being sold as a medicinal cure-all has become one of man's most essential needs.

The petroleum industry, born in 1859, has become the biggest of all the world's businesses. Oil in its myriad refined and processed forms is today one of the most vital commodities, used in some way or to some extent by practically every human being on the face of the earth.

Oil is still and will long remain the world's principal source of fuels and lubricants. I feel no hesitation in freely predicting that decades will pass before petroleum is supplanted to any appreciable degree as the world's principal source of power.

If anything, the demand will continue to grow. Already industrialized nations will continue to increase and expand their plants and factories; underdeveloped nations will come into their industrial own. Oil will be the principal source of energy for all.

Oil will provide heat for more and more homes, fuel for more and more vehicles, ships, and aircraft. Scientific and technological advances will not only increase and improve the potentials and uses of petroleum and its products but will also continue to find entirely new uses through petro-chemical processes. One needs only to remember that the demand for petroleum increases every time an automobile rolls off an assembly line or an oil furnace is installed in a new house, or even when a youngster gets a new bicycle or electric train, both of which need oil for lubrication.

The demand and uses for natural gas are also increasing. Markets for natural gas increased more than 400 per cent in the last twenty years. By 1955, natural gas had already begun to outstrip coal as an energy source in the United States.

The classic search for new oil and natural gas sources will go on. So will the search for newer and more efficient refining processes and for new uses and applications for petroleum and petroleum products. I feel that demand will increase greatly in the years to come, and I also feel that whatever the demand, it will be met as it has always been met.

I am no less optimistic about the outlook for my own business interests and the companies I own or control. These are thriving, but I know that there are no such things as final or ultimate successes or triumphs. Like any veteran businessman, my aims and ambitions are to make a continuing success of my career. I know that the only way in which this can be accomplished is by continuing to expand, by achieving a continuing series of successes.

The businessman who wants to reach the top can afford to be pleased and gratified when he manages to accomplish this or that end against the greater or lesser odds he inevitably and invariably faces. But he cannot afford to allow any of his achievements to make him complacent and self-satisfied. He cannot rest on his laurels, no matter how lush and verdant their foliage.

While the successful businessman recognizes his notable achievements for their importance and value, he regards them primarily as road-markers which serve as invaluable aids in guiding the further course of his business operations and career.

In my own case, I firmly determined to stay in the oil business after my initial success with the Nancy Taylor Allotment Lease. Subsequent successes as a wildcatter provided me with additional experience, produced more profits which I could use as working capital to expand my opera-tions, and gave me more confidence in my business judgment and ability. Each of my milestone successes also served to whet my appetite for facing increasingly greater challenges and for solving increasingly more complex problems.

By the time I started my campaign to gain control of the Tide Water Associated Oil Company, I felt that I had served a hard and instructive apprenticeship in the oil business. I had learned my oil-man's trade from the bottom.

I believed that I'd learned my lessons successfully and well. I wanted to apply my knowledge and experience to projects of greater depth and broader scope. I was convinced that by implementing ideas and plans I had formulated in the oil fields, I could direct the operations of Tide Water Associated more efficiently and profitably—more successfully—than they were then being directed by the company's incumbent management.

I did, of course, eventually succeed in my campaign to gain control of Tide Water Associated, but only after a long, tough, uphill fight against odds which look frightening even in retrospect, long after the battle was won. Yet, I consider my victory only a minor achievement compared to the far more important and meaningful success my associates and I achieved in building and expanding the company after I had gained control of it.

Nevertheless, I do not consider even these achievements to be anywhere near final. In my opinion, the company still has far to go and grow.

My attitudes toward the operations of the Getty Oil Company in the Neutral Zone conform to similar patterns. Obtaining the Neutral Zone concession, locating the area's vast oil deposits, and eventually attaining high levels of oil production there are all achievements that can be considered milestone successes in my career. But the job in our Middle East oil fields is far from finished. There is room there, too, for expansion and improvement, room for more and bigger successes. I feel the same about all my other business interests and enterprises.

I believe that to be truly successful, the businessman must first discard, or, at the very least, greatly discount, most traditional definitions and concepts of success. And he should critically examine and evaluate whatever preconceived theories he may have about gauging or achieving it.

There is nothing constant or static about business. The business world is a constantly changing one; the business scene shifts and varies from day to day and even from hour to hour. Thus, no single achievement or triumph will long retain its initial importance, significance, or value.

The only way in which any businessman can hope to achieve anything remotely approaching lasting success is by striving constantly to achieve success in everything he attempts, and by building new and greater successes on the foundations provided by old ones.

Sooner or later, nearly every businessman has his opportunities to achieve substantial successes. He must be able to recognize them when they present themselves, and he must also possess the imagination, ability, and willingness to work hard—the elements needed to make the most of his opportunities.

He must also remember that the true measure of success is not how much money he amasses, but what his money is doing. I've said it before, and I say it again. The best thing one can do with money is to invest it in businesses and enterprises which provide jobs and produce more and better materials or goods or perform more and better services for more people at lower prices.

That is what I have done with my money, and those are the aims and goals of the companies in which I have invested the money.

Therein lies the justification for wealth, and therefrom does the successful working businessman derive the greatest sense of accomplishment and satisfaction.